THE BEST OF THE INDEPENDENT
RHETORIC AND COMPOSITION JOURNALS

The Best of the Independent Rhetoric and Composition Journals

Series Editor: Steve Parks

Each year, a team of editors selects the best work published in the independent journals in the field of Rhetoric and Composition, following a competitive review process involving journal editors and publishers. For additional information about the series, see http://www.parlorpress.com/bestofrhetcomp.

THE BEST OF THE INDEPENDENT RHETORIC AND COMPOSITION JOURNALS

2012

Edited by Julia Voss, Beverly Moss, Steve Parks, Brian Bailie, Heather Christiansen, and Stephanie Ceraso

Parlor Press
Anderson, South Carolina
www.parlorpress.com

Parlor Press LLC, Anderson, South Carolina, USA

S A N: 2 5 4 - 8 8 7 9

ISSN 2327-4778 (print)

ISSN 2327-4786 (online)

1 2 3 4 5

Cover design by David Blakesley.
Printed on acid-free paper.

Parlor Press, LLC is an independent publisher of scholarly and trade titles in print and multimedia formats. This book is available in paper and digital formats from Parlor Press on the World Wide Web at http://www.parlorpress. com or through online and brick-and-mortar bookstores. For submission information or to find out about Parlor Press publications, write to Parlor Press, 3015 Brackenberry Drive, Anderson, South Carolina, 29621, or email editor@parlorpress.com.

Contents

The Journal of Teaching Writing

Kairos

KB Journal

Pedagogy

Reflections

Introduction

Questioning, Challenging, and Advocating: Advancing Knowledge in Composition and Rhetoric

Julia Voss and Beverly Moss

In his 2012 *Kairos* webtext "Views from a Distance: A Nephological Model of the CCCC Chairs' Addresses, 1977-2011" (featured in this collection), Derek N. Mueller uses word clouds as a way to make sense of composition and rhetoric as a field, to systematically notice trends, patterns, connections. Mueller suggests that "there is a value in *network sense*: an aptitude enriched by this tracing of linkages across an assortment of people, places, things, and moments." In the introduction to this anthology, we attempt a sort of *network sense* on a smaller scale. That is, the articles collected here create a snapshot of one year's trends, questions, themes, people, places, and moments in the field. Though the eleven articles in this collection vary in topic, questions, and methodology, there are ties—linkages—that bind them, painting a larger picture of current discussions in composition and rhetoric.

Although we offer a visual representation of these linkages through our own word cloud near the end of this chapter, our introduction focuses on the connections that emerge from the articles that follow. The pieces featured in this collection coalesce around key rhetorical moves that 1) question and challenge accepted practices and beliefs; 2) move from questioning and challenging to advocacy; and 3) illustrate and propose new methods and approaches for advancing the field. As we suggest below, most of the featured articles make at least two of these rhetorical moves. And while the scholars whose work is showcased here employ multiple methods (empirical, historical, discourse analysis, philosophical) and concern themselves with a variety of locations (classrooms; writing centers; and community, digital, and discursive spaces) their work consistently pushes composition to re-examine its boundaries and its purpose.

The articles in *Part 1: Questioning and Challenging Accepted Practices and Beliefs* cause us to stop, reflect, and re-see the field. The scholars featured in this section challenge philosophical, pedagogical, and curricular practices that have dominated our field. Matthew Pavesich, in "Reflecting on the Liberal Reflex: Rhetoric and the Politics of Acknowledgment in Basic Writing," challenges what he identifies as the prevailing liberal ideology found not only in colleges and universities, but especially in basic writing programs. He suggests that liberalism's commitment to the "equal treatment of everyone" ignores historical and current inequities that make the equal treatment approach complicit in perpetuating inequities and injustice. Pavesich examines how Roosevelt University, an institution committed to social justice, interrogated the liberal ideology underpinning its basic writing curriculum and has begun taking steps to differentiate its writing curriculum in response to the varied needs of a diverse student population. This case study models one way to incorporate a rhetorical approach—long endorsed in composition and rhetoric—in the basic writing subfield.

Advocacy on behalf of basic writing students who enter with fewer resources than many of their peers is fundamental both to the questions Pavesich raises about the liberal ideologies in basic writing curricula and to the rhetorical solution he proposes. He calls for a pedagogy that repositions the students and the work they do. We see Kelly Bradbury doing similar interrogation and re-situation work in "Positioning the Textbook as Contestable Intellectual Space." Bradbury challenges the messages conveyed to students by textbooks, a longtime staple in writing classrooms and a billion-dollar industry in the United States, pointing out how the ideological control textbooks exert over student learning runs counter to the "libratory and 'student-centered' pedagogies we employ in our classrooms." In the classroom-based study she describes, Bradbury asked students to assume responsibility for and control of their own learning by creating the textbook for their composition course. Having students choose their own readings and write their own discussion questions makes the textbook a "contestable space" for Bradbury. Doing so repositions both students and textbooks: students are elevated to the role of intellectuals, and textbook authors and contents are redefined. By questioning the role of the text-book, Bradbury calls us to see first-year writing students as intellectuals capable of "co-authoring classroom pedagogy."

Like Pavesich and Bradbury, in "Writing Time: Composing in an Accelerated World" Jeanne Marie Rose challenges the way that English Studies, and composition in particular, understands, interprets, and uses time as a concept and tool in the writing classroom. She argues that while process pedagogy tends to view time as a limitless resource, the global capitalist world in which we live places considerable demands on writers' time. As a result, Rose calls compositionists to "situate time in the context of our students and classes" and "examine the material realities of time." Rose proposes that composition teachers rethink process pedagogy. She argues that the classic version of process assumes that students have more time than they actually do in today's fast-paced global society. Therefore, Rose suggests that

> students need to examine the materiality of time and weigh its consequences for their lives as writers, students, workers, and citizens. We as teachers, meanwhile, need to be open to learning about our students' particular ways of experiencing time, and we need to bring this awareness to our course design and delivery.

Rose calls us to question typical classroom approaches to process pedagogy as well as to cultivate students' awareness of time as a valuable resource that is sought after by multiple audiences (capitalist, media, educational, et cetera).

Rose's questioning of how writing teachers and writing process pedagogy make use of time is, at its very core, a question about how we, students and teachers, are socialized to use time and efficiency. We also see this focus on socialization practices in the articles in *Part 2: From Questions and Challenges to Advocacy*. In "'So what are we working on?' Pronouns as a Way of Re-Examining Composing," Kate Pantelides and Mariaelena Bartesaghi analyze the use of pronouns in writing center consultations to challenge how writing center scholarship has socialized its consultants to think about collaboration in the writing center session. Dissatisfied with the way that collaboration has been characterized in previous writing center scholarship, Pantelides and Bartesaghi argue that "rarely are [writing center consultants] presented as they are in practice—chameleons that change their colors dependent on the moment-by-moment requirements of the consultation." The authors assert, in other words, that collaboration in the writing center consultation is a dynamic process that cannot be dictated by rigid guidelines about how directive/non-directive a consultant should be. In their semester-long study of graduate student consultants and clients in the writing center, Pantelides and Bartesaghi examine how consultants and clients use pronouns—especially *we* and *I*—to indicate shifts in authority throughout the session. The authors propose that consultants' use of *we* to refer at various times to themselves and the client, to the writing center as an organization, and to academic writing as a discipline is "multifunctional: signaling collaborative affiliation and disaffiliation by sharing and distancing oneself from a text." The relationship Pantelides and Bartesaghi draw between collaboration and asymmetry in writing center sessions ultimately challenges the field to extend its ongoing thinking about collaboration (reflected, for example, in Andrea Lunsford and Lisa Ede's twenty-year engagement with the concept) to the writing center.

While the articles we've introduced so far question and challenge accepted practices in traditional educational sites like composition classrooms and writing centers, the remaining essays in Part 2 move these challenges beyond the university classroom to alternative sites, namely community and corporate spaces. In doing so, these articles continue the field's interest in community literacies and composing in the public sphere. In some instances, by virtue of linking literacy to particular community spaces, these scholars challenge traditional views of literacy. Melvette Melvin-Davis's "Daughters Making Sense of African-American Literature in Out-of-School Zones" introduces readers to the group of 9th and 10th grade African American girls who participate in the Umoja Book Club, a community-based organization that meets outside of school space. Melvin-Davis argues that the out-of-school space and the reading activities that take place there offer these African American youth "homeplaces—spaces where diverse, relevant, and realistic African American experiences are shared and validated[.]" She demonstrates how culturally relevant pedagogy delivered in such homeplaces expands the girls' literacy identities, "giv[ing] voice to the young, gifted, and Black girls of the Umoja Book club and demonstrat[ing] to community and academic circles the value in connecting and cultivating young people's literacies in out-of-school spaces." Thus, while implicitly challenging the ability of traditional school spaces to meet the needs of certain marginalized populations, Melvin-Davis positions community spaces as valuable pedagogical sites, spaces where members of marginalized communities can use culturally relevant literacy artifacts—African American literature—to advocate for their own needs.

Similar to Melvin-Davis, in "Rhetorical Recipes: Women's Literacies In and Out of the Kitchen" Jamie White-Farnham highlights the importance of another alternative literacy site. White-Farnham focuses on domestic space, examining the literate lives of members of the Rhode Island branch of the Red Hat Society, a social club for women over fifty. Society members surprised White-Farnham by questioning the value of their everyday literacies, instead placing a premium on the traditional literacies they practice(d) in school and workplace settings. White-Farnham suggests that aspirational identities—in this case, the professional identities the women aspired to rather than the domestic identities traditionally associated with their gender—act as a filter according to which individuals value different literacies. More to the point, White-Farnham argues that while these research participants, deeply influenced by second-wave feminism, see little value in everyday literacy practices, they value traditional academic literacies, especially writing, very highly. These findings remind researchers and teachers who place a premium on the everyday literacies that emerge from and dominate non-traditional spaces not to underestimate the investment people have in traditional literacies, especially those from groups who have historically occupied subordinate positions. To respect and accurately represent participants' self-perception of their literate identities, researchers may, at times, need to reevaluate the non-traditional community practices they seek to study.

Where Melvin-Davis and White-Farnham interrogate the connections between literate identities and community literacy spaces, Heidi McKee introduces corporate spaces into the literacy conversation, focusing on the increasingly digital nature of contemporary literacy. The title of McKee's article—"Policy Matters Now and in the Future: Net Neutrality, Corporate Data Mining, and Government Surveillance"—identifies three key national-level policy issues that already affect writing and the teaching of writing, the importance of which will only increase over time. We need only note the political and cultural uproar over Edward Snowden's 2013 exposé of the U.S. government's covert practice of recording metadata about Americans' phone conversations to demonstrate the significance of these issues. By linking net neutrality, corporate data mining, and government surveillance to concerns about freedom of speech/information, personal/financial security, and warrantless seizure, McKee argues the field must deal with them as research and teaching in composition and rhetoric increasingly takes place in networked digital environments ranging from the World Wide Web to corporate social media platforms like Twitter, Google Docs, and YouTube. Finally, McKee calls on members of the field to get involved in these issues outside the classroom by joining organizations that monitor and agitate against the loss of net neutrality, the rise of corporate data mining, and the covert practice of government surveillance.

While the pieces in Part 2 question existing values and practices in composition and rhetoric and call us to advocate for change at the level of personal, educational, and social policy and beliefs, the work featured in *Part 3: New Methods and Approaches for Advancing the Field* offers new methods and approaches to research, composing, and teaching that can help to realize this kind of change. These pieces, all of which, interestingly, were published in webtext format only, represent novel ways to view the subject matter(s) of the field, canonical figures and texts, and the field itself. In "The Meaning of the *Motivorum*'s Motto: '*Ad bellum purificandum*' to '*Tendebantque manus ripae ulteriorisamore*'" Richard H. Thames re-examines the relationship between rhetoric and dialectic and how the "nature of poetics (which weaves the two together) [is] discerned." Thames analyzes the etymology of Latin words found in the epigraph and text of Burke's *Motivorum* to redefine the relationship between rhetoric and dialectic. He reads the history of these terms against the body of work surrounding Burke's unfinished *Motivorum* text, including letters, articles, and annotated versions of Burke's manuscripts to uncover the theorist's conception of language. Thames' two-part approach helps him re-open the classic text to argue that in the *Motivorum*, language depends on the pursuit of beauty through dialectic (as in Plato's *Symposium* and *Phaedrus*) as well as on the pursuit of war (as rhetoric has traditionally been defined). This combination of etymological inquiry and close reading allows Thames to reread the *Motivorum*, providing a new perspective on one of the field's major theorists.

Like Thames' reappraisal of Burke, Rex Veeder's "Re-reading Marshall McLuhan: Hectic Zen, Rhetoric, and Composition" examines what another major figure, Marshall McLuhan, has to offer the field of composition and rhetoric as a whole. Although McLuhan's influence on the field has thus far focused on media and cultural change, Veeder argues that McLuhan's approach to textual production has much to offer the wider field. Specifically, his "artistic, complex, and holistic form of exploration, writing, and thinking" provides Veeder with a model for what he calls "Hectic-Zen" composing. Hectic-Zen reflects the "allatonce"ness of media-saturated contemporary life by drawing out and documenting the patterns that emerge from this ubiquitous din. Veeder offers mosaic as an example of how Hectic-Zen composition might work. Because mosaics are made up of bits and pieces from various sources, they contain multiple perspectives that represent patterns found in the chaos from which their disparate elements are drawn. Furthermore, Veeder argues that a mosaic's modular nature embodies Hectic-Zen methods because it lets composers "suspend judgment" as they work piece by piece without having to envision the whole, allowing composers to resist totalizing understanding and explanation in favor of playful exploration. Veeder's essay itself models the mosaic-style, Hectic-Zen mode he advocates by 1) interspersing references to McLuhan and the other scholars who populate Veeder's intellectual universe (such as Burke, Ann Berthoff, and Gloria Anzaldúa, whose work embodies the Hectic-Zen mode) and 2) breaking up his written text with playful doodles that abstractly illustrate his concepts.

The exploratory, experiential composing method Veeder derives from McLuhan reflects the kind of rhetorical environment Noah H. Roderick describes in "Analogize This! The Politics of Scale and the Problem of Substance in Complexity-Based Composition." He argues that the complex adaptive network or ecological world view found in recent composition scholarship that draws on complexity theory (seen in the work of Byron Hawk, Sidney I. Dobrin, and others) ushers in a new kind of writing subject, the eco-subject. The eco-subject is not a self-contained, autonomous being but the nexus of social, material, and biological factors that distribute activity across multiple components of the physical and virtual networks within which we are embedded. Roderick's rhetorical ecologies parallel the patterned, allatonce mediascapes from which Veeder's Hectic-Zen compositions emerge. Both describe complex adaptive systems in which "relationships between writing subjects, media audiences, institutions, and kairotic moments" and the texts they produce "are constantly co-evolving." Roderick argues that the co-evolution Veeder describes results from the connections that feedback loops create between seeming disparate material and cultural elements ranging from "information flows, [to] social networks, [to] animal metabolism." For Roderick, these linkages between local and global conditions offset the neoliberal agenda some critics ascribe to network theory and complexity theory. Tying together micro and macro concerns allows for the "continuous invention of [eco-]subjectivity," in which humans function as participants in complex networks that help shape other network components, even the large ones like institutions and ideologies, through mutually influential feedback loops. These feedback loops allow Roderick to argue for a postmodern ethical dimension of posthuman network culture, presenting a new philosophical and pedagogical point of departure for composition and rhetoric.

The patterns which Roderick and Veeder focus on bring us back to Mueller's article, where this introduction began. Mueller analyzes the annual CCCC Chairs' speeches from 1977 to 2011, using word clouds generated from the published versions of their speeches in order to examine when various terms appear, rise, and recede in these "views from the center," which Mueller uses as barometers of the field's intellectual climate. The word cloud methodology Mueller describes allows for a "distant reading" practice that focuses strictly on patterns of word use without examining their context. Word clouds' "distance" from the meaning of the source texts distinguishes them from Ellen Barton's and Duane Roen's thematic analyses of the same texts, providing for a new, digital humanities approach to the field's intellectual history. Mueller also compares word cloud-based distant reading to article abstracts, which seek to capture the essence of a piece, attempting the kind of explanation Veeder discourages. Because word clouds measure term frequency, Mueller argues that they can capture the "gestural build-ups, micro-turns, and anomalies to the larger patterns" that close thematic reading can miss, thereby harnessing the data-processing power McKee associates with corporate data mining for the benefit of the field. Such a distant reading method offers, therefore, one way to represent and investigate the complex rhetorical situations Roderick describes and even embodies the kind of exploratory (rather than explanatory) Hectic-Zen mode of composition that Veeder advocates. Finally, because Mueller uses customized software to create his word clouds, he includes a detailed description of his methods, providing a model for how to introduce new research tools (whether digital or analog) into rhetoric and composition scholarship.

By way of bringing the eleven articles highlighted here into conversation with each other, we followed Mueller's lead and created our own word cloud based on the articles. Some of the major terms across these articles are expected: students, writing, work, rhetoric, Burke. Others, however, are surprising, for example "time," which may support Rose's claim that time is becoming an increasingly important consideration for the field. Some of the small-sized "trace"-words—such as Facebook, users, sciences, personal—that come up are illuminating as well in their seeming marginalization, indications of future concerns for the field. As you peruse the collection, consider, as Mueller suggests, what these different snapshot methods say about the current state of the field.

A Note on Selection Criteria and Methods:

These eleven articles advance knowledge in composition and rhetoric because they question, challenge, innovate, and re-imagine the field. It is those qualities that reviewers used as criteria for ranking the nominated articles. The major criteria for ranking and selecting the articles are threefold:

1. Article must demonstrate a broad sense of the discipline, demonstrating the ability to explain how its specific intervention in a sub-disciplinary area intersects and addresses broad concerns of the field.
2. Article must make an original contribution to the sub-disciplinary field, expanding or rearticulating central premises of that area.
3. Article must be written in a style which, while disciplinary-based, attempts to engage with a wider audience.

The editor of each participating journal was invited to submit two articles for consideration. Both articles were reviewed by reading groups at several colleges and universities across the United States. These groups consisted of full-time and part-time faculty, lecturers, and graduate students who read the articles and, according to the criteria listed above, ranked the articles on a scale of 1 to 4 (4 being an article that meets the highest criteria). The editors used these scores to select the final articles that appear here.

We owe a great debt to our reading groups, whose work made this project possible. We thank them for their careful reading and rankings of the articles. Specifically, we thank all of the associate editors who participated in the reading groups: Sarah Antinora, UC Riverside; Francesca Astiazaran, CSU San Bernadino; Paige V. Banaji, Ohio State University; Jessica Best, UC Riverside; Lindsey Banister, Syracuse University; Chase Bollig; Ohio State University; Matthew Bond, UC Riverside; Bridgette Callahan, CSU San Bernadino; Joanna Collins, University of Pittsburgh; Clare Connors, University of Pittsburgh; Katherine M. DeLuca; Ohio State University; Chloe de los Reyes, CSU San Bernadino; Jennie Friedrich, UC Riverside; Brenda Glascott, CSU San Bernadino; Rochelle Gold, UC Riverside; Ashley Hamilton, CSU San Bernadino; Joel Harris, CSU San Bernadino; Jennifer Herman; Ohio State University; Deborah Kuzawa; Ohio State University; Annie S. Mendenhall; Ohio State University; Peter Moe, University of Pittsburgh; Kristin Noone, UC Riverside; Tamara Isaak, Syracuse University; Emily Maloney, University of Pittsburgh; Lauren Obermark; Ohio State University; Jess Pauszek, Syracuse University; Anne Schnarr, UC Riverside; Karrieann Soto, Syracuse University; Frances Suderman, CSU San Bernadino' Noel Tague, University of Pittsburgh; Jaclyn Vasquez, CSU San Bernadino.

The Best of the Independent Rhetoric and Composition Journals

COMMUNITY LITERACY JOURNAL

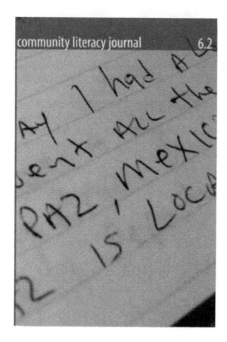

Community Litearcy Journal is on the Web at http://www. communityliteracy.org/

The *Community Literacy Journal* publishes both scholarly work that contributes to the field's emerging methodologies and research agendas and work by literacy workers, practitioners, and community literacy program staff. We are especially committed to presenting work done in collaboration between academics and community members.

We understand "community literacy" as the domain for literacy work that exists outside of mainstream educational and work institutions. It can be found in programs devoted to adult education, early childhood education, reading initiatives, lifelong learning, workplace literacy, or work with marginalized populations, but it can also be found in more informal, ad hoc projects.

For us, literacy is defined as the realm where attention is paid not just to content or to knowledge but to the symbolic means by which it is represented and used. Thus, literacy makes reference not just to letters and to text but to other multimodal and technological representations as well.

Rhetorical Recipes: Women's Literacies In and Out of the Kitchen

We think that Professor White-Farnham's article presents an excellent and compelling interview methodology for inquiring into "women's lived experience and the significance of everyday life" and reveals how social and everyday literacies function in several overlapping social and personal spheres and contexts.

1 Rhetorical Recipes: Women's Literacies In and Out of the Kitchen

Jamie White-Farnham

Drawing on interview data regarding literacy practices done in tandem with housework, this article presents an array of recipe uses among retirement-age women. Given their backgrounds as professionals who came of age during second-wave feminism, the women see little value in "domestic" practices such as cooking literacies (Barton & Hamilton). However, the women's uses of recipes for a variety of rhetorical purposes, in and out of the kitchen, are valuable material and social reflections of the women's success in acquiring traditional literacies in school and at work.

"Resources? For cleaning?! That's the last thing I think of!" When my research participant Sandra scoffed at the possibility that literacy and housework could intersect, she exemplified the general response of each of my six research participants to my questions about the literacy practices they use in housework: a somewhat protective attitude towards literacy, as if its use to facilitate mundane chores might debase it. Sandra's reaction is but a single example of the decisive and dichotomous opinions shared in my recent interview study of women of retirement age regarding the relationship between housework and literacy: "I'm a terrible housekeeper. If you had asked me about career, I could have helped you."

Sandra, like Emme, Edna, Donna, Anna, and Dee[1], is a member of the Red Hat Society (RHS), a national social club for women over age fifty, which describes itself as a way for women to "let go of burdensome responsibilities for a little while" (Red Hat Society). The growth of the group since its inception in 1997 is impressive; reportedly, its membership has exceeded one million women worldwide. According to Sue Ellen Cooper, the California woman who founded Red Hat Society, the group's primary appeal "is our determination to find the joy in life, to grasp the fun there is to be had at this age—fifty and beyond" (8). Cooper describes the recruitment base of RHS as former "wives, mothers, and, often, career women [who] have survived the busiest, most hectic years," and the official website promotes the social activity of the group as "an opportunity for those who have shouldered various responsibilities at home and in the community their whole lives, to say goodbye to burdensome responsibilities and obligations for a little while" (Cooper 8; Red Hat Society).

There have been an untold number of press accounts of the group as it has attracted attention in each new community where chapters have formed. The archives of the *The Providence Journal* have chronicled RHS's growth in Rhode Island since chapters began cropping up in the state between 2002 and 2003. A profile of a South County chapter emphasizes its new members' enthusiasm to become part of the national trend, "in search of a silly state of mind" (Fleming C3). Among the reasons they participate in the group, the Rhody Red Hatters count making new friends, taking trips, participating in cultural events, and generally breaking up the monotony of daily routines and feelings of isolation a person can experience at and after retirement age.

In addition to this notoriety, the group has also drawn critique. A 2008 editorial comment by Paula Span in *The New York Times* denigrates the role that the hats, as a piece of the organization's savvy merchandising tie-ins, play in the RHS's claim on fun. Span writes: "I think I'll do my socializing bare-headed. When I'm old, I'll probably wear mostly black, the way I do now. And I'll call the group I have dinner with 'my friends'" (9). Span's position hints at a problem more significant than style, however. Like many social clubs of which the purpose is leisure, RHS requires of its members expendable income and time; it therefore suffers from a correlative lack of diversity in the classes and races of its members. Though RHS publicity documents use the phrase "all walks of life" to describe its members, there is little evidence of a wide scope of participation by women who are other than white and middle-class in my research experience (Red Hat Society). Other accounts of the organization, including leisure studies research by Careen M. Yarnal et al, describe a similar lack of difference among the women in their survey samples (152). My study, open to all eighty members of RHS in Rhode Island, attracted only white, middle-class participants. This perhaps reflects the state's overall demographics: 88.5% white with an 11% poverty rate (United States Census Bureau).

And, while the group's several corporate sponsorship and licensing agreements have come under some critique, they are also a reflection of the RHS's growth and influence (Span 9). In its manual of sorts, *Fun and Friendship After Fifty*, RHS founder Cooper explains the reason such a group is warranted in the US, particularly for aging women: "middle-aged women have gotten used to going unnoticed, to being invisible" (9). Sandra and the other participants' reasons for belonging to RHS resound with this claim; they joined RHS as an "antidote" to the conditions of living as retired, aging women, which include loneliness, complacency, and—above all—mundanity.

In combating complacency, these women live anything but mundane lives. Data drawn from my interviews with them reveal that literacy permeates their activities from everyday writing and reading in the kitchen to formal literacy endeavors such as taking college courses and teaching enrichment classes in community centers. The women are very proud of the latter undertakings since they value literacy greatly in its traditional forms, especially writing and reading for educational and professional purposes. At the same time, the women see little value in the everyday literacy practices they undertake. Specifically, *literacies* such as the processes and practices of cooking are held in lower esteem than more visible and text-based *Literacy* comprised of, for these women, personal and public writing projects. In taking up a variety of recipe uses in my participants' literacy experiences both in and out of the kitchen, this article addresses a debate resulting from the "social turn" in literacy studies, which shifted traditional notions of literacy from a text-based, formally-taught set of skills learned during one's childhood and useful in institutional settings to an extratextual set of sociocognitive practices acquired throughout a person's life useful in a variety of contexts (see Deborah Brandt, David Barton & Mary Hamilton, and Deborah Williams Minter et al, among others). While these characteristics of literacy are generally agreed upon, a divide exists among social practice literacy theorists regarding the potential for social power that literacy affords its users. Some (Paulo Freire, Morris Young, and Jacqueline Jones Royster, for instance) ascribe literacy the power to overcome oppression, inferior status, and unjust conditions. Others (Sylvia Scribner, as well as Brandt & Katie Clinton) are highly cautious in ascribing literacy such power, given that access to literacy is usually in the hands of the powerful, whether or not users know it.

This debate frames my participants' experiences in acquiring professional literacies, which helped them resist the conventional domestic roles and responsibilities they faced as young women in the late 1960s and early 1970s. As professionals who came of age during second-wave feminism, the participants in this study struggled to pursue and achieve their educations and professions. Sandra is a retired English and ESL teacher with a master's degree in Education. The contexts in which she and the other women acquired their formal literacies necessitated pitting their home lives, which included homemaking and child-drearing, against their personal and professional goals. An attendant result of their experiences is the women's simultaneous undervaluing of everyday literacies and especially those useful in housework. As this article will describe further, the cooking practices of two women in particular—though rife with the type of decision-making, material, and sociopolitical effects that characterize social practice literacy—are downplayed, unrecognizable even to the women themselves. Sandra's sound bites offer one reason why. In describing patterns surrounding the women's uses both in and out of the kitchen of a traditionally "domestic" text, the recipe, this article demonstrates how the women both align themselves with professional, community, and personal pursuits and simultaneously denigrate the idea of intentional, motivated participation in housework.

Playing It By Ear: Donna and Edna

Rather than referring to recipes in cookbooks or on websites, Donna and Edna each compose original recipes. However, in describing their cooking practices, Donna and Edna actually have nothing—no artifacts, that is—to share. Rather than relying on websites, cookbooks, or recipe cards, they compose *in situ*, or work from ingredients on hand to address the demands they face in their immediate, rhetorical situations. In this way, the women's practices are comprised of basic rhetorical principles: they must consider their audience (children? adults? how many?), purpose (to nourish? to impress?), genre (simple lunch? Sunday dinner? party?), and material conditions (various ingredients and tools, money, and time). All of these elements vary, of course, according to the woman and the situation.

Donna, a semi-retired nurse who has four adult children, says she uses "no writing, no recipe cards," but instead engages in "instinctive cooking" of fresh foods, eschewing canned fruit, vegetables, and beans. Calling her cast iron griddle her "second hand," she goes into detail about the preparation of potatoes: "I do them boiled and sliced and fried until they're crispy and then added to beans—from scratch." Donna calls this meal good for "clean energy, a perfect balance." Partially in response to the material conditions in which she cooked while living overseas, where varieties of packaged and canned foods popular in the US were unavailable, Donna also counts among her motivations to use fresh ingredients her daughter's sensitivities to preservatives in processed, packaged foods. Importantly, Donna describes the values that underscore her interest in fresh foods and home cooking: health and nutrition. As a nursing professional and a mother who believes in a child-centered parenting style, she says, "I think I cook with respect to the kids."

Similarly creative, Edna's cooking faces stricter material impositions, including a tight budget and accommodating three "big eaters," her husband and two sons (when they were teenagers). Edna also works only with a limited number of traditional ingredients appropriate within her knowledge of Italian cooking, listing onions, garlic, and homemade breadcrumbs as the base of most recipes. She is proud of keeping these ingredients on hand all the time, storing lentils and breadcrumbs in re-purposed glass jars in the pantry. Although these material conditions are inflexible, Edna describes her everyday cooking for her family of five as very flexible, emphasizing that: "I play it by ear. I don't worry about recipes because everything calls for garlic and onions." She credits her mother-in-law with "giving" her lots of recipes, but when I ask if I can see them, she says that "they show you or tell you, they don't write them down...not a recipe, something you wrote down, but a pinch of this or that..." To Edna, recipes are things one might "worry" about, adding complication to something that comes naturally to her.

Discussing Donna's and Edna's recipe production in rhetorical terms runs counter to the ways in which the women themselves describe and perceive these practices. Between Donna's "instinctive" cooking and Edna's "pinch of this or that," the women reflect their confidence in the kitchen, though they also resist generally accepted social theories of literacy as a powerful "social practice" or "set of practices" (Barton and Hamilton 6; Minter, Gere, and Keller-Cohen 671), which is neither solely text-based nor tethered to traditional literate institutions such as school, work, or church (see also Brandt, Hogg, Royster, Rumsey, Sohn, and Young, among others). The work of Barton and Hamilton on "cooking literacies" in particular highlights the decision-making of their participant Rita to exemplify the "tangible, observable" aspects of social practice literacy, whether or not the writing or reading of texts is involved:

> Rita does not always go through the same set of activities in making the pie [from a well-used recipe]. Sometimes she makes double the amount described in the recipe if more people will be eating it […] Rita does not always follow recipes exactly, but will add herbs and spices to taste; sometimes she makes up recipes; at one point she describes making a vegetable and pasta dish similar to one she had as a take-away meal. (8)

Barton and Hamilton's description of Rita is echoed in Donna's and Edna's practices, also notable for their extra textual, though rhetorical natures: the production of a meal rendered from material work with ingredients, amounts, and tools alongside flexibility in the wake of changing rhetorical elements such as purpose, audience, and available means.

Donna and Edna's practices also exemplify what Barton and Hamilton call the "interpretive" aspect of literacy, or the "attitudes, values, and other social meanings which lie behind these activities" (151). On one hand, Edna's motivations for her cooking literacies are ingrained through her cultural affiliation as an Italian-American and her experience in poverty as a child. Edna's mother was widowed during the Depression after her and her husband's grocery store went under. Edna was ten, and until she began work at a wire factory after her high school graduation, she, her mother, and three siblings at home lived on Social Security and an elder brother's army wages. Edna and I discovered several similarities between her and my grandmother Helen, who sponsored my affinity for housework and whose practices inspired this project, in that they hail from the same culture and generation, each of them Rhode Island-raised daughters of Italian immigrants who themselves raised children in the 1950s and 1960s. Edna describes making "a triple batch of red sauce using five pounds of hamburg and three pounds of sausage on Sundays." This Italian cooking shorthand—"red sauce" and "hamburg"—along with the very large quantities match the ways my grandmother both cooked and talked about cooking. Here, literacy is a tool to uphold traditions, her aims being the maintenance of practices, materials, and key cultural values of her New England Italian-American family.

On the other hand, Donna has rejected her family's ways of cooking and available printed recipes based on her values of health and wellness gleaned from her professional knowledge. Donna pursued a nursing career in the midst of raising four children, and today she continues her education at the state college, along with staying current with the nursing literature of the day. Having resisted the expectations and scorn of her and her husband's family to pursue her career, Donna imbued her housekeeping practices with her professional values of health and wellness. By doing so, she countered the philosophical underpinnings of her mother's and her in-laws' takes on, specifically, parenting and cooking.

For example, Donna prioritized playing with and reading to her children over a housework routine. She involved them in some chores through play, such as helping wash dishes or prepare meals. But she describes her commitment to their growth and development over household chores through a memory of walking with her children to the library every few days to fill their red wagon with twenty-five books at a time, the lending limit. She considers her way of caretaking "child-centered at the expense of housework," while her European in-laws "put neatness over children." In another instance of resisting ways of homemaking within her family, Donna shifted the focus of feeding her children from their discipline to their health. Since she grew up to resent her own mother's model of feeding children based on a reward/punishment system, Donna drew from her nursing education to focus on food, as her original recipes exemplify, as an element of one's health. Donna resisted these conservative values through her cooking literacies.

Whether or not literacy practices uphold or resist a particular value system or ideology is a central question in the study of social-practice literacy. While some contemporary scholars highlight the potential for critique and political action in literacy practices, such as Young's "resistant literacy," others are more cautious since they recognize that literacy endeavors can be halted by users' subject positions and/or material resources (112). For instance, Brandt & Clinton are skeptical of the agency some scholars believe literacy affords its user because sponsors of literacy are often not at the scene of literacy and extend their influence without users' awareness of them (349). Scribner also sees a need for this type of caution when she describes the metaphor of "literacy as power." She writes: "the expansion of literacy skills is often viewed as a means for poor or politically powerless groups to claim their place in the world [...] yet the capacity of literacy to confer power or to be the primary impetus for significant and lasting economic and social change has proved problematic in developing countries" (11-12). Indeed, while Donna's and Edna's original recipes offer evidence of how literacy affords its users the power to sustain or resist a value system, the fact remains that neither woman ascribes this type of social or ideological power to her cooking.

Recently, the work of Rumsey on "heritage literacy" has emphasized the importance of context and change in her study of Amish women's "home-based or indigenous" literacy practices such as cooking and quilting ("Heritage" 584). Interested in how changing tools and technology affect these types of literacy practices, Rumsey highlights the recursive process that literacies undergo both in their routine performances and their longevity (or lack of) within a culture. She writes:

> Connection of object to context is always evolving and always growing because objects change and the context changes over time. The object changes because people adopt and adapt new or different technologies and literacies, such as my mother getting an electric mixer or a wider variety of ingredients being available in grocery stores. Further, heritage literacy is recursive. As contexts and objects change, people adapt to these changes and change how they pass on their intellectual and literacy inheritances. ("Passage" 92)

Rumsey's attention to how and not whether dominant social forces and groups of literacy users affect each other moves beyond considering literacy "as a dichotomous variable, perceived either as conservative and controlling or as liberating" (Graff xix). That is, rather than seeing literacy as a stable variable that exacts changes (or not) within a context, Rumsey sees literacy practices and tools themselves as flexible and changeable, working in contexts for users in specific, though perhaps fleeting, ways. This takes the onus off of literacy to be the game-changer that Brandt and Scribner have argued that it cannot be. A question therefore arises: if literacy users themselves do not see their sociocognitive practices in everyday settings as important or powerful beyond the scope of their kitchens, where and with what practices do they see themselves contributing, via change or simply cooperation, to their communities or the world? The answer for the women in this study: traditional literacies, and especially writing.

MORE INTERESTING THINGS TO DO:
DEE, ANNA, AND DONNA

Dee, Anna, and Donna are each semi-retired women who fill their free time with continuing education, community volunteerism, babysitting grandchildren, and social events. These women shared experiences with me regarding recipes that had a lot to do with their literate abilities, though nothing to do with cooking. Each coming of age during second wave feminism, or the time that Dee remembers as "women's lib," the three women balanced caring for their families with attending college and building their careers. They value their accumulated literacies greatly, having acquired them in spite of expectations of their families to assume traditional domestic roles and responsibilities as young women.

These experiences and their reasons for joining the Red Hat Society cast a long shadow on perceptions of "home" as a productive or even pleasant place to be. As such, Dee, Anna, and Donna are prone to dismissing and belittling housework as a concern appropriate for a study on women. In relying on a key principle of Kathleen Weiler's feminist research methodology, I aimed to emphasize "women's lived experience and the significance of everyday life" and resist approaching the study of women from "a male hegemonic ideology or language" (58, 61). Weiler instead suggests that women's consciousness:

> is grounded in actual material life. What focusing on the everyday life of women should do instead [of dichotomizing the public and private] is reveal that connection between public and private, between production and reproduction. In

> socialist-feminist research, the everyday world is not a self-contained world; quite the contrary, it is an integral part of the social whole. (61)

Yet, as will become evident in this section, the dichotomy was palpable. Clearly, the differences between the women's and my experiences, material circumstances, and generations were at play. Women like my participants contributed to the broad-scale social changes that removed "housework" as a fraught and gendered social expectation of many children of my generation. Thus, my freedom to embrace or reject housework in my everyday life allows me to consider it a subject of interest. The differences between our perspectives resulted in some uncomfortable moments during our interviews, and I suspect the women felt disappointment in what I was describing as feminist research.

Despite having agreed to participate in the study and signing an IRB consent form, Donna, Dee, and Sandra were disconcerted by my interest in housework, and their reactions to some questions ranged from curiosity to disdain to ridicule. However, using an interview approach advocated by John Creswell comprised of "unstructured and generally open-ended questions that are few in number and intended to elicit views and opinions from the participants," I followed the women's leads as I learned more about them and their literacy practices (188). Moreover, according to Stephen Doheny-Farina & Lee Odell, "the researcher's goal is not simply to confirm the researcher's own intuitions or conclusions but to find out what the participant thinks—to stimulate the interviewee to express the meanings that he or she attributes to the topic at hand" (522). Dee, Anna, and Donna, in describing their uses of recipes in family history projects, self-sponsored writing projects, and community fundraising, were stimulated to express their disdain for the domestic and affirm their esteem of literacy in a traditional, text-based sense. Perhaps more importantly to them, discussing recipes also resulted in data that I did not anticipate: the questioning and critique of a (my) positive stance towards housework.

Painting a mutually exclusive relationship between housework and one's career, Dee and Donna both use the word "boring" to describe housework, and perhaps rightfully so given the variety of their interesting activities and commitments. Alongside contingent work as nurses, the two women volunteer at organizations as varied as the Providence Performing Arts Center, a nursing home, hospice care, and the city zoo. At the time of our interview, Dee was also enrolled in a Spanish class at her local senior center, an effort aimed at improving her communication with patients at an adult care center where she worked. Her prioritization of education and career and her concomitant attitude towards housework stem in part from her experience in at least one consciousness-raising group. Dee stated:

> Housework…it's boring. I have more interesting things to do, and now I don't have to keep clean for anybody in particular. I think people who don't have much of an education might make more of it because that's what they can be proud of. But, when you're working and you're educated, you want to be known for more than a clean house. I was, when women's lib first started, I was in those groups…it was 'where are you going in your life?' rather than 'what are you doing at home?' It was more than just raising kids. And I actually didn't stay home that long with my kids, I was either going to school or working part-time when they were young, like when we adopted my oldest daughter I was getting my bachelor's degree and then I got my masters when my youngest was a baby.

In support of these accomplishments, Dee delegated housework, sometimes employing cleaners, au pairs to watch the children, and, when they were older, her children for a few extra dollars. Dee didn't—and doesn't now—cook much, so she is hard-pressed to recognize the usefulness of recipes in a traditional sense, saying: "I planned ahead because I was working full time. My daughter says she learned to cook by herself because 'my mother was working.' I used the crock-pot a lot because I could throw things in in the morning." Dee sees this type of planning and organizing to feed her family as a way to minimize housework, allowing her to expend more of her time and energy on her career and educational goals.

Yet, recipes remain important to Dee in a far different capacity than cooking; her main use of them comes in the form of preserving her family history. She keeps "two little [recipe boxes] with all the recipes I have in the kitchen…I have some of my mother's that I keep because they're in her handwriting. And, I have my sister's cookie recipe." As static texts, the recipes serve a memorial function, like heirlooms for Dee to save and pass down. They are reminders of the important women in her life, though not necessarily their cooking. And, while the recipes are artifacts of Dee's mother's and sister's cooking literacy,

Dee prizes them for their sentimental, and not practical, value. The material aspects of the writing—he handwriting, the boxes they are stored in, and their daily presence in Dee's life—are most important for Dee, who values texts over cooking.

Like Dee, Anna has prioritized other interests and responsibilities over housework, including her long-term babysitting commitment to her granddaughter, her main hobby of gardening, and her talent for creative writing. She compares the relative importance of housekeeping and pursuing a career, suggesting that women who have careers don't or can't focus on housework. She herself is retired Air Force administrative personnel, who worked mainly at a data entry job while her children were growing up. She also spent time volunteering in her children's schools. In Anna's experience, women like her who have careers and especially those with children hire help for housework. She explained her own attitude:

> I'm not into being like, super particular about everything because housework is boring. There's a lot more interesting things to do than housework…I keep up the standards, but, you know, there's too many more other things that are more interesting than just housework.

For Anna, creative writing is one of those things. As a writer, she is known for composing rhyming tribute poems that celebrate, entertain, and sometimes poke fun at her friends and family members: "Sometimes it's just to cheer somebody up, making fun of something so that it's not a dreary event for someone, seeing the lighter side of something. Sometimes these little ditties just go through my head, so I sit down and write them and then later I'll go to add something or change them." Anna sent me an example of her personalized specialty poems shortly after our first interview:

> One day in my e-mail I was surprised to see
>
> That someone actually wanted to interview "little 'ole me"
>
> The young lady was a student and was working on her PhD
>
> So, in the interest of education I thought "why not me?"

Anna's hobby and talent explains some rhetorical aspects of her recipes, which exist as entries in a hand-written cookbook she is at work compiling. Anna laments the loss of some artifacts, including recipes and housework instructions she wrote for her daughter many years ago: "My daughter has been out of college for over ten years so [the recipes] that I wrote for her are long gone." Therefore, Anna has rewritten what she calls "the college recipes," including the one pictured here for Tuna Noodle Casserole.

> Tuna Noodle Casserole
> ½ pkg. egg noodles   or   2 cups macaroni
> 1- 6oz can of tuna (drain off the liquid)
> 1- can of cream of mushroom soup
>
> Cook noodles or macaroni until tender
> While noodles are cooking- open & drain the
>   tuna & open the cream of mushroom soup
>   and combine them in a medium size
>   casserole dish add 1 can of milk to the
>   mixture and stir
>
> Also preheat oven to 350°
>
> Drain the noodles & add to soup & tuna mixture
> Top with bread crumbs or left over potato chips
>   to make a crunchy topping to your casserole
>
> Bake for about 30 minutes

The influence of Anna's creative writing is evident in this example, as the recipe tends toward narrative form rather than practical instructions. As well, its presentation is attractive, centered on the page and written in pretty handwriting. Since she doubts that her daughter actually cooked this meal in the dorm, Anna writes the recipes to commemorate her daughter's coming-of-age and not necessarily to keep the recipe in circulation as a cooking practice. In handwriting recipes out again, Anna revives the memories for both of them. Of the cookbook project, Anna says: "It's still in the works…not very accessible right now. It needs to be organized," highlighting the presentation of the document, its suitability to be considered a "book," rather than the recipes' potential for their typical use in the kitchen. The writing of this cookbook out of Anna's own collection of recipes, which may have once guided her cooking practices in this kitchen, but don't now, is a contribution to her writerly identity and legacy in her family.

Finally, Donna also regards the importance of literacy in terms of writing; however, her recipes are directed toward an audience not only outside the kitchen, but also outside her family. As a member and former president of several community groups—a women's church group, parent volunteer committees at her children's schools, and a local hospital committee—Donna participated in compiling, publishing, and selling cookbooks as fundraisers for four different community organizations over the years, a fairly common fundraising activity. As I have described, Donna's literacy efforts have been directed largely toward education: her children's literacy learning, her own career training, and her continuing education in Women's Studies coursework. Therefore, despite her impressive cooking literacies, Donna notes that the recipes themselves were not her main contribution to these projects. Instead, she emphasizes other elements central to the cookbooks' production, including tasks that drew on her own and other group members' professional skills:

> Jamie: Did yours or the other women's professional experience lend a lot to [the cookbook]?
>
> Donna: Yes, we were very organized. All the women in one capacity or another worked outside the home. One woman especially, who was another RN, was definitely an advantage. She knew how to find a publisher to keep the cost reasonable and still be able to turn a profit. That [committee] was more structured, more direct. It took three or four months with a firm deadline. Others I've seen took over a year.

Donna's late 20th century education and professional life are evident in her praise of the committee on which she served, especially the importance of organization, collaboration, and follow-through. Here, Donna aligns her work with "recipes" not with the domestic duty of cooking, but with her professional experience and knowledge. This corresponds with Donna's underlying motivation in the creation of her original recipes—her value of education. She is proud of her contribution to the projects not as an authority with recipes, but as a commodifier of them, taking advantage of recipes' material value in support of communities built on traditional Literacy. Perhaps it is not so surprising that committees such as Donna's consider a book a worthy item to help maintain institutions of literacy such as schools and churches. I find it ironic, however, that given the strength of resistance to cooking and housework among the women in the study, of Donna's generation and demographic, the committee would choose to sell cookbooks. Yet, Donna describes these projects as successful. The communities surrounding these institutions may not use the recipes for cooking literacy; however a book represents Literacy in its traditional form, and is therefore worth the community's money, time, and respect. In undertaking projects for which recipes serve a public function, Donna sees the community groups she served as sites for which the process of writing and her expert literacies are more appropriate and impactful than in her home.

Dee, Anna, and Donna's experiences acquiring professional literacies during second-wave feminism have shaped their views on what forms of literacy matter—writing and reading—as well as the limiting effect the "domestic" can have on those forms. Accordingly, since the women have little interest in the notion of cooking, or any chores they consider housework, as a set of practices worth their time and attention, recipes are mainly valuable to them when their purposes are other than simply practical and their audiences are located outside of the kitchen. In these capacities, recipes have provided each woman with an opportunity to leave a mark on her family and/or community, audiences far wider and far more important to these women than a single cook—especially if that cook is meant to be her. The women's rhetorically diverse use of recipes as family histories, self-sponsored writing, and community service projects reflect Dee, Anna, and Donna's commitment to and appreciation for the goals and contexts they see as most appropriate for Literacy.

A CASE OF BIFURCATION?

Perhaps the most striking account of the women's struggle between literacy and housework in this study is articulated by my participant Emme, the Queen of the Red Hatters, a single mother who put herself through college while caring for her two children. While Emme's main contribution to the study concerns her leadership role in RHS outside of this account of recipe use, a brief story she shared with me speaks volumes about the home/work dichotomy present in the data.

Balking at the idea that housework could be a priority for her while pursuing a career by way of a college degree, she says: "My housework consisted of opening a can of food up for the kids, dropping them at the babysitter, going to class, and then coming home to pick them up sleeping and lug them up the stairs." A former military reservist, Emme has a reputation as the most fun-loving and "wild" Red Hatter. If Emme's priority is to have fun and let loose, it is not only to escape from "various responsibilities at home and in the community," as the Red Hat society mission statement suggests, but also to counteract a work history that, like the other women's, pulled her in many directions and made housework a laughable non-issue (Red Hat Society).

One way to understand the strength of the women's anti-housework conviction is the concept of bifurcated consciousness, which may account for the women's simultaneous undervaluing of housework and their pitting the domestic against the professional, even when their commitment to a variety of literacy-rich pursuits is evident. According to rhetorical scholar Mary M. Lay, "a bifurcated consciousness potentially affects a woman's ability to appreciate her own experiences and to interpret their meaning outside the gender role assigned to her" (Lay 85). For example, in her study of midwives' arguments for their practice's legitimacy in public policy, Lay asserts that the spokesperson for direct-entry midwives (as distinct from certified nurse midwives) was forced to leave out of her argument the fact that midwives rely often on their instincts and feelings, which comprise a strong knowledge base and successful practices. The reason for the omission was not only because experience-as-knowledge wasn't "scientific" enough for her audience, but also because even when such instincts and experience work well, midwives have often downplayed their authority as knowers and therefore examples of their success are not powerful enough for a public policy argument.

In one instance, an apprentice midwife prevents a baby from bleeding to death simply by checking on him, but doesn't give herself credit for saving his life: "I don't like to think what might have happened if *someone* hadn't investigated the little noises he was making" (86, my emphasis). In discussing the apprentice's undervaluation of her role in the episode, Lay writes: "[the spokesperson's] challenge, then [...] was to legitimize midwives' knowledge to establish the midwives as knowers despite cultural assumptions and individual perceptions that might discredit their knowledge based on experience" (86). Midwives, like other professional feminist communities, value "women's ways of knowing," but don't present the known as if it were a solid truth, an effect that Lay suggests results from a bifurcated consciousness.

Extending the concept of bifurcation to my participants' stances offers at least one reason why Dee, Sandra, Donna, and Anna tend to focus on a work/home dichotomy, even amid the obvious variety of their talents and interests. Must home and work mutually exclude each other? Perhaps it did for these women, since housework remained, even while enrolled in college or working full time, their own individual responsibilities. The women, each of whom in this case are/were married to men, point out that while their husbands were supportive of their professional goals in terms of financial and moral support, few of them provided specific help in terms of housework. Anna relates that sharing household duties is part of a learning process for married men today. She sees a more balanced attention to housework within heteronormative families such as her daughter's and describes the arrangements for cooking, cleaning, and childcare of her daughters and sons-in-law: "Younger men expect to help with housework since their wives have careers. There was a strict gender division for housework in my time, for my generation, but not now."

Though their responses to questions regarding housework and literacy prioritize the professional over the domestic, none of the women solely identify themselves as professionals; indeed, their interesting variety of experiences is one of the reasons many of them enjoy the Red Hat Society so much. However, the women take similar stances regarding housework as an obstacle to more worthwhile professional, social, and personal pursuits: as Dee puts it, "more interesting things to do." In disparaging housework, the women distance themselves from the site of domestic roles and responsibilities that, in their experiences, does not command respect in the same way other sites do. Sandra enumerates housework's place in her life, which includes her marriage, her teaching career, Red Hat events, and avid travel: "Housework is not even secondary for women—more like 100th."

RHETORICAL RECIPES

In terms of the sociopolitical effects attributed to literacy in its traditional sense, the women who focused their literate energies on their professional success and personal interests have indeed made significant changes on both broad and personal scales. The broader anti-sex-ist social changes to which my participants have contributed include the blurring of gender roles within families, wide-spread acquisition of professional literacies by women under daunting material circum-stances, and wresting traditional domestic practices away from narrow conceptions of homemaking into sites of personal interest and satis-faction. The knowledge and skills the women have acquired in their range of literate experiences reflect Brandt's view of literacy acquisition as a response to large-scale technological and social changes such as the proliferation of the service economy, women in professional settings, and digital technology ("Accumulating" 660). In fact, the pursuit of higher education and professional literacy by these women and others like them not only respond to, but *constitute* such social change. One can understand the prioritization of the women's literacy practices.

Yet, the question of what to do with the theorized sociopolitical potential of everyday literacies remains. That is, how do expanded notions of "literacy as power," especially in regards to social practice literacy, help users if they themselves don't recognize them as even worthy of a brief conversation? In this case, inquiry into housework literacy and recipes occasioned an at-times uncomfortable re-telling of the women's struggles between housework and literacy, and I believe the women's descriptions of their literacy practices interrupt what oth-erwise threatens to become a seamless feminist progress narrative. It certainly reminds me that my opportunities to study, write about, and do (or not do) housework exist because of the experiences of women like my participants—including my own mother, whose acquisition of professional literacy constitutes a similar story—to which I am in-debted.

The women's struggles also offer support to Scribner's "literacy as power" myth, since they manifest limits of the power that practices of both everyday and institutional literacies can afford their users. On one hand, Edna's and Donna's uses of recipes reflect their commitments to certain value systems that motivate their practices and afford the women opportunities to contribute to and/or change the lives of their families and communities—Italian-Americans for Edna, the health profession for Donna. However, the women render these contributions almost meaningless by chalking their proficiencies in the kitchen up to "instinct" and "playing it by ear." One could also argue that these are such small and individual examples that there is no model that might be extrapolated and systematically employed to help those who are oppressed, as Brandt and Clinton have noted.

Additionally, consider the element of disregard that my participants bring to discussions of housework and literacy, evidenced by Sandra's scoffing and Dee's description of housework as the drudgery of the uneducated. While these stances align with a long-standing feminist argument against housework traceable to Charlotte Perkins Gilman's "sexuo-economic imbalance," or the connection between women's financial and social dependence on men, they also suggest emotional scars. The difficulty in pursuing literate success in the face of oppressive, gendered traditions has a long-lasting effect; not only has it minimized the participants' esteem of "home-based practices," but they continue to see housework as a threat to the rich lives they lead (Rumsey "Heritage" 584). Traditional literate success has not mitigated their resentment, even forty years after the fact.

In providing an account of the literacy practices of the Red Hat Society, a community of women who have banded together based on their common and difficult work histories, this study does not seek simply to celebrate domesticity with an uncritical "girl power" stance. That is, I want to honor the women's experiences while also conducting inquiry into what I see as a productive, though perhaps unpopular, context. Discovering the variations of the women's recipes for a number of rhetorical purposes and audiences within the women's families and communities unearthed very broad and flexible conceptions of what "recipe" can mean: cooking practices, interesting writing projects, or even a joke. For Donna and Edna, recipes are not a set of instructions, but an inventional resource for rhetorical decision-making in what is so often considered a limiting context. And, in their textual forms as relics and novelties, recipes comprise opportunities for Dee, Anna, and Donna to put their considerable knowledge and talents to the best uses they see fit, including to support traditional literacy institutions. The women whose professional literacies obscured the domestic obstacles in their way today enjoy a relative freedom to employ the literacy practices they wish in the contexts they wish, choosing to embrace, denounce, or ignore cooking and housework altogether.

NOTES

1. These names are pseudonyms the participants chose for themselves.

WORKS CITED

Barton, Mary and David Hamilton. *Local Literacies: Reading and Writing in One Community.* New York: Routledge, 1998.

Brandt, Deborah. "Accumulating Literacy: Writing and Learning to Write in the 20th Century." *College English* 57.6 (1995): 649-68.

Brandt, Deborah and Katie Clinton. "Limits of the Local: Expanding Perspectives on Literacy as Social Practice." *Journal of Literacy Research* 34.3 (2002): 337-56.

Cooper, Sue Ellen. *The Red Hat Society: Fun and Friendship After Fifty.* New York: Warner, 2004.

Creswell, John W. *Research Design: Qualitative, Quantitative, and Mixed Methods Approaches.* Thousand Oaks: Sage, 2003.

Doheny-Farina, Stephen and Lee Odell. "Ethnographic Research on Writing: Assumptions and Methodology." *Writing in Non-Academic Settings.* Ed. Lee Odell and Dixie Goswami. New York: Guilford, 1985. 503-535.

Fleming, Arline A. "Time for a cup of fun: Head to the Red Hat Society." *Providence Journal.* 8 Feb. 2002, C3. Web. 4 Jan. 2010.

Gilman, Charlotte Perkins. *Women and Economics: A Study of the Economic Relation Between Men and Women as a Factor in Social Evolution.* Boston: Small, Maynard & Co., 1898. *A Celebration of Women Writers.* Ed. Mary Mark Ockerbloom. Web. 18 December 2008.

Graff, Harvey J. *The Literacy Myth: Cultural Integration and Social Structure in the Nineteenth Century.* 1979. New Brunswick, NJ: Transaction, 1991.

Hogg, Charlotte. *From the Garden Club: Rural Women Writing Community.* Lincoln: University of Nebraska Press, 2006.

Lay, Mary M. *The Rhetoric of Midwifery: Gender, Knowledge, and Power.* New Brunswick, NJ: Rutgers University Press, 2000.

Minter, Deborah Williams, Anne Ruggles Gere, and Deborah Keller-Cohen. "Learning Literacies." *College English* 57.6 (1995): 669-687.

Red Hat Society. "About Us." 2009. 15 Mar. 2010. <http://www.redhatsociety.com>.

Rumsey, Suzanne Kesler. "Cooking, Recipes, and Work Ethic: Passage of a Heritage Literacy Practice." *Journal of Literacy and Technology* 10.1 (2009): 69-94.

_____. "Heritage Literacy: Adoption, Adaptation, and Alienation of Multimodal Literacy Tools." *College Composition and Communication* 60.3 (2009): 573-586.

Royster, Jacqueline Jones. *Traces of a Stream: Literacy and Social Change Among African American Women.* Pittsburgh: University Press, 2000.

Scribner, Sylvia. "Literacy in Three Metaphors." *American Journal of Education* 93.1 (1984): 6-21.

Sohn, Katherine Kelleher. "Whistlin' and Crowin' Women of Appalachia: Literacy Practices
Since College." *College Composition and Communication* 54.3 (2003): 423-452.

Span, Paula. "Hatless, and Aging on My Own Terms." *New York Times* 26 Oct. 2008. L19. Web. 21 Mar. 2010.

United State Census Bureau. "Rhode Island." *State and County Quick Facts.* 16 Aug. 2010. Web. 20 Sept. 2010.

Weiler, Kathleen. *Women Teaching for Change.* New York: Bergin and Garvey, 1988.

Yarnal, Careen, Deborah Kerstetter, Garry Chick, and Susan Hutchinson. "The Red Hat Society: An Exploration of Play and Masking in Older Women's Lives." *From Children to Red Hatters: Diverse Images and Issues of Play.* Ed. David Kuschner. Lanham: U Press of America, 2009. 144-165.

Young, Morris. *Minor Re/Visions: Asian American Literacy Narratives as a Rhetoric of Citizenship.* Carbondale: SIU Press, 2004.

COMPOSITION FORUM

Composition Forum is a peer-reviewed journal for scholars and teachers interested in the investigation of composition theory and its relation to the teaching of writing at the post-secondary level. The journal features articles that explore the intersections of composition theory and pedagogy, including essays that examine specific pedagogical theories or that examine how theory could or should inform classroom practices, methodology, and research into multiple literacies. *Composition Forum* also publishes articles that describe specific and innovative writing program practices and writing courses, reviews of relevant books in composition studies, and interviews with notable scholars and teachers who can address issues germane to our theoretical approach.

> *Composition Forum* and this article are on the Web at http://compositionforum.com/

Analogize This! The Politics of Scale and the Problem of Substance in Complexity-Based Composition

Noah Roderick's "Analogize This! The Politics of Scale and the Problem of Substance in Complexity-Based Composition" article addresses the debate over how much composition studies can or should align itself with the natural sciences. The author concludes that complexity-based descriptions of the writing act do align the discipline with the sciences, but that composition scholars must also be able to critique the neoliberal politics which are often wrapped up in the discourse of complexity. This article demonstrates *Composition Forum*'s unique focus on the intersections of composition theory and practice, as well as the journal's commitment to interdisciplinary research and scholarship.

2 Analogize This! The Politics of Scale and the Problem of Substance in Complexity-Based Composition

Noah R. Roderick

Abstract: In light of recent enthusiasm in composition studies (and in the social sciences more broadly) for complexity theory and ecology, this article revisits the debate over how much composition studies can or should align itself with the natural sciences. For many in the discipline, the science debate—which was ignited in the 1970s, both by the development of process theory and also by the popularity of Thomas Kuhn's *The Structure of Scientific Revolutions*—was put to rest with the anti-positivist sentiment of the 1980s. The author concludes, however, that complexity-based descriptions of the writing act do align the discipline with the sciences. But the author contends that while composition scholars need not reject an alignment with complexity science, they must also be able to critique the neoliberal politics which are often wrapped up in the discourse of complexity. To that end, the author proposes that scholars and teachers of composition take up a project of critical analysis of analogical invention, which addresses the social conditions that underlie the creation and argument of knowledge in a world of complex systems.

Any scan of the major rhetoric, composition, or literacy journals over the past ten years or so will show that complexity and ecology are rapidly becoming dominant metaphors in those fields. Given its position as a nexus between technology, communication studies, and the humanities, it is no surprise that many in composition studies, in particular, have eagerly taken up the banners of complexity science and ecocomposition. The epistemic and pedagogical possibilities of open-ing up scholarship and teaching in composition to complexity science and ecology studies are the subjects of countless dissertations, articles and books. Early overtures include Marilyn Cooper's article, "The Ecology of Writing" and Margaret A. Syverson's book, *The Wealth of Reality: an Ecology of Composition*, which took the crucial step of align-ing the epistemology of complexity with the ethics of ecology. More recent works, such as Byron Hawk's *A Counter-History of Composition: Towards Methodologies of Complexity* and Sidney Dobrin's *Postcomposi-tion*, continue to more fully develop the radical philosophical implica-tions of appropriating the discourse of complexity science. Combining recent insights from the physical sciences with the post-humanist phi-losophies of, among others, Martin Heidegger, Gilles Deleuze, Mark C. Taylor, and Gregory Ulmer, these more recent arguments for com-plexity are examining the deep relationship between information tech-nology, rhetoric, and the emergent properties of subjectivity, calling even for a post-subjective rhetoric.

In this essay, I revisit the relationship between science and com-position studies, claiming that the question of whether or not it be-longs to the sciences or to the humanities was not settled with the decline of the internalist- cognitivist movement associated with 1970s process pedagogy, as Robert Connors argued. I claim that composi-tionists need to take seriously the potential of complexity science to describe the writing act, not because the past decade has yielded any positive knowledge about, for instance, the writer's mind, but because the interface between the natural and social sciences has been radically altered. In other words, the interesting questions for when natural sci-entists and scholars in the humanities and social sciences talk are no longer so much about what the mind is or how to understand human-ity through the mind, but on how, for example, information flows, social networks, and animal metabolic rates can occupy the same on-tological field. Science, I argue, has traded in the metaphysics of the mind (as coherent unit) for the metaphysics of the eco-subject—a sin-gular field where seemingly unrelated phenomena become indistinct in their processes of emergence and transformation. Under this new metaphysical goalpost, then, the writing act can be described as being a function of network behavior rather than an effect of generalizable mental processes.

Briefly, the science of complex systems concerns itself with the way seemingly simple things or actions emerge from a multitude of actors, actions, and interactions. Complex systems emerge out of positive feedback loops, rather than linear, cause-and-effect relationships. In its origins, the study of complex systems is a composite of a diverse group of theories that date back over the past 130 years or so, including James Clerk Maxwell's *kinetic theory*, Kurt Gödel's *incompleteness theorem*, Friedrich von Hayek's *microeconomics*, and Claude Shannon's *information theory*, to name only a few. Objects of complexity science commonly include what we would normally think of as networks or systems, such as animal metabolic systems, aviation hubs, fractal topography, internet search algorithms, morphological computation environments, and information economies. It also offers descriptions of metaphysical phenomena (in that they are beyond spatial and temporal apprehension), such as consciousness, cognition, intelligence, experience, as well as questions of origins and existence (natural theology, natural history, evolution, cosmology). Indeed, as I will argue, its existence as a *science* of complex systems, beyond the sum of its composite theoretical parts, can hardly be conceived of without the exigency of such metaphysical questions to call it into being.{1}

The study of complex systems should not be conflated with quantum physics or chaos theory, because although the fields often share common theoretical origins and interact seamlessly, they differ in the range of things they attempt to explain. Chaos theory tends to refer to the way small actions or actors can have large or cascading effects inside of dynamic systems. For example, Edward Lorenz's famous butterfly flaps its wings in Brazil and effects a tornado in Texas. That kind of dynamic is indeed part of emergence in complex systems. But what those who study complexity are more interested in are how the many random actions of multiple actors regularly produce simple actions on a different scale (e.g., when a school of fish suddenly changes direction without a central command). This interest in the emergence of wholes also distinguishes (but does not separate) complexity science from the study of quantum mechanics. The latter is more fascinated by the way the physical world operates in qualitatively different ways at the subatomic level. Complexity science, too, is interested in such qualitative differences between the behaviors of a system and those of its component parts; however, complexity science extends its focus to comparisons of qualitative differences between emergent systems and their component parts. Complexity science therefore emphasizes a univocal view of reality, so that, for instance, as long as neural networks and social networks can be conceptualized as complex-adaptive systems, they are essentially the same substance—they just operate on different scales. Insofar as composition studies goes, rhetorical ecologies such as genre and activity systems may also emerge and behave as complex-adaptive systems. That point becomes particularly salient as the composing of texts, both inside and outside of the classroom, happens in a multimedia environment. Such digital and virtual forums act as accelerants in the proliferation of genres (by means of feedback loops), wherein relationships between writing subjects, media, audiences, institutions, and kairotic moments are constantly co-evolving.

A return to science is nothing for compositionists to shy away from, but as our knowledge-making practices become part of the constellation of complexity sciences, we should also develop a means to identify and critique the ideological baggage that the discourse of complexity carries with it. This essay represents the groundwork for such a critique. I shall argue that complexity science need not be a post-political project that naturalizes status- quo neoliberal capitalism, as many of the important voices of complexity science have presented it as doing. To the contrary, I will argue that composition studies has an opportunity to play an important role in describing how knowledge is produced and argued in a world of complex systems while offering new ways of critically examining the social conditions which make complexity-based knowledge claims valid and exigent.

COMPOSITION STUDIES AND SCIENCE

The first temptation in a critique of a complexity science of literacy and writing might be to argue that appropriating descriptions and methodologies of complexity in the natural sciences for the social sciences or for the humanities constitutes a misunderstanding or misuse of legitimate scientific knowledge, just as Robert Connors argued vis-à- vis cognitive science and process theory. His 1983 attack on the scientific claims of process theory ("Composition Studies and Science") provides what I would argue is an instructive example of the failure of such an argument. In her 1982 *CCC* article, "The Winds of Change: Thomas Kuhn and the Revolution in the Teaching of Writing," Maxine Cousins Hairston claimed that process theory, with its empirical methodology and scientific discourse, signaled the emergence of composition as a normal science. Composition, she claimed, had experienced a genuine paradigm shift from the disparate practices of current-traditional rhetoric to a relatively coherent, consensus-validated set of epistemological assumptions in process theory. Connors's response to Hairston not only disputes the idea that composition had entered any such paradigm, but further denies that science could ever offer the discipline anything except useful metaphors. Connors saw the enthusiasm in composition studies for the Kuhnian paradigm as being no more than part of a larger fad:

> Many have taken heart at Kuhn's description of the arrival of the first natural-science paradigms, which transformed chaotic, inchoate fields into orderly, normal-science endeavors over night … . The field of composition studies is by no means the only disciplinary area to be attracted to the image of the sciences and inflamed by Kuhn's explanation of them. (4)

At a most basic level, says Connors, compositionists are enamored with the elegant image Kuhn presents of the ossification of scientific knowledge being an inherently social process. But most powerfully, Connors argues that a Kuhnian description of the field offered compositionists "terms that were suitably vague," for "the implicit promise of universal scientific maturity" (17). In other words, a properly scientific description not only offered the still young discipline the assurance of a coherent definition of what constitutes legitimate knowledge in scholarship, but it also offered scientific credentials at a time when the humanities had all but lost its ability to offer privileged insight into the human condition.

Connors is happy to entertain empirical research for theoretical context, or to provide descriptive metaphors, but he warns that empirical context and scientific metaphors can never make the leap to applied scientific knowledge. Connors believes that making institutional practice work for descriptive, scientific analogies is not only deeply unscientific but it also leads to—and here I have a lot of sympathy for his argument—an erosion of the spirit of free inquiry, which, for Connors, the humanities embody:

> The push toward science in our field at the present time can lead all too easily to scientism, placing methodology at the heart of rhetorical education and tilting composition studies

> toward the sort of mechanistic concerns with neutral "tech-
> niques" that we wish in our best moments to transcend... .
> We should not in our search for provable knowledge forget
> that the essential use of all knowledge is in aiding humanity
> in the search for consensually arrived at truth. (19)

It is important to first of all parse out the different ways in which
Connors argues composition studies cannot be scientific. He is quite
correct in that *teaching* writing cannot be scientific any more than
teaching physics or chemistry can be scientific. But his assertion that
descriptive knowledge about the writing act cannot be scientific is problematic. First, his argument against positivistic descriptions of writing
is actually tautological, since the argument itself rests upon a logical-
positivist definition of scientific knowledge. Connors borrows directly
from Kuhn's famous positivist rival, Karl Popper, to define exactly
what scientific knowledge is, and therefore, why the theory choices
of a discipline like composition studies could never be understood as
being scientific. Connors's third "gate" criterion for the existence of a
genuine science states, "Hypotheses in scientific fields should be falsi-
fiable and should result in successful predictions, the success of which
should be explicable" (6). One of Kuhn's main objections to Popper,
however, was precisely that the grounds on which a theory is falsifi-
able are historically determined, and furthermore, that the establishment of a normal science can be described by the potentially falsifying
anomalies to its theories that it chooses to overlook (until, of course, a
paradigmatic crisis finally occurs).

Connors's other problematic objection to an accord between composition and the sciences is that the very status of cognitive science—to
which process theorists attached their research—as a science is doubtful. Connors once again locates the essence of a science in its experimental methodology rather than in the metaphysical phenomena (the
mind, evolution, etc.) it seeks to systematically describe. Experimental
method, then, is where he locates the shortcomings of psychology as a
science. Connors claims that some of the observational methods psychology has borrowed from the physical sciences were borrowed before
psychology "had any definite content":

> The natural science experimental method presupposes objec-
> tivity, an ideal whose meaning in the human sciences is ex-
> ceedingly problematical... . Psychologists have found much

to their chagrin, however, that the transaction between two atoms of hydrogen is not necessarily an accurate analog for the transaction between two human beings. (11)

But an analog between such micro- and macro -processes is precisely what methodologies of complexity attempt to do to studies of cognition and human interaction. Indeed, complexity science proposes nothing less than a fundamental reevaluation of our concept of analogy so that phenomena which would be essentially distinct in a mind-body epistemology occupy a single ontological plane, at least in terms of how they emerge. In his foundational text, *Gödel, Escher, Bach: The Golden Braid*, Douglas Hofstadter famously analogizes the relationship between individual neurons and cognition to individual ants and the ant colony. Each neuron, like each ant, reacts not to a central command, but to the activity of the neurons around it. What emerges from that recursive process then appears as if a response to a central command. The important insight of Hofstadter's view of complexity is that the self-organization of neurons/ants is not a single chain of responses from an external stimulus but rather a continual up-scaling of multiple chains of responses, a general process applying to all self-emergent phenomena. What's more, the same models of hierarchical clustering that describe self-organization at the cellular level are being directly analogized to systematically describe what we would more readily recognize as network phenomena, such as social organization and market behavior (Barabási 238). Given that it does call upon us to reconceive of analogy in ontological terms (in which case, *isomorphism* is more appropriate than analogy), it is not hard to see how externalist or post-process theories of literacy and rhetoric could be not just in productive conversation with complexity, but actually incorporated into the general matrix of a complexity science.

THE ETERNAL RETURN OF COMPLEXITY

Outspoken critic of sociological complexity science, Steve Fuller, dismisses the discourse of complexity in the social sciences as "metaphorical gas," unfavorably comparing it to nineteenth-century positivism. Indeed, the chief difference between the two movements, for Fuller, is that positivism was originally an anti-jargonist movement that was meant to provide some measure of public accountability for claims made in the social sciences, whereas complexity science, he claims, is actually a turn inwards, *towards* jargon. Moreover, Fuller argues that the social sciences's embrace of complexity theory has yielded no epistemic gains. Citing Émile Durkheim's theory of population and the division of labor, among others, as an example of what could be recast as in the light the popular complexity concept, tipping point, Fuller concludes, "these metaphorical extrapolations [from complexity science] that we make in social science are ones we already have." The question, then, is why, if complexity theory does not tell social scientists much they do not already know, has it been so enthusiastically adopted in the first place ? Fuller gives two explanations, with the first being a simple question of funding. Natural sciences are prestige knowledges, both in terms of state and of corporate funding. And among the natural sciences, genomics and cybernetics—from which a large section of complexity knowledge emerges—tend to generate the most excitement, both for the general public, and for their potential for several industries to generate new wealth. It is only natural that the social sciences would want to attach themselves to those revenue sources. Furthermore, Fuller argues that there is an "elective affinity" between postmodern politics and the rhetoric of complexity. {2} Social scientists have, by and large, abandoned the grand narratives of the nation-state and class struggle to explain social phenomena, instead embracing the permanence of global capitalism. And complexity science appears in most cases to affirm the economic wisdom of Friedrich von Hayek and Milton Friedman.

Fuller is absolutely correct in both of his explanations for the enthusiasm for complexity science in the social sciences, and the remainder of this paper will focus upon that elective affinity between neoliberal ideology and the appropriation of complexity in writing and literacy studies. But he is wrong to say that complexity science is just positivism in a sleek, new package. I argue complexity science cannot be the same thing as positivism, first of all because positivism, as it were, has no *positive* content to it as complexity science does. Positivism is a stance towards methods of knowledge making rather than a particular theory of natural processes. Furthermore, as I have indicated with regards to Connors's claims about cognitive science, positivist methods in the social sciences attempt to understand and predict individual and collective behaviors by building systematic descriptions of the mind, which, as a metaphysical object, is irreducible to the sum of its parts. {3} I argue that complexity science must be understood and critiqued through its own metaphysical foundations, and not by the metaphysics of the mind. The first challenge of critiquing complexity science in the social sciences is, therefore, not to try to prove how unoriginal it is but to identify precisely where and how it becomes new knowledge.

We could, for example, take a key concept for complexity compositionists, such as the *screen* (Bay; Hawk, "Toward"; Taylor, *Moment*; Hayles) and claim that it is merely a repackaging of Kenneth Burke's well-known concept of *terministic screens*. Consider one of the attributes of the terministic screen Burke gives against Mark C. Taylor's definition of the screen:

> Even if any given terminology is a *reflection* of reality, by its very nature as a terminology it must be a *selection* of reality; and to this extent it must function also as a deflection of reality ... . Here the kind of deflection I have in mind concerns simply the fact that any nomenclature necessarily directs the attention into some channels rather than others. (Burke 45)

> A screen, then, is more like a permeable membrane than an impenetrable wall; it does not simply divide but also joins by simultaneously keeping out and letting through. As such, a screen is something like a mesh or net forming the site of passage through which elusive differences slip and slide by crossing and criss-crossing. (Taylor, *Moment* 199-200)

From the outset, these two identifications of the screen match up pretty well. They both claim that any selection or ingress of reality/information is simultaneously a deflection into multiple contextual channels or passages. The difference lies in the context into which each of those identifications is articulated. For Burke, the screen extends— and extends from—what he already gives as his description of the human: "Man is a symbol-using animal" (3).

Against any previous definitions of the human as an inventor or communicator, he provides the example of a wren, who exhibits "genius" by using a bit of food as a way of baiting a reluctant chick out of its nest. Although other birds might be able to imitate the behavior, the wren would not be able to abstract the invention into a symbol in order to set off a chain of communication across the wren world. Communication, for Burke, both makes humans one with, and distinct from animals: "When a bit of talking takes place, just what is doing the talking? Just where are the words coming from? Some of the motivation must derive from our animalality, and some from our symbolicity" (6). The terministic screen provides Burke with a description for how his human-defining concept of "symbolicity" works in practice. Burke's screen is, therefore, thrown into and is reproducing his humanist ideology, but it also adds new knowledge about the human, which Burke's humanist ideology then comes around to legitimate. Similarly, Taylor's definition of the screen is thrown into a posthumanist ideological scheme: "In network culture, *subjects are screens* and *knowing is screening*" (200). Taylor's is an ontological notion of the screen in which humans are information interfaces among other interfaces, and in fact, are composed of self-similar, micro- interfaces. For Taylor, screens are not, as Burke would have it, modes by which we interact with reality; screens *are* reality. Drawing upon Claude Shannon's *information theory*, Taylor argues that being always exists at the apertural screen of noise and information (110 -11). Again, this concept of the screen is both reproducing and being legitimated by a posthumanist ideology, but it is also helping composition scholars to think of non-epistemic modes of rhetoric, particularly in network environments.

Even within arguments for an ontological description of rhetoric and communication, the same line of discontinuity should be drawn. For instance, in his 1978 article, "An Ontological Basis for a Modern Theory of the Composing Process," Frank D'Angelo talks a lot about evolution and complexity. Specifically, he writes, "the composing process is analogous to universal evolutionary processes, in which an original, amorphous, undifferentiated whole gradually evolves into a more complex, differentiated whole" (143). It quickly becomes apparent, however, that D'Angelo is working with evolution as a *metaphor* for consciousness. The ontological unity D'Angelo is arguing for exists between individual consciousness and the composing process. The kind of evolution D'Angelo conceives of is "teleological" (141). Leaving behind for a moment the fact that Darwinian natural selection is resolutely anti- teleological, D'Angelo's argument does not (actually, cannot) consider the mind itself as an assemblage, nor could it consider the monism of the mind and external stimuli. Complexity, instead, is here a product of the mind, which itself works through a kind of self-recognition process reminiscent of Hegel's master-servant dialectic:

> In the composing process, it seems that both conscious and
> subconscious processes take part. The subconscious mind
> provides the design, and the conscious mind provides its de-
> velopment.... ... Since the subconscious part of the mind is not
> always accessible for invention, the writer must aid the sub-
> conscious as much as possible by a deliberate and conscious
> effort, by defining the problem, by filling in the details, by
> carefully working out the design—in brief, by preparing the
> mind so that the subconscious can take over. (142 -43).

For a complexity theorist, such as Douglas Hofstadter, the very idea of
self-recognition is anathema. It is anathema not only because empirical
observation does not support the existence of separate realms of the
conscious and subconscious, but because the metaphysical foundations
from which complexity science attempts to systematically describe a
metaphysical problem like consciousness are univocal, as opposed to
the equivocalism of the subconscious-conscious dialectic. Again, when
comparing complexity theory to prior theories
that may have used similar metaphors, it is important to resist the
temptation to see complexity science as either a resurrection of an old
idea for fashionable purposes or as being part of a progressive continu-
ity of knowledge.

The danger here is that while a critic like Fuller might dismiss the
appropriation of complexity science as recycled or repackaged knowledge, complexity science advocates can use that same claim for indis-
tinction in order to advance a messianic notion of complexity, which
reifies the very logic of the neoliberal economics Fuller denounces.
Taylor, whose *The Moment of Complexity* inspired a special 2004 issue
of the *Journal of Advanced Composition*, argues that the emergence of
network culture absolutely closes the door on any form of cultural
analysis that does not begin with self-organization as a precept. Like
Francis Fukuyama (*The End of History*), Taylor places an all -encom-
passing historical break in 1989, when both the Berlin Wall fell and
when the Santa Fe Institute hosted its conference on "Complexity, Entropy, and the Physics of Information," which would become a major
entry point for complexity science in the social sciences (*Moment* 99).
At this point, "[t]he social and economic problems Marx and Engles
[sic] detected and the cures they prescribed reflect an industrial society
and its corresponding form of capitalism, which are passing away in
the moment of complexity" (100). Finally, Taylor proclaims that "[o]

ther than in certain corners of the university where the news of 1989 does not seem to have arrived, Marx has become irrelevant" (100). As a matter of fact, Taylor is more of a Fukuyaman than Fukuyama in his pronouncement. For Fukuyama, liberal democracy merely signaled the end to the ideological struggles that began with the French and American revolutions (4-5). But Taylor sees the emergence of network culture as constituting a unification of historically contingent cultural and economic practices with the timelessness of natural processes:

> One of the arguments in *The Moment of Complexity* is that physical, biological, social and cultural systems are bound in intricate loops of codependence and coevolution. This means that the cultural influences the natural as much as the natural influences the cultural.... . We are coming to understand that physical, biological, economic, and political processes are to a large extent information processes. ("An Interview" 809)

Taylor is here referring to Shannon's information theory, as well as to subsequent work on information in complex adaptive systems, which cast biological processes (at both the levels of micro-mutation and of macro -speciation) in terms of the random, recursive transformation of information and noise (*Moment* 136-37). The random, recursive transformation of information and noise is, in turn, governed by the thermodynamic process of entropy. Thus, mutations in an individual organism are random noise until they are realized as information when they connect with their ecological networks, the possibilities of which are conditioned by macro -species contacts. (This process constitutes a positive feedback loop, which, originally an information trope, has become one of the most important terms in complexity science.) Evolution is here not a matter of a successful individual organism filling a niche and so distinguishing itself from its species. Evolution in a feedback loop model is a convergent rather than a divergent process; it depends upon both network formation and competition, or a "marriage of self-organization and selection" (*Moment* 190). This noise/information loop model not only eschews the Darwinian arboreal model of evolution, but in terms of its implications for economic and cultural phenomena, it also supersedes the simple analogy between natural selection and Adam Smith's invisible hand of the market. Taylor argues that the natural selection/ invisible hand analogy was based upon a "doctrine of divine providence rewritten as economic theory" (180). However, it is clear that for Taylor the noise/information model demonstrates that thermodynamic processes, biological evolution, and market behavior are ontologically indistinct. This discovery that information threads through everything in nature not only makes the global information economy inevitable, but such an advanced state of capitalism simultaneously brings us to "the moment of complexity," giving us a special insight into the nature of reality that we could not have had before. In other words, "Like it or not, global capital is the reality with which we have to deal and simply bemoaning that fact or devising futile strategies of resistance will accomplish nothing" ("An Interview" 811).

THE MIND AND THE ECO-SUBJECT

The messianic arrival of network culture and complexity knowledge, for Taylor, calls upon us to conceive of expanded notions not only of information, but also of subjectivity and writing ("An Interview" 809). The sense that literacy and mediated communication can no longer be accounted for in terms of grammatical structures and universal processes has been growing for decades, as both a complement to process theory and as an argument against it. Post -process theory is probably the most notable example of the rejection of a coherent, internal account of literacy and writing. Thomas Kent, with whom post-process is most closely associated, applies to the writing act Donald Davidson's notion of "externalism," which functions "in opposition to internalist Cartesian conceptions of the world" (103). Clearly, this represents a departure from the metaphysics of the mind, of which earlier cognitive scientists tried to construct a systematic description. In addition to Davidson and Richard Rorty's neo-pragmatism, Kent draws heavily from Jean-Francois Lyotard's theory of postmodern knowledge (from whom he gets the *paralogy* in "paralogic rhetoric") and Lyotard's claim that the master narratives which provided legitimacy for universalist/objectivist scientific knowledge, such as nationalism and Marxism, are in irreversible decline. The consequence of this decline for Kent is a "grand aporia that lies at the heart of the master narrative of objectivity: the impossibility of representing an objective world through the subjectivity of language"—in other words, Lyotard is announcing the decline of the autonomous subject (71). For postmodernists in the humanities, the decline of grand legitimating narratives and the autonomous subject was generally something to be celebrated. Lyotard's proclamation represented a kind of liberation from the homogenizing constraints of scientism, which was particularly attractive to compositionists who, like Connors, were suspicious of scientific prescription in the humanities. Although he would later make it clear that the decline of grand narratives was something worth affirming, Lyotard's actual position in *The Postmodern Condition*—and this is something much less talked about— was not that science realized it could no longer account for the big metaphysical questions, but that it simply lost interest in them because of the divergent capitalistic interests that began providing most of the support for science's growing price tag in the late-twentieth century.{4} The inability to pose metaphysical questions for systematic description was not, therefore, the defeat of scientism, but the failure of the humanities to develop such questions for science.

The externalism of post-process theory, with its deep roots in neo-pragmatism, would certainly not forward a metaphysical phenomenon around which to build a systematic description that the writing act could be included in.

As Byron Hawk argues, Kent is still mired in an epistemic conception of rhetoric and "a reified notion of language use" (Counter-History 222). Hawk asserts that paralogic rhetoric cannot work beyond the linear, if not recursive, relationship between the "reader, writer, language, and text," in the communication triangle (221). Kent, therefore, reproduces the "subjectivity of language" that his anti-Cartesian stance is supposed to move beyond. There is indeed a growing consensus in composition studies (particularly among New Media specialists) that the increasing, post-genomic interconnection between technology and nature, as well as the rapid proliferation of rhetorical genres is exceeding our ability to account for the communicative act by language alone, even by such open-ended interpretive strategies such as Kent's. As Jennifer Bay puts it: "Taking complexity theory into consideration means we can no longer envision rhetoric as merely verbal, visual, and oral. Rather, rhetoric is networked among all three components through the ultimate screening device that is the body" (30). Thus, it is clear that it just will not do to drop the metaphysics of the mind without asking new kinds of metaphysical questions. This is why I don't think it is enough to characterize this new stance towards making knowledge as being "post-humanist," the term with which Katherine Hayles, Mark C. Taylor and others identify. Indeed, the "post- humanist," in this case appears to signify a negation of humanism, which is itself a very modernistic, dialectical stance. Rather than a negation of metaphysical boundaries (in this case, the parameters of the human), I prefer to think that we are in the midst of an epistemic break, in which new metaphysical boundaries are being drawn. In other words, we can think of ourselves as post-human, as long as we don't go thinking we're post-metaphysical.

I would argue that the metaphysical object that is emerging in the sciences in general, and to which complexity- and ecology-based theories of writing are attaching themselves is not a negation of the human subject ("Man") that gave rise to modern sciences, but an expansion of the reflexive subject. Instead of the human subject, we can perhaps call it the *eco-subject*, but it shares many of the key attributes that helped European science develop as a relatively coherent project (what Lyotard might include as a grand narrative of human progress) from the seventeenth century onwards. It must be noted first of all that the modern sciences of language, economics, and government, as well as the physical sciences, could not have developed as they did without a general understanding of the mind (as transcendent to the brain) as the core of the human subject. Michel Foucault argues that seventeenth- and eighteenth-century knowledges (collectively, the "Classical" episteme) were governed by the Cartesian idea that the human, with its ability to represent through language an already tabularized world, was exceptional in its relationship to nature. Furthermore, in "Classical thought, man does not occupy a place in nature through the intermediary of the regional, limited, specific 'nature' that is granted to him, as to all other beings, as a birthright" (310). At the end of the eighteenth century, however, Foucault claims that the relationship in the *cogito* between "I think" and "I am" became opaque, as the human became not just an outside observer of nature, but an object in nature to be observed as well (311-12). The idea of the mind as being opaque to the self, but nonetheless constitutive of Man within nature, provided the moderns with what Foucault termed an "empirco-transcendental doublet," which was a subject capable of making truth about the objective world only by rendering itself knowable as a historical object (318). This "finitude" of the mind served to productively limit what was and was not possible to know about the objective world, as well as how knowing was itself possible (i.e. epistemology).

Like Man, the eco-subject is the locus of knowledge, and as it is opaque to itself, it is also an object of knowledge. In other words, like Man, the eco-subject is a fully self-reflexive being. However, in the case of the latter, knowledge production is no longer the exclusive property of the mind. Additionally, the mind itself is no longer an organic brain which embodies a self-conscious and autonomous being.{5} The brain instead is immanent to the environment around it, a self-organizing collection of neural networks wherein thoughts happen as a result of individual neurons perceiving "signals from other individuals, and a sufficient summed strength of these signals causes the individuals to act in certain ways that produce additional signals" (Mitchell 6). The conscious mind is no more a centralized unit than a colony of ants or a traffic system. But that is not to say that consciousness is no more than the sum of the brain's neurons. Instead, consciousness is actually extended to stimuli the body experiences as it connects to its environment and other bodies. If consciousness is a series of complex networks that transcend the individual body, then thought is affect, rather than a dialectic between an immaterial unit and a material body. But although the eco-subject makes no distinction between the mind and objective reality, it is still a metaphysical unity because there remains an assumption that even phenomena which we have not apprehended operate on the same plane on which thought operates. It is, therefore, not so different from the Newtonian universe, which operated under the singular logic of God's mind, which itself was only different from the human mind as a matter of degree rather than substance.

CONSEQUENCES FOR COMPOSITION STUDIES

One of the consequences of the natural and social sciences galvanizing around the eco-subject, for composition studies, is that epistemology is being jettisoned in favor of ontology in the description of writing. Under this new knowledge regime, for instance, it is anathema to conduct research on topics such as the psychology of rhetorical invention, as process theorists had once done. Furthermore, the search for generalizable foundations of knowledge or for the conditions in which knowledge is created, which was at the heart of James Berlin's socio-epistemic rhetoric, are not interesting for complexity theorists, because in self-emergent, adaptive networks, those foundations are in such flux so as to be unobservable in any synchronic way. A further consequence of jettisoning epistemology is that the critical categories of race, class and gender are subsumed under the onto-political category of ecology. Sidney Dobrin and Christian Weisser argue, for instance, that ecology is just as valuable a critical category as the others (567), whereas Hawk goes further to claim that "race, class, and gender are reductive inventional topoi … which may or may not connect to students' local lived lives" (*Counter-History* 214). This is not a reactionary stance, but rather an expression of Deleuzean micro-politics, which is particularly well- suited to posthumanist complexity science. For Berlin, the power of race, class, and gender to produce social subjectivity is exerted though language, and so it is through critique of language that they are resisted. But from a micro-political perspective, resistance is exercised against totalization and sameness. This is achieved by the continuous invention of subjectivity by means of linking up desires between individuals, which, in turn, is experienced in terms of affect instead of as the result of a dialectic. In the classroom, this means that students "would need to, and be encouraged to, work out their own constellations that would mix our curriculum with their context, our theories and methods with their own political interests—should they have them" (Hawk, *Counter- History* 219). Thus in the place of politics and critique, the sciences of ecology and complexity gives us the ethics of linking and locality.

To the extent that a socio-epistemic understanding of writing is merely politically prescriptive without actually describing anything new about the embodied or localized conditions of knowledge production, the desire to leave it behind is understandable. But I argue it is equally undesirable to take a post-political stance, wherein we simply focus on developing pedagogical strategies which adapt and conform to the sciences of complexity and ecology. In order to cultivate a more productive interface with those sciences, composition studies should not only be engaged with the new knowledge regime concomitantly, but critically as well. Therefore, in addition to experimenting with eco- and complexity-based pedagogies, compositionists should also focus on (a) researching and teaching how knowledge is argued and produced under the regime of the eco-subject, and (b) critiquing the ideological assumptions of that knowledge regime.

Where I see work in rhetoric and composition making a critical contribution to the constellation of complexity sciences is on the question of invention. If indeed the cognitivist -process movement constituted a Kuhnian paradigm, the necessary crisis that called that paradigm into existence was the persistent lack of a coherent way to describe invention. It was the problem of invention that turned research in rhetoric and composition towards the writer's mind, and which led to a general consensus in the discipline that the relationship between mental processes and the writing act is recursive. Furthermore, as Anis Bawarshi argues, in understanding invention as internal to the mind, the cognitivist -process movement also "'invents' the writer as the primary site and agent of writing," therefore circumscribing agency to within the writer (51). That rhetorical invention is a non-linear process is not in question, but the fact that the mind as the agent of invention is being superseded by the eco-subject means that invention, and, therefore the writer's agency, are, once again, in need of coherent descriptions. The discourse of complexity seems to be able to provide such descriptions. A complex-ecological understanding of invention maintains that it happens through the emergence of *schemata*, in which experience is adapted to new contexts (Taylor, *Moment* 206). Hawk argues that in turn, "[e]nvironment, rhetoric, texts, and audiences are complex adaptive systems in themselves and together form other complex adaptive systems," and so "[w]hat we have are networks linked to other networks" ("Toward" 150). The convergence of singularities that create these contexts thus have as much part in the moment of invention as the writer does. Whereas a writer's agency in a cogntivist understanding was conditioned by her ability to gather objective knowledge about her audience and genre (a kind of *gestalt*), the writer's agency in a complex ecology depends on her ability to successfully adapt to new settings by making analogies to her experience of prior settings. That analogy is both the foundation of descriptive knowledge in complexity science (e.g., the analogy between traffic patterns and ant colonies) and also the means by which rhetorical invention occurs in complex networks actually affirms the disciplinary ethos of rhetoric and composition—that argument is not simply an arrangement of knowledge, but is inseparable from the very creation of knowledge.

While it is obviously valuable to teach students about the connection between analogy and invention as they negotiate their way through multimedia and multi-disciplinary environments, it is also essential that we not ignore the political dimension of analogy. Analogy is potentially political because it can provide the bridge between descriptive and prescriptive knowledge—in other words, what is and what should be. On one level, analogical invention could mean moving between texts in a genre, such as encyclopedic writing, in order to write a successful Wikipedia article. But it could also mean something more radical. For example, researchers from the University of Arizona's *Institute of the Environment*, working with agencies such as the

U.S. Department of Homeland Security, are developing a science of analogy between animal immune systems and global security against the decentralized threats of global terrorism and pandemic disease. The research team behind the project, Sagarin et al., claims: "The most potent biological analogy for human security is the immune system, which shifts from early, generalized responses to more adaptive responses as pathogens become more threatening" (293). Using a metaphor like "pathogen" to describe threats to security is nothing new. But Sagarin et al. are not, as propagandists and political leaders have done in the past, forwarding the comparison in order to strip the security threats of their humanity so that they can have license to treat them in inhumane ways. The question of humanity simply does not arise, as the difference between cell-level pathogens, global pandemics, and international security threats is a matter of scale rather than one of substance. The descriptive claim that global disease pandemics and terrorist groups organize and reproduce like pathogens in the body *causes* the prescriptive statement that those threats to security should be dealt with in ways analogous to the ways in which antibodies respond to pathogens. The overall descriptive analogy is incomplete without conceiving of the existence of scaled antibodies for both global pandemics and for people considered terrorists.

The student writing the Wikipedia article and the Sagarin team's study on global terrorism are both examples of invention because they are forging new links between phenomena in order to make new knowledge. But in neither case is there necessarily a historical understanding of the conditions that make those analogies valid or exigent, such as the revival of an Enlightenment project to make the world's knowledge universally accessible in the case of Wikipedia, or the phenomenon of post-nation-state sovereignty in the case of the pandemic/terrorist analogy. In order, therefore, to understand the social conditions that make an analogy valid or exigent, it is necessary to continue to call upon those sometimes reductive critical categories of class, race, gender, sovereignty, etc.

While I strongly reject Mark C. Taylor's assertion that a big political project like Marxism is an anachronism in the age of complex systems, it must be conceded that much of our talk in the humanities and social sciences about ideology and language falls on deaf ears, as far as the physical sciences are concerned. But this is not because complexity science can now explain social structures, communication, and lived experience ways that make social critique obsolete. Rather it is because for the past thirty years or so, basic science has been regarded and funded not as a big social project, but as a means to the fractured ends of the applied sciences. (In this respect, compositionists and those in the basic sciences already have a lot in common.) But with global economic and ecological catastrophes looming, capital "S" Science may again become a coherent, social project. That can only be a good thing for the humanities and social sciences, provided that we ask interesting questions which guide the project. Critical analysis of analogical invention, I believe, is the best way to start that conversation.

NOTES

1. Throughout this essay, I will talk about complexity "science" instead of "theory." Although "theory" is the currency of the realm n the humanities and the social sciences, my interest is in the moment at which composition studies appropriates the science of complexity, and in the social conditions that enable that moment.

2. Fuller uses the term, *elective affinity* knowing that it has strong resonance for sociologists. It was used in eighteenth century science to describe and predict chemical reactions. Max Weber later took the term up (from Goethe) in *The Protestant Ethic and the Spirit of Capitalism.*

3. In his *The Rules of Sociological Method* (one of the foundational texts in the social sciences), Durkheim goes to great pains to make a sharp distinction between sociology as a "science of institutions," and psychology, which is the science of the individual mind (lvi). However, Durkheim's central and very influential idea of the collective consciousness—radically different though it may be from individual consciousness—is still subject-object orientated, and is, therefore, just as tied into the Cartesian conception of the mind as was the field of psychology against which Durkheim was defining sociology.

4. "The State and/or company must abandon the idealist and humanist narratives of legitimation in order to justify the new goal: in the discourse of today's financial backers of research, the only credible goal is power. Scientists, technicians, and instruments are purchased not to find truth, but to augment power" (Lyotard 46).

5. Descartes is famous for his dualistic formulation of the human, being both animal body and eternal soul; however, he could not imagine the two entities co-existing without meeting in a real, physical space. He guessed, therefore, that the body and soul intermingle in the pineal gland, which is located at the base of the brain. This was, perhaps, an even more materialistic take on the mind than the one developed in nineteenth and

twentieth century psychology, wherein the unconscious was not located anywhere spatially, but was nonetheless immanent to the brain.

Works Cited

Barabási, Albert-László. *Linked: How Everything is Connected to Everything Else and What it Means for Business, Science, and Everyday Life.* NY: Plume, 2003. Print.

Bay, Jennifer L. "Screening (In)Formation: Bodies and Writing in Network Culture." *Plugged In: Technology, Rhetoric, and Culture in a Posthuman Age.* Ed. Lynn Worsham and Gary A. Olson. NY: Hampton P, 2008. 25-40. Print.

Burke, Kenneth. *Language as Symbolic Action: Essays on Life, Literature and Method.* Berkeley: UP of California, 1963. Print.

Connors, Robert J. "Composition Studies and Science." *College English* 45.1 (1983): 1-20. Print.

D'Angelo, Frank J. "An Ontological Basis for a Modern Theory of the Composing Process." *Cross-Talk in Comp Theory.* 2nd ed. Ed. Victor Villanueva. Urbana: NCTE, 2003. 141-50. Print.

Darwin, Charles. *The Origin of Species.* Alachua, FL: Bridge-Logos, 2009. Print. Dawkins, Richard. *The Selfish Gene.* 2nd ed. Oxford: Oxford UP, 1989. Print.

Deleuze, Gilles, and Felix Guattari. *Anti-Oedipus: Capitalism and Schizophrenia.* Trans. Robert Hurley, Mark Seem, and Helen R. Lane. Minneapolis: UP of Minnesota, 1983. Print.

Dobrin, Sidney. *Postcomposition.* Carbondale, IL: Southern Illinois UP, 2011. Print.

Dobrin, Sidney I. and Christian R. Weisser. "Breaking Ground in Ecocomposition: Exploring Relationships between Discourse and Environment." *College English* 64.5 (2002): 566-89. Print.

Durkheim, Émile. *The Rules of Sociological Method.* 2nd ed. Chicago: UP of Chicago, 1938. Print.

Flower, Linda, and John R. Hayes. "A Cognitive Process Theory of Writing." *Cross-Talk in Comp Theory.* 2nd ed. Ed. Victor Villanueva. Urbana: NCTE, 2003. 273-98. Print.

Foucault, Michel. *The Order of Things: An Archeology of the Human Sciences.* NY: Vintage, 1970. Print.

Fukuyama, Francis. *The End of History and the Last Man.* NY: Free P, 2006. Print.

Fuller, Steve. "Is Complexity Theory Just Postmodern Positivism?" Steve Fuller, Audio Lectures. University of Warwick, Department of Sociology. 12 Sep. 2005. WAV file. 8 Jan. 2012.

Graves, Heather Brodie. "Marbles, Dimples, Rubber Sheets, and Quantum Wells: The Role of Analogy in the Rhetoric of Science." *RSQ: Rhetoric Society Quarterly* 28.1 (1998): 25-48. Print.

Hairston, Maxine Cousins. "The Winds of Change: Thomas Kuhn and the Revolution in Teaching of Writing." *The Norton Book of Composition Studies.* Ed. Susan Miller. NY: Norton, 2009. 439-450. Print.

Hawk, Byron. "Toward A Rhetoric of Network (Media) Culture: Notes of Polarities and Potentiality." *Plugged In: Technology, Rhetoric, and Culture in a Posthuman Age.* Ed. Lynn Worsham and Gary A. Olson. NY: Hampton Press, 2008. Print.

———. A Counter-History of Composition: *Toward Methodologies of Complexity.* Pittsburgh: UP of Pittsburgh, 2007. Print.

Hayles, N. Katherine. *How We Became Posthuman: Virtual Bodies in Cybernetics, Literature, and Informatics.* Chicago: UP of Chicago, 1999. Print.

Hofstadter, Douglas. *Goedel, Escher, and Bach: An Eternal Golden Braid.* NY: Basic Books, 1999. Print.

———. *Fluid Concepts and Creative Analogies: Computer Models of the Fundamental Mechanisms of Thought.* NY: Basic Books, 1995. Print.

Kent, Thomas. *Parlogic Rhetoric: A Theory of Communicative Interaction.* London: Lewisburg-Bucknell UP, 1993. Print.

Krauss, Lawrence M., and Robert Sherrer. "The End of Cosmology ?: An Accelerating Universe Wipes out Traces of its Own Origins." *Scientific American* (Mar. 2008): 23-26. Print.

Kuhn, Thomas. *The Structure of Scientific Revolutions.* Chicago: UP of Chicago, 1970. Print.

Lyotard, Jean-Francois. *The Postmodern Condition: A Report on Knowledge.* Trans. Geoff Bennington and Brian Massumi. Minneapolis: UP of Minnesota, 1984. Print.

Marx, Karl. *Capital Volume I.* Trans. Ben Fowkes. London: Penguin Classics, 1990. Print.

Mitchell, Melanie. *Complexity: A Guided Tour.* Oxford: Oxford UP, 2009. Print.

Pinker, Steven. *The Blank Slate: The Modern Denial of Human Nature.* NY: Penguin, 2003. Print.

Sagarin et al. "Decentralize, adapt and cooperate." *Nature* 465 (2010): 292-93. Print.

Shannon, Claude E., and Warren Weaver. *The Mathematical Theory of Communication.* Urbana: UP of Illinois, 1998. Print.

Syverson, Margaret. *The Wealth of Reality: An Ecology of Composition.* Carbondale: Southern Illinois UP, 1999. Print.

Taylor, Mark C. "An Interview with Mark C. Taylor." *JAC* 24.4 (2004): 805-19. Print.

————. *The Moment of Complexity: Emerging Network Culture.* Chicago: UP of Chicago, 2001. Print. Ulmer, Gregory. *Internet Invention: From Literacy to Electracy.* NY: Longman, 2002. Print.

COMPOSITION STUDIES

Composition Studies is on the Web at http://www.uc.edu/journals/composition-studies.html

The oldest independent periodical in the field, *Composition Studies* is an academic journal dedicated to the range of professional practices associated with rhetoric and composition: teaching college writing; theorizing rhetoric and composing; administering writing related programs; preparing the field's future teacher-scholars. We welcome work that doesn't fit neatly elsewhere.

"So what are we working on?" Pronouns as a Way of Re-Examining Composing

This piece is an excellent example of the value of situated research methods to the field of writing studies. The authors examine power relationships in a writing center by theorizing from practice, an anchored research approach that is rooted in one of the major tenets of *Composition Studies*: practitioner knowledge matters.

3 "So what are *we* working on?" Pronouns as a Way of Re-Examining Composing

Kate Pantelides and Mariaelena Bartesaghi

The encounters of writing center tutors and clients, this essay argues, are tensional, asymmetrical, and productive negotiations of a coauthored *we*. As authorship and authorization are discursive processes, we offer an empirical examination of how personal pronouns mark important shifts in the dynamic creation of a shared academic manuscript in writing center consultations. Though it is tempting to analyze the work of *we* as simply inclusive, our analysis proposes that *we* is multifunctional, periodically signaling collaborative affiliation and disaffiliation, marking the negotiation of coauthorship, implying shared identity, and acting as an indicator of institutional discourse.

The fictitious notion of the perfect writing consultant (who is neither too directive nor too hands-off) or perfect composition instructor seems to loom large—a destructive figure who inhabits the discourse of theory. He or she is an ideal whose invocation encourages a narrative of guilt that does not get told at the center of writing center scholarship, but remains at the periphery, whispered in conversations about praxis. Although empirical work lays bare ways in which writers and consultants negotiate work, authorship, and responsibility, the question remains how these behaviors should be construed. How can and should praxis be adapted? Can we do better at defining our expectations for this continuum of interaction for consultants and clients to alleviate the inevitable guilt that comes with the binary presented in literature?

To answer these questions and better understand the actual complexity of writing center collaboration—collaboration that is neither purely "peer," non-interventionist, nor authoritative, colluding expert—we approach the issue discursively, seeking to illuminate what lies between institutional discourse and interactional practice and to open up possibilities for an alternative discourse of praxis to take its place. We base our analysis on an empirical study of writing consultations over the course of a semester at a large RU/VH institution. The selections considered here are derived from ten writing consultations between graduate student consultants and graduate student clients at our university's writing center that were recorded and transcribed by the first author. The writing consultants are all MA and doctoral-level students from the English, World Languages, and Communication departments, and the clients are graduate students from across the disciplines. We find graduate student interaction analytically compelling, and the consultation serves as a privileged site for an exploration of their institutionally hybrid status, both with respect to each other and to the context that the consultation both invokes and (re)produces

The encounters of writing center tutors and clients, this essay argues, are tensional, asymmetrical, and productive negotiations of a co-authored we. As authorship and authorization are discursive processes, we (also as coauthors) offer an empirical examination of how *we*, *I*, and *you*, mark important shifts in the consultants' and clients' dynamic creation of a shared academic manuscript. In analyzing coproduction and coauthorship, we do not, however, subscribe to the idea of *collaboration* as it presently appears in writing center and composition metadiscourse. We do not add to the robust literature where the term is evaluated as an activity which consultants (and ironically, for a term which includes two people, that is where the blame falls) in the writing center don't do *well* or could do much better or indeed engage in *badly*. By disengaging from the present view of collaboration, which has been part of writing centers since the work of scholars such as Stephen North and Jeff Brooks, we propose two things.

The first is to wrest praxis from the constant evaluative oscillation of writing center disciplinary terminology (i.e., good-bad, collaboration-collusion, symmetry-asymmetry, consultant or peer; see review of literature which follows) which can condemn or (more rarely) praise, but offers no lingo for productive analytical discussion, or transferal of a way to do things in terms of skills and bona fide strategies. What we offer in its place is an empirical examination of what it is that writing practitioners and writing center participants actually *do* when enacting the practice of composing. The second is to encourage a re-articulation, or a way to relanguage our doings—to an audience within and beyond the writing center itself—in a way that better represents and values the complexities of our work. *Collaboration* may serve well as an interpretive shell for a complex interactional sequence, but it is a gloss, and it does little to help us understand the dynamic itself.

A good place to start our examination of writing center discourse is with the figure of the consultant. As a primary character in writing center helping narratives, the writing consultant appears to clients and the university at large under several guises. Most writing center models oscillate between conceptualizing consultants as helpers in an authority dynamic structured in top-down fashion (Shamoon and Burns 140-48); we find them cast in various roles, as coaches, teachers, and even therapists (Harris 35-40). Conversely, consultants can be portrayed as cheerleaders on the sidelines (Brooks 2). Rarely are they presented as they are in practice—chameleons that change their colors dependent on the moment-by-moment discursive requirements of the consultation.

To add a new (dark) twist to this plot, a recent empirical study of writing center praxis argues that the relationship between consultants and client-writers is based on *collusion*, defined as a consultant-enacted, client-disempowering array of practices of "the same old authoritarian control" (Lunsford qtd. in Rollins, Smith, and Westbrook 122), masquerading as collaboration. The critique might be renewed but its discursive backdrop is familiar. Indeed, the idea(l) of collaboration as "textual nonintervention" (Clark and Healy 36) has guided composition praxis in the writing center since North's 1984 treatise "The Idea of a Writing Center." In a relationship defined by helping, North drew a counterintuitive boundary between consultants' actions and writers' expectations, facilitation, and intervention. In a political relationship defined by helping, inscribed in helping discourse (see Edelman) where one party defines the terms in which what becomes known as help will be understood and delivered to the other (Bartesaghi 16), North drew an uncertain binary between peerdom and directiveness, writer's work and consultant's help. For, if as North saw it, consultants "are not here to serve, supplement, back up, complement, reinforce, or otherwise be defined by any external curriculum" (79), consultants' help is done by "talk[ing] to writers." However, despite North's subsequent willingness to reconsider his line in the sand (see North, "Revisiting"), not to mention others' arguments as to the complexities and practical impossibility of textual nonintervention in writing center interaction (see Ede and Lunsford), the existence of a "legitimate and illegitimate collaboration" discourse is, as Wittgenstein famously wrote, a picture that holds us captive (Clark and Healy 39). It is in our language, and our language repeats it to us, helps us reconstruct it, subscribe to it and, subsequently, even prescribe it.

Though we primarily refer to them as consultants and clients, thus choosing a metaphor from counseling of a various nature, writing center interlocutors in our data are both graduate students. They both orient to particular material realities within the academy,[1] and do so discursively. That is, graduate student-clients bring their writing to the center to ensure that they can speak the language of their respective academic discourse communities (see Berkenkotter and Ravotas), a linguistic accomplishment that most graduate writing consultants are also desperately trying to finesse. Both student-consultants and clients still struggle with many of the same issues that undergraduates do—meeting the requirements of assignments, structuring arguments, polishing manuscripts—but often these struggles are magnified, in writing theses and dissertations, developing IRB protocols, and trying to construct professional ethos. Because we propose to opt out of the binary that paints authority and collaboration as oppositional, we instead focus on the asymmetrical complexities that collaboration entails by examining how graduate student consultants and clients use pronouns when talking about composing.

Collaboration in Writing Center Practice: A Reconstruction

Within writing center studies, scholars have explored what collaboration entails by examining consultant-client discourse in terms of the dynamic of asymmetry implicit within helping relationships where "those who self-define as giving help set the parameters of the relationship defined as helping; within that relationship, helpers and helped have different access, rights, and duties in the negotiation of its terms" (Bartesaghi 16). In "Scaffolding in the Writing Center: A Microanalysis of an Experienced Tutor's Verbal and Nonverbal Tutoring Strategies," Isabelle Thompson defines scaffolding as strategies which "[support] students while they figure out answers for themselves" (423). She examines a "successful" tutorial in terms of the asymmetrical practices that take place in this interaction: direct instruction, cognitive scaffolding, and motivational scaffolding, signaled in both talk and gesture. Urging the writing center community to not mark directiveness as inherently problematic, Thompson cites its appropriate use as one of the most important facets of a successful tutorial. She writes that a student must be "motivationally ready ... [for] tutors [to] be productively directive. If tutors are too directive too early, before students are motivated to be active participants, the conference is not likely to be successful" (447).

Similarly, in her article "Dominance in Academic Writing Tutorials: Gender, Language Proficiency, and the Offering of Suggestions," Terese Thonus examines tutors' directives, accepting them as a natural and necessary part of writing center action, and she seeks to tie the strategies by which tutors enact dominance to gender and language ability. In her study of 16 consultations, she charts the frequency and type of suggestion as it correlates to gender and speakers' language status. While Thonus acknowledges that writing consultants' position within the institution provides them with shaky authority, she concludes that more than any other variable, institutional affiliation grants dominance most visibly (244).

As useful as Thompson's and Thonus's findings are, they intensify the metadiscursive disconnect between what we theorize and practice and *how we theorize what we practice.* Consider how writing centers employ the discourse of "collaboration" to situate themselves within their universities. A case in point is the authors' university writing center website, which characterizes writing center interaction in the following way:

> Writing Center consultations are fifty minutes long and begin at the top of each hour. Consultants do not offer proofreading or editing services; instead, sessions are conducted collaboratively, and consultants make suggestions to help writers develop their *own* work. ("Writing Center")

Such a preface leaves consultants and clients unsure of what the consultation will actually entail. What is the magical interaction that is not proofreading, not editing, but instead—appropriate collaboration?

Given this disconnect, it is up to consultants and clients to interpret and negotiate the meaning of "collaboration" in the moment-by-moment exchanges of the consultation as it occurs. In contrast to instructors, consultants' identities as collaborators are languaged in symmetrical terms; they are non-experts, non-evaluators, helpers that simply allow students to free themselves from writer's block. As graduate students helping other students—who are often going through the same milestones of university education—consultants occupy a hybrid "status that is equal yet somehow unequal" (Williams 38). Since writing center consultations usually begin with a discussion of the writer's project, the writer reading her work out loud, and then a move to Socratic discussion regarding what the writer would like to change, praxis can easily be construed as "textual nonintervention." But the idea(lization) of the consultant as a ventriloquist of sorts, who merely provides students access to their "voices," tricks consultants into being taken in by a (metadiscursive) Wittgensteinian picture that is incoherent with practice. And it tricks us, as writing center users and theorists, into imagining consultants as not actually doing anything other than enabling a process that pre-existed the consultation: a monologic vision which allows scripting of the very process and its characters. Discursive work adds actual voices to this monologue, suggesting that opting out of the picture is an empirical project, from the inside out.

Brooke Rollins, Trixie Smith, and Evelyn Westbrook explore the discourse of writing center praxis in terms of interactional ethos. In their study of graduate consultations, they examine how consultants use tools that, they argue, covertly deny authority: claiming ignorance, using embedded directives, and relying on the inclusive pronouns *we* and *us*. They write that:

> inclusive pronouns ... suggest that the client is actively involved in issuing directives. This use of inclusive pronouns is the most simplistic, yet perhaps most representative method of disguising the assistant's authority. ... For example, when an assistant uses the phrase "We decided..." rather than "I decided...," she insists that the decision is a joint one. (128)

Thus, for Rollins, Smith, and Westbrook, tutor contributions are directive, but covertly so: they are based on collusion. What is troubling about their analysis is that, by focusing on so-called tutor's authority, they do not take into account the dynamic, back-and-forth features of interaction, or how clients also use pronouns in the consultation.

We are interested in showing how in spoken discourse, or talk-in-interaction, pronouns reveal a speaker's positioning toward the topic at hand. This allows us to examine both the immediate context of the relationship of consultant and client and the broader frame of institutional discourse of composing within which this relationship takes place. In contrast, Communication scholars Kathleen Haspel and Karen Tracy have examined pronoun usage as a productive site for understanding speakers' strategies of affiliation and disaffiliation to what they are speaking about. In their examination of a disagreement at a school board meeting in "Marking and Shifting Lines in the Sand," the authors consider how varied the work of *we* and *they* can be. Alternately used as inclusive, disaffiliative, and accusative, Haspel and Tracy see how *we*, especially, is used by speakers to successfully claim a particular identity and strengthen their claims. Like Haspel and Tracy, our study values the insight pronoun use provides into discursive collaboration, and we use them to detail the nature of the asymmetrical relationship enacted within writing center consultations (as suggested by Thompson).

DISCOURSE ANALYSIS

In his recent contribution to *Composition Studies,* Paul Walker proposes discourse analysis as a method for reconstituting Composition's theoretical metavocabulary—terminology, enactment, and practical consequentiality. In also adopting a discursive approach, we continue Walker's reflexive move. As a method, DA involves recording, faithfully transcribing, and analyzing talk. An important metatheoretical assumption of this process of recording and transcription is that, though DA focuses on problematic communication settings, answers are not known ahead of time, but derived inductively from the data. Authority, or what is known in critical theory as power, is seen in DA as a dynamic of talk in interaction: it has to be claimed, and authorized, by participants in the talk, within a particular context. By focusing on clients' and consultants' use of pronouns, and their switches between the singular *I* to the inclusive *we*, our analysis emphasizes speakers' available resources (see Fairclough; Haspel and Tracy) for claiming singular and shared ownership of a text. Invoked by these claims are relationships of identity and responsibility which themselves speak of the discursive context of the consultation as helping interaction in an institutional setting. Our transcription notation is at an intermediate level of detail (see Gilewicz and Thonus); we capture pauses, simultaneous or overlapping speech, vocalizations, emphases, false starts, and non-verbal features of the interaction (see Appendix for transcription notation).

ANALYSIS: PRONOUN USE IN WRITING CENTER INTERACTION

In the sections that follow, we present four extracts from writing consultations to show how graduate students—as both consultants and clients in the writing center—avail themselves of pronouns to coproduce new meanings, a new textual composition, and reflexively share the work of composing. We offer this examination as an opening to set aside what is presently argued about collaboration and offer a way to reconsider it as a multifaceted interactional praxis along a continuum of asymmetric helping strategies.

WE AS INFLUENCE

As a practice which materializes and reformulates its institutional context, the writing center consultation is a dynamic of what Bazerman and Paradis define as influence, "a means of inducing or enrolling outsiders into an insider's view and commitments" (7). Pronouns influence by negotiating speaker's positions of insider and outsider as institutional members, or experts, raising questions of who may influence whom and whose commitments about the writing process are more important in an exchange. We illustrate this use of pronouns in an extract from a consultation, below, in which a graduate student client working on her dissertation in Education (G) meets with a graduate student writing consultant (T). Although G has decided to use the writing center throughout her dissertation process and she has scheduled appointments throughout the semester, this is one of her first consultations, as is made clear by her unawareness of writing center praxis:

Extract 1

```
55   G:   You don't have to read it like (.) you can read it quietly. I mean,
56        I've got other stuff that I can do.
57   T:   Well maybe what we can do is actually (.) to make sure that your
58        meaning and intentions are clear. So maybe I'll read the first ten lines out
59        [loud
60   G:   [O.K.
```

61   T: And we can make sure we're on the same um (.) paycheck.

In line 57, the consultant uses *we* as a corrective response to the student's *I* and *you* presentation. Since the student has agreed to work on her project in the writing center but has not worked with a consultant before, she sets the terms of the helping relationship as one in which she and the consultant will take turns developing her work independently. His *we* reconstructs the student's terms within the appropriate institutional discourse of the consultation, reframing both the immediate praxis (i.e. how things will go) and inducting her into the discourse of writing center ideology.

In line 61, the consultant uses humor to mitigate his directive, encouraging the student to be on the same "paycheck" as opposed reading the work "quietly" to himself (Line 55); this deliberate use of *we* signals a "complex transformation, involving shifts of meaning and new perspectives," that asks the student to conceive of the helping relationship in a different way (Linell 148). Rather than simply signaling tutorial "collusion," the use of the inclusive pronoun functions as a creative way to induct the student into an institutional way of seeing and reconstructing the meaning of praxis from a client-led to a consultant-led dynamic. Instead of sitting idly by while the consultant does the work of the consultation, *we* invites the student to partake in writing center praxis, that of reading the paper out loud. The fact that the extract is sealed with an "OK" in a cooperative overlap (lines 59 and 60) suggests that the student accepts the consultant's invitation.

WE AS COAUTHORSHIP

Once they are presented to consultants at the writing center, client manuscripts become part of a cycle of talking and writing (see Labov and Fanshel) where the lines between suggestions for improvement and composing become blurred. This very tension, which involves the amount of responsibility toward the shared text, is signaled in consultants' strategies of affiliation and disaffiliation toward the manuscript they are working on with a client. Accordingly, *we* is used to signal the consultant's accountability toward the text as a shared, coauthored institutional product. Conversely, the consultant also shifts pronouns to distance himself from its coproduction and render the student accountable for it. As Haspel and Tracy argue, "In using a reference term, speakers state or imply their membership in one category (we) and, at the same time, their nonmembership in a contrast category (they)" (148). In the context of the charged school board meeting that they observe, Haspel and Tracy examine how a speaker begins his discussion by using *we* to "initially [position] himself as someone speaking on behalf of his wife and himself," and then soon turns to *they* when addressing the troublesome material at the center of the meeting (148-152). The following extract follows a similar pattern.

In this exchange, the pair is engaged in considering the client's response to an article. Since the client, a Higher Education MA student, is a frequent user of the Writing Center, she quickly recognizes the troublesome aspect of her request to work on a paper hours before it is due. From the outset, there is a tension between what the client (S) wants to work on and the consultant's (T) agenda for the paper.

Extract 2

16	T:	And when is this paper due?
17	S:	(4.0) ((laughter))
18	T:	Today?
19	S:	Today.
20	T:	To<u>day</u>? Oh my goodness. We'll see what we can do. Okay um.
21		What I'd like you to do (.)
22		You mind reading this out loud?

Notice how the consultant reacts to this common occurrence in the writing center: the challenge of an imminent deadline. He immediately introduces *we* in Line 20, signaling that the challenge of the due date might be something that they can confront together. In line 17, the student responds to the consultant's question about the deadline with a long pause and laughter, which signals her hesitation to introduce the troublesome material (see Jefferson). The trouble is reinforced by the consultant's correct guess that the paper is due "today" (line 18) and the student's emphatic repetition (line 19). In lines 20-21, the consultant orients to this trouble with an interesting pronominal switch, outlining the tension between what is doable and accountable as shared product and what is, instead, positioned individual academic accomplishment. In this short extract, pronouns already accomplish quite a bit of work, first signaling solidarity, then suggesting how the student is responsible for the work at hand.

The tutor reinforces the shared plan for the session in line 20 with "okay" and the subsequent vocalization "um." In this case, the discourse marker "okay" acts as a repair, that is, it allows the consultant to "take back" his prior version, in which he would be directly accountable for a paper "due today." Not finishing his utterance, he then switches to *I*, to do something he is solely accountable for. Here the singular pronoun marks the consultant's invocation of the ideological tenet of textual responsibility, where the student's role is to be solely responsible for the academic text and the consultant's role is not to intervene. Note, however, that this ideology can only be enacted by means of a clear directive on the consultant's part (line 21), though the additional backtrack in the following turn, "You mind?" hedges and mitigates the force of his instruction. This short extract encapsulates thirty seconds when the consultant oscillates between degrees of responsibility, demonstrating the complexities of working at the boundary of, and embodying, the liminal "equal yet somehow unequal" role.

WE AS SHARED IDENTITY

Whereas *we* may mark shifts in the helping asymmetry, it can also display clients' and consultants' co-orientation to the academic text as an emergent institutional product and their co-incumbent position as graduate students within the academy. Their orientation to a joint identity is exemplified in the following exchange between a graduate student consultant (T) and client (S), an MA student in Criminology, where the two are focused on the matter of correct APA citation. We present the beginning of the consultation (lines 1-3) and then move to a later segment of the exchange (lines 36-45) to continue our analysis.

Extract 3

```
1   T:   Okay, so what are we working on?
2   S:   Um, so we're looking at a paper for this course and she basically
3        suggested that everybody come, basically, you know for APA style
[[...]]
36  T:   Alright, let's find those headings. They're all so weird.
37  S:   Yeah, I was just looking at the (website).
38  T:   Yeah, that's frustrating because it can be like really confusing. Because
39       you don't know [which to trust
40  S:                  [Exactly
41  T:   Definitely.  [That's no fun
42  S:                [((laughter))
43  T:   I think that's the right page, we've got seven different options there.
44       (10.0) ((read paper)) Okay
45       yeah (5.0) ((read paper))
```

The consultant begins the interaction with an invitation to work on the task of correct citation together, beginning the dialogue with "What are we working on?" (line 1). The student accounts for her place in the writing center in an interesting way; by explaining that her professor encouraged "everyone" to come and that she just needs help on citation (lines 1-3), she modifies the consultant's *we* by making her professor responsible for her need to "work on" something. Additionally, she makes "everyone" part of the collective who needs writing center help and herself as needing assistance on APA style (line 3). The consultant's uptake of the client's response introduces a new grouping of *we* to the consultation: a "let's" (line 36), that includes the consultant and the client. This *we* marks a shared task between the two, which the consultant expands in the second part of her turn in line 36 regarding APA rules: "They are all so weird." With this small self-disclosure that reveals the consultant as also a graduate student miffed by APA citation, the tutor brings about a shift in the consultation. This is a discursive shift materialized in praxis, as we now see the pair engaged in reading the text together (an action not instructed by the consultant) and looking up information toward a common goal.

The consultant's additional contribution in line 38 illustrates how shared identity can be cultivated by graduate students working together in a collaborative asymmetry. The tutor's introduction of confusion and issues of "trust" (lines 38-39), with respect to information about correct citation, are direct claims of her identity as a novice or learner within the academic setting that she and her interlocutor occupy. The sincerity of this identity construction notwithstanding, we see by the client's overlapping speech in lines 40-41, and the laughter at the tutor's humor (line 42), that it functions as a bridge for the client to meet the consultant in a shared space.

WE AS MARKER OF INSTITUTIONAL DISCOURSE

In this final example, the tutor (T) begins the consultation with the usual question, "what [are we] working on today?" (line 1). The student (J), an ELL doctoral student in Education, reads this question as a prompt for her writing center literacy narrative, describing her work with other writing consultants and the focus of her project in the writing center (lines 8-13). Although she answers the initial request for information with *I* (line 2-3), the client switches to *we* in her own narrative (line 12), signaling the coconstruction of discourse in the center and her knowledge of the writing center consultation as a specific genre of helping relationships, complete with expected writing center "talk" and requests. As Jessica Williams suggests, writing center interaction functions as a type of institutional discourse (37). Although it is distinct from "workplace talk," writing center discourse stands at the "intersection" of two types of institutional discourse, expert-client, as in commercial settings, and expert-novice, as in educational settings (39).

Extract 4

1	T:	Ok, ((clears throat)) so what exactly is it we're working on today?
2	J:	I've been—I've been meeting for a couple of weeks with the other tutors.
3		I've been meeting many people really [((laughter))
4	T:	[((laughter))
5	J:	I've been working on this proposal and I almost submit
6		submit it next week (.) aaand I'm just trying to see what I can do.
7	T:	((laughter))
8	J:	Definitely, I have limited time. I cannot really (2.0) uh (2.0) have fixed.
9		everything fixed. But for myself (.) I've told the other tutors.
10		I go to improve my writing skills, umm, I know that right now
11		I'm doing my dissertation, so uh, I'm just going to come
12		regularly here, so we will work on many other things (.) not only (2.0)
13		dissertation.

Initially, the student explains her goals for visiting the writing center, commenting that although she is now focusing on specific materials for her dissertation (line 11), she wants to improve her writing skills generally with regular visits to the center (lines 9-10). Through her narrative, the student displays knowledge of writing center philosophy and the idea of writing as a process. Her comments can be read as the student's acceptance of what she has come to know of the center; she has embraced the pervasive writing center maxim, "become a better writer, don't just produce a better paper." During the whole of the student's successful literacy narrative, the consultant agrees and laughs (lines 4 and 7) to affirm the student's acknowledgment of the particular relationship invited in the center.

In the four exchanges presented above, *we* is explored within a dynamic of talk-in-interaction, where both consultant and client strategies are taken into account. Our analysis shows that *we* and *I* have different functions in negotiating consultant and client goals within a *collaborative asymmetry*, a phrase that enables a both/and productivity for analyst and participants alike as they coconstruct the shifts and reformulations of an institutional helping relationship.

Conclusion: What Comes Next

Once the putative dichotomy of collaboration and authority is set aside, we are invited to opt out of its discourse and the relational terms that it prescribes for the praxis of composing. We may instead consider the ways in which a collaborative asymmetry involves a productive and creative tension between ideology and praxis, which participants both acknowledge and resist at will as they orient to each other, the text they both wish to improve upon, and the institutional context of the consultation. Though it is compelling to analyze the work of *we* as inclusive, and therefore a means for the consultant to encode so-called collaboration while, in fact, colluding, our analysis proposes that *we* is itself multifunctional: signaling collaborative affiliation and disaffiliation by sharing and distancing oneself from a text; marking the negotiation of coauthorship; implying shared identity by acknowledging a common status within the institution through the act of composing; and acting as an indicator of institutional discourse by acknowledging shared assumptions and constraints of the particular community. All these discursive acts embody collaboration, for collaboration itself consists of strategies of asymmetry by which writing consultants, as helpers in a dynamic, conduct interaction with their clients.

Our analyses, our critiques, and the metadiscourse of collaboration we have reconstructed in order to set aside here, do not remain in an epistemological bubble that floats separated from the ontology of our praxis. That which we define as "illegitimate" or "collusion," cannot but re-enter the conversations of our praxis as training, self-assessments, gossip and value judgments, affecting both clients and consultants. In the case of consultants, whose work the writing center depends on, we wonder what kind of resources this languaging of what is as opposed to what should be offers for them to build their own characterizations as professionals within the academy. Tutors either feel they are too non-directive and, as a result, frustrating in their suggestions to clients, or too directive, and thus misbehaving (see Pantelides; Blau and Hall) in their roles as helpers.[2] The frequent manifestation of tutor fear (Lidh 9) and anxiety (see Chandler), suggests that the discursive toolbox of "writing center orthodoxy" (Clark and Healy 36) could offer consultants more effective tools. If asymmetry is part and parcel of writing center collaboration (see Latterell; Thompson; Thonus; Rollins, Smith and Westbrook), as conversation scholars show that it is indeed a feature of any exchange (see

Drew), then it should be an accepted part of the way writing centers present themselves outside of their own discourse community, to clients and to the university at large.

It may be that recognizing and detailing the kind of interaction that takes place in the writing center is not politically expedient. As opposed to the dubious words "coproduced" and "asymmetrical," and the fuzzy categories of what actual writing center interaction entails, the assertion that students develop "their own work" in the Writing Center is a non-threatening, symmetrical peer interaction that is much simpler and easier to defend to administrators focused on the dangers of plagiarism and academic dishonesty, especially those already suspicious of writing center work. Writing center administrators purposely simplify this relationship and define it in terms of what it isn't—a relationship with an expert, an editor, an instructor—in order to occupy a safe political space. Surely this argument has been made before, that writing centers must resist unfair university policies (see Kail and Trimbur; Clark and Healy; Grimm), but they've made this argument for different reasons, for institutional value change.

We hold, however, that a representation of writing center interaction as complex collaborative asymmetry is more in keeping with writing center ideology than playing passive defense, and eliminating the disconnect between practice and theory will help consultants feel more at ease with the requirements of their occupation. More broadly, Compositionists of all stripes can benefit from acknowledging the fuzziness of our roles and the lack of clear demarcation between who the university wants us to be, who we say we are, and what actually happens in classrooms. To acknowledge the discourses we enact in our relationships means to move away from the narrative of guilt that frequently plagues both our practice and our scholarship.

NOTES

1. We thank one of our anonymous reviewers for pointing this out to us.

2. These are worries that numerous tutors have expressed to the first author in post-session discussions.

WORKS CITED

Bartesaghi, Mariaelena. "How the Therapist Does Authority: Six Strategies to Substitute Client Accounts in the Session." *Communication & Medicine* 6.1 (2009): 15-25. Print.

Bazerman, Charles, and James G. Paradis. *Textual Dynamics of the Professions: Historical and Contemporary Studies of Writing in Professional Communities.* Madison: U of Wisconsin P, 1991. Print.

Berkenkotter, Carol, and Doris Ravotas. "Genre as Tool in the Transmission of Practice Over Time and Across Professional Boundaries." *Mind, Culture, and Activity* 4.4 (1997): 256-74. Print.

Blau, Susan, and John Hall. "Guilt-Free Tutoring: Rethinking How We Tutor Non-Native-English Speaking Students." *Writing Center Journal* 23.1 (2002): 23-44. Print.

Brooks, Jeff. "Minimalist Tutoring: Making the Student Do All the Work." *Writing Lab Newsletter* 15.6 (1991): 1-4. Web. 1 Jan. 2011.

Clark, Irene L., and Dave Healy. "Are Writing Centers Ethical?" *WPA: Writing Program Administration* 20.1-2 (1996): 32-48. Print.

Chandler, Sally. "Fear, Teaching Composition, and Students' Discursive Choices: Re-thinking Connections Between Emotions and College Student Writing." *Composition Studies* 35.2 (2007): 53-70. Print.

Drew, Paul. "Asymmetries of Knowledge in Conversational Interaction." *Asymmetries in Dialogue.* Ed. Ivana Marková and Klaus Foppa. Hemel Hempstead: Harvester Wheatsheaf, 1991. 29-48. Print.

Ede, Lisa, and Andrea A. Lunsford. "Collaboration and Concepts of Authorship." *PMLA* 116.2 (2001): 354-69. Print.

Edelman, Murray. "The Political Language of the Helping Professions." *Politics & Society* 4.3 (1974): 295-310. Print.

Fairclough, Norman. *Language and Power.* London: Longman, 1989. Print.

Gilewicz, Magdalena, and Terese Thonus. "Close Vertical Transcription in Writing Center Training and Research." *The Writing Center Journal* 24.1 (2003): 25-50. Print.

Grimm, Nancy M. *Good Intentions: Writing Center Work for Postmodern Times.* Portsmouth: Boynton/Cook-Heinemann, 1999. Print.

Harris, Muriel. *Teaching One-to-One: The Writing Conference.* Urbana: NCTE, 1986. Print.

Haspel, Kathleen, and Karen Tracy. "Marking and Shifting Lines in the Sand." *The Prettier Doll: Rhetoric, Discourse, and Ordinary Democracy.* Ed. Karen Tracy, James P. McDaniel, and Bruce E. Gronbeck. Tuscaloosa: U of Alabama P, 2007. 142-75. Print.

Jefferson, Gail. "On the Organization of Laughter in Talk About Troubles." *Structures of Social Action: Studies in Conversation Analysis.* Ed. J. M. Atkinson and John Heritage. Cambridge: Cambridge UP, 1984. 346-69. Print.

Kail, Harvey, and John Trimbur. "The Politics of Peer Tutoring." *WPA: Writing Program Administration* 11.1 (1987): 5-12. Print.

Labov, William, and David Fanshel. *Therapeutic Discourse: Psychotherapy as Conversation*. New York: Academic P, 1977. Print.

Latterell, Catherine G. "Decentering Student-Centeredness: Rethinking Tutor Authority in the Writing Center." *Stories from the Center: Connecting Narrative and Theory in the Writing Center.* Ed. Lynn Craigue Briggs and Meg Woolbright. Urbana: NCTE, 2000. 104-20. Print.

Lidh, Todd M. "Nothing to Fear But Fear Itself." *The Writing Lab Newsletter* 17.4 (1992): 9. Web. 15 Jan. 2010.

Linell, Peter. "Discourse Across Boundaries: On Recontextualizations and the Blending of Voices in Professional Discourse." *Text* 18.2 (1998): 143-57. Print.

North, Stephen M. "The Idea of the Writing Center." *Landmark Essays on Writing Centers*. Ed. Christina Murphy and Joe Law. Davis: Hermagoras, 1995. 71-85. Print.

—. "Revisiting 'The Idea of a Writing Center.'" *The Writing Center Journal* 15.1 (Fall 1994): 7-19. Print.

Pantelides, Kate. "Invisible Expectations and Hidden Agendas: Behaving Badly in the Writing Center." Florida Regional Writing Center Conference. University of South Florida, Tampa. 17 April 2009. Conference Presentation.

Rollins, Brooke, Trixie D. Smith, and Evelyn Westbrook. "Collusion and Collaboration: Concealing Authority in the Writing Center." *(E)merging Identities: Graduate Students in the Writing Center.* Ed. Melissa Nicolas. Southland: Fountainhead P, 2008. 119-40. Print.

Shamoon, Linda K., and Deborah H. Burns. "A Critique of Pure Tutoring." *The Writing Center Journal* 15.2 (1995): 134-51. Print.

Thompson, Isabelle. "Scaffolding in the Writing Center: A Microanalysis of an Experienced Tutor's Verbal and Nonverbal Tutoring Strategies." *Written Communication* 26.4 (2009): 417-53. Print.

Thonus, Terese. "Dominance in Academic Writing Tutorials: Gender, Language Proficiency, and the Offering of Suggestions." *Discourse & Society* 10.2 (1999): 225-48. Web. 15 Jan. 2010.

Walker, Paul. "(Un)Earthing a Vocabulary of Values: A Discourse Analysis for Ecocomposition." *Composition Studies* 38.1 (2010): 69-87. Web. 15 Jan. 2010.

Williams, Jessica. "Writing Center Interaction: Institutional Discourse and the Role of Peer Tutors." *Interlanguage Pragmatics: Exploring Institutional Talk.* Ed. Kathleen Bardovi-Harlig and Beverly Hartford. Mahwah: Lawrence Erlbaum, 2005. 37-65. Print.

Wittgenstein, Ludwig. *Philosophical Investigations*. Trans. G. E. M. Anscombe. New York: Blackwell, 1953. Print.

"Writing Center." University of South Florida

APPENDIX A: TRANSCRIPTION NOTATION

(.)	An audible pause, like drawing a breath
(.2)	A timed pause, in fraction of a second
[	Marks the beginning of overlapping or simultaneous speech
–	Speech that is abruptly cut off
(word)	Inaudible speech, with the transcriptionist's best guess between parentheses
((laugh))	Transcriptionist's rendition of non-phonetic material
Underline	Underline a word or part of a word marks emphasis

COMPUTERS AND COMPOSITION

Volume 28, Number 4, December, 2011   ISSN 8755-4615

ELSEVIER

Composition 20/20: How the Future of the Web
Could Sharpen the Teaching of Writing

Guest Editors: Randall McClure, Janice R. Walker

Editor
Kristine L. Blair
Bowling Green State University

Computers and Composition is online at http://www.jour-nals.elsevier.com/computers-and-composition

Computers and Composition is devoted to exploring the use of computers in writing classes, writing programs, and writing research. It provides a forum for discussing issues connected with writing and computer use. It also offers information about integrating computers into writing programs on the basis of sound theoretical and pedagogical decisions, and empirical evidence. It welcomes articles, reviews, and responses that may be of interest to readers, including descriptions of computer-aided writing and/or reading instruction, discussions of topics related to computer use of software development; explorations of controversial ethical, legal, or social issues related to the use of computers in writing programs; and to discussions of how computers affect form and content for written discourse, the process by which this discourse is produced, or the impact this discourse has on an audience.

Policy Matters Now and in the Future: Net Neutrality, Corporate Data Mining, and Government Surveillance

Heidi McKee's "Policy Matters Now and in the Future: Net Neutrality, Corporate Data Mining, and Government Surveillance," draws from work in composition, interdisciplinary studies on privacy, information sharing, surveillance on the Internet, analyses of applicable policies and laws, and the advocacy efforts by organizations to make recommendations for how writing instructors and their students more fully control the visual, verbal, aural writing they read and produce online. In an era in which tweeting, Facebooking, and other social media usage have become action verbs, it is vital that citizens and academics understand the ethical responsibilities of incorporating these tools of communication, and admittedly surveillance, into our pedagogies. McKee's work superbly synthesizes these issues in ways that fit the mission and scope of *Computers and Composition*.

4 Policy Matters Now and in the Future: Net Neutrality, Corporate Data Mining, and Government Surveillance

Heidi A. McKee

In this article, I will detail three key policy issues that have a profound effect on the future of the World Wide Web and Internet-based communications: net neutrality, corporate data mining, and government surveillance. Focusing on policy issues in the U.S., I will describe not only current practices and cases, but future possibilities for writers and teachers of writing. I will draw from work in composition, interdisciplinary studies on privacy, information sharing, and surveillance on the Internet, analyses of applicable policies and laws, and the advocacy efforts by organizations. Issues I will examine include the importance of and threats to net neutrality; how data mining and (so-called) privacy agreements currently work, specifically at social networking sites often used in writing classrooms; and how government and institutional surveillance is far more prevalent than many realize. I will close with recommendations for what writing instructors (and students) can do to try to craft a different future, one where writers and the visual, verbal, aural writing they read and produce online will not be collected, scrutinized, and controlled (or, realistically, at least not as much).

Imagine...

> ... For homework, you ask students to review sites discussing digital divides, including the Electronic Frontier Foundation and the Digital Divide Institute. But because of the tiered content delivery systems in place for the Web, students get tired of waiting "forever" (their words) for those sites to

load, so they just read and watch the information available at FoxNews.com, a site that loads quickly because Fox News Corporation has the funding to pay the steep fees to secure prioritized delivery service.

... Students in class roll their eyes when they hear you—for the umpteenth time—lament the passage of whitespace and, more importantly, the passage of privacy or, at least, the illusion of privacy. They've come of age immersed in ubiquitous advertising and don't seem to mind (or even notice) that the texts they compose are laden with ads. It's just not a big deal to them that the software they use (including word processing programs) and the online sites they visit data mine every word they write and every link they click in order to provide targeted advertising.

... One afternoon you get a visit to your office from Homeland Security agents who confiscate your digital devices and want to talk with you about your possible ties to terrorist organizations. It seems your inquiry unit on the rhetorics of terrorism and the blogs and tweets (or other 2020 communications) that your students have composed have attracted some attention.

Unfortunately, these scenarios are not that far in the future. In fact, some of them, as I describe below, are actually happening now. From behavioral profiling and paid prioritization to the warrantless seizure of digital communications, the extent of overt and covert Web surveillance, data mining, and corporate takeover of the Internet already occurring is mind-boggling—and scary. Scarier still is the thought of what could happen in the future if some of the more disturbing trends continue to develop as they are.

As writers, teachers, and researchers who use the Web extensively in our work, we need, in Cindy Selfe's (1999) words, to pay attention to policy. And we need to provide venues for students to learn about policy as well. The negotiations and decisions that government agencies make (or fail to make) regarding legal and regulatory oversight of the Internet matter tremendously. The decisions made now about the Internet will have a profound effect on its development. By 2020 the Web could be completely controlled by corporations with what user-generated content there is being packaged by commercial sites and closely watched by government agents. Fortunately, it is not too late.

Working individually and collectively, we can help ensure a different future for the Web. The first steps are to become more informed and then to aim to become more involved.

In this article, I will detail three key policy issues that have a profound effect on the future of the Web and Internet-based communications: net neutrality, corporate data mining, and government surveillance.[1] Focusing on policy issues in the U.S., I will describe not only current practices and cases, but future possibilities for writers and teachers of writing. I will draw from work in composition, interdisciplinary studies on privacy, information sharing, and surveillance on the Internet, and analyses of applicable policies and laws and the advocacy efforts by citizen and educational organizations. Issues I will examine include the importance of and threats to net neutrality; how data mining and (so-called) privacy agreements currently work, specifically at sites often used in writing classrooms such as Facebook, Google, and Twitter; and how government and institutional surveillance is far more prevalent than many realize. I will then close with recommendations for what writing instructors (and students) can do to try to craft a different future, one where writers and the visual, verbal, aural writing they read and produce online will not be collected, scrutinized, and controlled (or, realistically, at least not as much).

I begin with what is the greatest threat to the Web and to all who read, write, and share media on the Web: the efforts by corporations to undermine net neutrality.

1. Dirt roads and super highways: The need to preserve net neutrality

One of the founding principles of the Internet is net neutrality—that the Internet would be an open system where all content delivered across networks would be treated equally in terms of transmission. Larger files and encrypted files would, of course, take longer to transmit but all would have the same access to the network. As explained in the mission statement of the Open

> "I will take a back seat to no one in my commitment to network neutrality. Because once providers start to priv- ilege some applications or websites over others, then the smaller voices get squeezed out and we all lose. The Internet is perhaps the most open net- work in history, and we have to keep it that way" –Barack Obama (2007)

Internet Coalition (2010), a coalition of Internet companies who support preserving an open Internet (or, as in the case of some companies such as Google, *claim* to support):

> Internet openness (network neutrality) means that users are in control of where to go and what to do online, and broadband providers do not discriminate among lawful Internet content or applications. This is the fundamental principle of the Internet's design. It shouldn't matter whether you're visiting a mainstream media website or an individual's blog, sending emails or purchasing a song. The phone and cable companies that provide you with the access to the Internet should route all traffic in a neutral manner, without blocking, speeding up, or slowing down particular applications or content.

In the U.S., net neutrality was understood to be an essential part of what the Internet was (note the past tense). But then a series of events happened that now challenge net neutrality as a founding principle and put the future of the Internet in jeopardy.

In 2005, the Federal Communications Commission (FCC), working with the antiregulatory policies of President George W. Bush's administration, chose to classify the Internet as an information service rather than as a telecom- munications service. The FCC has far fewer regulations it can enforce on information services because information services are not "common carriers" subject to more stringent Title II regulations (FCC, 2005). At about the same time as classifying the Internet in this lower regulatory category, the FCC did adopt four policy statements about network neutrality that would guide its regulatory oversight under Title I, including that "consumers are entitled to access lawful Internet content of their choice" (FCC, 2005, p. 3). At first glance, the adoption of these policy principles would seem to ensure some protection for net neutrality. But policy principles are not regulations, as both corporations and courts were well aware.

Comcast was the first company to challenge the FCC's authority to regulate the Internet and Internet service providers. Beginning in 2007, Comcast throttled Bit-

> "But protecting an open Internet isn't just about developing new and enforceable net neutrality standards, it's also about making sure that the Internet is not effectively owned by a handful of companies"
> —Senator Al Franken (2010)

Torrent, a peer-to-peer file application, slowing the transfer of BitTorrent files to the point that users of Comcast's cable broadband could not send or receive files. The FCC chose to investigate on the grounds that because of their net neutrality princi- ples they had ancillary authority under Title I to regulate networks. In 2008 in a 3-2 ruling the FCC commissioners found Comcast in viola- tion of the law, requiring Comcast to cease-and-desist its discriminatory treatment of BitTorrent and to provide the FCC and consumers a detailed statement of how Comcast intended to manage information on its networks. Comcast chose to appeal the ruling to the federal courts, and in April 2010 the federal DC Circuit court ruled that the FCC had overstepped its authority in regulating Comcast. According to the ruling, "[b]ecause the Commission has failed to tie its assertion of ancillary authority over Comcast's Inter- net service to any 'statutorily mandated responsibility'" (Comcast Corporation v. FCC, 2010, p. 36)—because the Internet had been classified as an information service and not a common carrier (like telephones), the FCC had no authority to regulate Comcast's decisions about its network management (see also McCullagh, 2010; Weinberg & Bergmayer, 2010).

Unless federal regulations are changed, this court ruling will be the death knell for the Internet as we have known it, portending a future where a handful of corporations control what Internet users get to read and write online and effectively changing the Internet into a locked-down media, like cable television. But if the Internet were to be reclas- sified as a common carrier subject to more stringent regulatory oversight, then the FCC could enforce as *regulations* its current *policies* of net neutrality, thus, in theory at least, preserving an open Internet. But, as you can imagine, the battle over reclassification is raging.

In a much publicized—and skewered—legislative framework proposal, Verizon and Google in fall 2010 sought to preempt FCC reclassification (Verizon & Google, 2010). They proposed that wired ("wireline") Internet services abide by open Internet policies with exceptions for "reasonable network management," an ambiguous term that essen- tially covers any and all decisions they make about traffic on their networks. In addition, they proposed that because wireless Internet delivery is "unique," Internet services provided wirelessly to mobile devices do not need to abide by any principles for open networks or to "the transparency principle" where carriers must inform users of what services are blocked, tiered, etc. Given that currently

60 percent of Americans access the Internet via wireless and among Latinos and African Americans that percentage is even higher (Smith, 2010) and given that the Internet is the Internet no matter how you access it, to claim somehow that different regulations must exist for wireless networks is misguided at best and downright fraudulent at worst. As Craig Aaron (2010), the Managing Director of Free Press (an organization at the forefront fighting to preserve net neutrality), explained "The Proposal is one massive loop- hole that sets the stage for the corporate takeover of the Internet." And, as Joel Kelsey (2010), also of Free Press, noted:

> It [the Verizon-Google proposal] would open the door to out-right blocking of applications, just as Comcast did with Bit-Torrent, or the blocking of content, just as Verizon did with text-messages from NARAL Pro-choice America.[2] It would divide the information superhighway, creating new private fast lanes for the big players while leaving the little guy stranded on a winding dirt road [...] This is not real Net Neutrality. And this pact would harm millions of Americans.

But Verizon and Google are not the only corporations seeking to undermine net neutrality. AT&T, one of the largest phone carriers in the U.S. has plans to implement "paid prioritization" where the company is paid by Internet content developers to deliver their content at variable rates. In a letter to the FCC in August, 2010, AT&T claimed that paid prioritization would still be an open Internet because all content would be delivered, just some at higher speeds and better service than others (Turner, 2010). But in actuality this would mean that those with money would be able to pay to get their content delivered at speeds and levels of service that users expect. Why wait minutes for the non-profit's blog to load when Fox News or MSNBC comes up in milliseconds?

> "This is not about protecting the Internet against imaginary dangers. We're seeing the breaks and cracks emerge, and they threaten to change the Internet's fundamental architecture of openness. [...] This is about pre- serving and maintaining something profoundly successful and ensuring that it's not distorted or undermined. If we wait too long to preserve a free and open Internet, it will be too late."—FCC Chair Julius Genachowski (2009, p. 18)

Recognizing that the Comcast ruling could lead to corporate take-over of the Internet, FCC chair Julius Genachowski spearheaded the FCC's efforts to protect net neutrality and to change government regulations. After hundreds of hours of meetings and public hearings, on December 21, 2010 the FCC voted 3-2 to enact new regulations that they argue will preserve an open Internet (FCC, 2010).[3] Unfortunately, the regulations do not reclassify the Internet as a telecommunications subject to more stringent Title II protections. Instead the order looks nearly identically to the Verizon-Google proposal, setting up differences between fixed and mobile broadband providers.[4] One of the only provisions that applies equally to both fixed and mobile broadband providers is the transparency requirement. Mobile broadband providers are allowed to block some content and, most importantly, *only* fixed broadband providers are required to abide by no unreasonable discrimination—mobile broadband providers may discriminate (that is throttle) whatever network communications they feel like:

1. **Transparency.** *Fixed* and *mobile* broadband providers must disclose the network management practices, perfor- mance characteristics, and terms and conditions of their broadband services;

2. **No blocking.** *Fixed* broadband providers may not block lawful content, applications, services, or non-harmful devices; *mobile* broadband providers may not block lawful websites, or block applications that compete with their voice or video telephony services; and

3. **No unreasonable discrimination.** *Fixed* broadband providers may not unreasonably discriminate in transmitting lawful network traffic. (FCC, 2010, p. 2, emphasis added)

Anyone who's ever tried to read a company's terms of service or privacy statements knows that these "transparent" statements are too often anything but, so the fact that companies are required to report how they manage their networks does not seem, ultimately, that helpful for the typical consumer. As for the differential treatment of fixed and mobile Internet access, this is incredibly troubling and problematic, as is too the failure of the order to explicitly ban "paid- prioritization." In addition, the loopholes are huge: nearly every provision contains an exception for "reasonable network management," which means under the guise of managing networks ISP's are allowed to restrict delivery and access to Internet sites and services. As Tim Karr (2010) of Free Press passionately argued:

> His [Genachowski's] rule, for the first time in history, allows discrimination over the mobile Internet, paving the way for widespread industry abuses [...] The FCC rule doesn't do enough to stop the phone and cable companies from dividing the Internet into fast and slow lanes. It doesn't stop them from splitting the Internet into two—one Internet for those who can pay to access special sites and services, and another neglected network for the rest of us. The rule fails miserably to protect wireless users from discrimination, a prospect that's especially troubling for African American and Latino communities who increasingly access the Internet via mobile devices.

The implications of this for all Internet users are troubling to say the least. As then-candidate Barack Obama (2007) said "The Internet is perhaps the most open network in history and we have to keep it that way." As writing teachers we may decry the volume of misinformation on the Internet—the way students sometimes end up citing ridiculously inappropriate sources for the purpose, audience and context of their arguments, but how much worse to have only filtered information avail- able? If net neutrality is not enforceable by government regula-

"The rules approved by the FCC would not protect these communi- ties [...] In effect, consumers of color, who are more dependent on wireless broadband to access the Internet, would have less govern-men- tal protection than Americans who can afford both wired and wireless connections."—Rep. Maxine Waters (2010)

tors, as it seems hardly to be with the December 2010 regulations from the FCC, we face a future where the Internet is like cable television where behemoth corporations control and produce the majority of content, controlling what we can see, read, hear, and write online. In addition, much has been made of how the current open networks on the Web enable students to become producers, not just consumers of content (Anderson, 2003; Bruns, 2008), but in a World Wide Web where authors must pay to deliver content, what audiences would students find for their work if what they produce languishes on the digital equivalent of slow, pot-holed, low-traffic back roads? I doubt a student's blog post about endangered species, for example, would receive comments from Greenpeace activists in Australia, for example, as happened for a student whom I taught. Preserving an open Internet (and, importantly, ensuring access, in all its senses, for all) are central priorities and efforts all of us need to engage in.

Part of the problem is, I think, that the idea of preserving openness through regulation seems a bit counterintuitive. Regulations, especially in this Tea Party moment where the networks are filled with anti-government fervor (except regarding social issues, but that's another article), are often (inappropriately) framed as restrictive, as preventing action rather than enabling it. But without regulation to preserve an open Internet, the Web as we know it will cease to exist.

Just as net neutrality is essential for the access and delivery of information, preserving some semblance of privacy online is essential for maintaining the Web as a venue for writing. As more and more communications move to the cloud—to being hosted and stored on remote servers—the amounts of data being collected and what can be done with that data is nearly unlimited. The present and future threats to privacy online are extensive.

2. All in the name of personalization: Data mining and privacy online

Even as you read this, data about you is being collected, packaged, shipped and sold all over the world. Data mining for "interest-based ads" (Google's term) and "instant personalization" (Facebook's term) is big business, pushing online companies stock values soaring and challenging the boundaries of what online users will accept. It's no wonder that Google has patents on portable data centers installed in shipping contain-

> "You have zero privacy anyway. Get over it."— Scott McNealy (1999), CEO of Sun Microsystems

ers and on floating island data centers (Claburn, 2009). In 2020, unless some efforts are made to rein in these megabusinesses, everything we write with any digital device may be data mined and "served" with "personalized content" (e.g., ads).

In the first-year writing program at Miami University where I teach, instructors and students frequently use the Web and Web-based services to both access information and to compose and publish online. Some of these sites are hosted locally or are directly contracted by the university so that university policies govern use of data (e.g., Blackboard, e-mail accounts and our program wiki hosted on a university server), but most are accessed from remote servers whose terms of use and privacy policies are governed by the corporations that own the site. Sites we often use where students write online include search engines, Prezi, Twitter, Google Docs, YouTube (a service of Google), WordPress.com, Ning, and Facebook. In our use of commercially available Web sites, I think our program is fairly representative of many writing programs at two-year and four-year institutions across the country. In an ideal world we would move to all open-source, non-commercial sites for writing and researching online but resource limitations, particularly of time and people, make it convenient to just head to Google Docs, for example, for collaborative writing or YouTube for extensive video hosting.'

But convenient does not always mean best choice, especially in relation to the privacy of communications and actions online. As we and our students write messages, post on walls, send tweets, upload photos, share videos, and "like" various items online, we're leaving identity trails com-posed of millions of bits of disparate data that corporations, in the name of targeted advertising and personalization, are using to track our every move.

> "We have a duty to ask whether these people—and the millions of Ameri- cans just like them—fully understand and appreciate what information is being collected about them, and whether or not they are empowered to stop certain practices from taking place."
> –Senator John D. Rockefeller IV (2010)

(Law enforcement is as well—see below.) That corporations seek this information is, of course, not new. Newspaper, radio, and television media have always sought information on users so as to deliver user demographics to advertisers. But with digital technologies—especially with how every keystroke and click online is able to be recorded and captured—the amount of data amassed and the speed with which it can be packaged, repackaged, transferred, and analyzed is unprecedented. Privacy practices established in the 1970's are simply not effective for protecting us now and they certainly won't be for doing so in 2020 when cloud computing and Web 3.0 technologies will be even more extensive (see Strickland, 2010). If we don't advocate now for more extensive (and effective) privacy policies, we will face a future with even more ubiquitous advertising and behavioral profiling fueled by ever-expanding data mining.

Concerns about privacy and data mining of information in computer networks are not new. In the late 1960's and early 1970's as the data processing capabilities of mainframe computers became clear, Alan Westin, a professor at Columbia University, published several key books about privacy and data protection where he argued that privacy is about the control of information and that consumers need to be able to control what information is revealed and shared about them to whom (see Westin, 1967; Westin, 1971; Westin & Baker, 1972).[5] From these discussions of privacy in relation to computing technology, a set of Fair Information Practice Principles were developed, principles that still shape the Federal Trade Commission's (FTC) enforcement of data protection regulations today. As Jon Leibowitz (2010), Chairman of the FTC, explained in Senate testimony:

> (1) businesses should provide **notice** of what information they collect from consumers and how they use it; (2) consumers should be given **choices** about how information collected from them may be used; (3) con- sumers should be able to **access** data collected about them; and (4) businesses should take reasonable steps to ensure the **security** of the information they collect from consumers. The Commission [FTC] also identified **enforcement**—the use of a reliable mechanism to impose sanctions for noncompliance with the fair information principles—as a critical component of any self-regulatory program to ensure privacy online. (p. 3, emphasis in the original)

A key word not bolded in that explanation is "self-regulatory." Currently, with the exception of data about children, finances, and health and with the exception for outright crimes such as identity theft, there is little legislation to protect the privacy of people's communications and actions online. Basically, corporations such as Google, Twitter, or Facebook are asked to self-regulate and to file once a year a statement with the FTC as to how their privacy practices align with the Fair Information Practices Principles. If it seems a company's policies are out-of-line or if consumer complaints are received, then the FTC may intercede on users' behalf.

But under President George W. Bush's administration, the FTC moved away from enforcing (the limited) compliance with the Fair

Information Practices and instead moved to a "harm-based" approach, where companies would only be investigated (and possibly fined and regulated) when "specific and tangible privacy harms" (Leibowitz, 2010, p. 2) occurred, "those presenting risks to physical security or economic injury, or causing unwarranted intrusions in our daily lives" (p. 5). Under this harm-based approach, the FTC focuses less on what data companies routinely collect and what they do with it and instead focuses on such clear crimes as identity theft and financial theft through spyware, etc. (p. 5). That corporations such as Facebook and Google collect every search, every post, every Web site visited by people online is not, under this harm-based approach, that much of a concern to the FTC provided that companies have publicly posted privacy policies that give customers notification and choice (even if the choice is simply, choose to agree to our privacy policies or don't use the site).

But in the actual, everyday usage of the Web, this belief in the feasibility of notification and choice is laughable. How many of you have actually read the privacy policies of the online sites you use or have asked your students to do the same? If you have, how long did it take you? How long did it take your students? According to Aleecia M. McDonald (2009), an online privacy researcher at Carnegie Mellon, if the average U.S. Internet user actually read the privacy policies of all the sites she visited online, the time required would be between 181 and 304 hours per year depending on how active an online user she was. And if you did bother to read the privacy policies, could you understand them? Primarily written by company lawyers, privacy policies and the terms of service (the two documents are often cross-referenced) often seem more geared to legally protecting companies rather than actually informing consumers. It could be that many are so hard to understand because once you spend the time to parse them, the loopholes of what individuals are actually giving companies permission to do is frightening. For example, Twitter's (2010) Terms of Service stated:

> By submitting, posting or displaying Content on or through the Services, you grant us a worldwide, non-exclusive, royalty-free license (with the right to sublicense) to use, copy, reproduce, process, adapt, modify, publish, transmit, display and distribute such Content in any and all media or distribution methods (now known or later developed).

And the privacy policy stated:

> When using any of our Services you consent to the collection, transfer, manipulation, storage, disclosure and other uses of your information as described in this Privacy Policy. Irrespective of which country that you reside in or create information from, your information may be used by Twitter in the United States or any other country where Twitter operates.

The content and information referenced in these statements include that which is by default public or that a user sets to public—tweets, profile, lists, etc. but they also include data gathered from cookies about Web usage, including pages visited, links visited, and interactions with third-parties. Now to be fair to Twitter, most of the information they log is publicly available. So

> "[D]ata collected for one purpose can be combined with other data and then used for purposes not anticipated by the consumer. Further, unbeknownst to many consumers, companies such as data brokers collect and sell such aggregated data on a routine basis."—Jon Leibowitz (2010), Chair- man of the FTC

what does it matter if they have the right to disclose your tweets if your tweets are already public? What matters is the lens that can be brought to bear. One tweet amid millions of other tweets is not probably going to garner that much attention, unless you're Lindsey Lohan. But if all of your tweets are gathered together, analyzed for your interests, political leanings, etc. and cross-referenced with your actions at other Web sites you visit, that massive aggregating of data enables Twitter to offer companies incredibly specific and targeted demographic information for the posting of ads. Like other social networking sites, Twitter emphasizes that it does not reveal "personally identifying information" but what is "personally-identifying" has changed as data reidentification gets easier and easier (Gross & Acquisti, 2005; Millar, 2009).

Facebook, the company with perhaps the most egregious record on privacy, does share personally-identifying information (or at least make it available for searching)—a policy change they put in place with no prior notification to users. One day you were able to control who could see your name, profile, and other directory information—the next day your name, profile picture, and gender were public (see Opsahl, 2010).[6] According to U.S. regulations, companies can change—or even suspend or cancel—their privacy policies with no required prior notification to users. Now when a person first creates a Facebook account almost all privacy settings are defaulted to "Everyone." Like most companies, Facebook structures its privacy "choices" as opt-out, not opt-in, which means a user's information is automatically set to the most permissive level unless the user changes his privacy settings to be more restrictive. As numerous consumer rights advocates have argued, setting privacy options to opt-out rather than opt-in means that many users do not change their settings (although this is beginning to change, see Lenhart & Madden, 2007). And it's hard to change your settings if you don't know a site's policies and practices have changed. For example, in 2007 Facebook launched Facebook Beacon without warning users that this feature would publicize the products they bought at third-party sites on their friends' news feeds. As you can imagine, Facebook users were outraged that purchases they thought were private were broadcast to all their friends, and the user uprising (for that's really what it was) led Facebook to shut Beacon down in 2009 (see Electronic Privacy Information Center, 2010). But even though the purchase information is no longer being broadcast to friends, Facebook is still collecting the information and sharing it with the many "third-parties" (i.e., marketers) with which they do business. Facebook's most recent privacy policy (April 22, 2010) explains what data they keep on users:

> Site activity information: We keep track of some of the actions you take on Facebook, such as adding connections (including joining a group or adding a friend), creating a photo album, sending a gift, poking another user, indicating that you "like" a post, attending an event, or connecting with an application. In some cases you are also taking an action when you provide information or content to us. For example, if you share a video, in addition to storing the actual content you uploaded, we might log the fact that you shared it.

Now some of this you'd expect. You are, after all, uploading content and they need to know which content belongs to what users. But their tracking of information is even more extensive:

> Access Device and Browser Information: When you access Facebook from a computer, mobile phone, or other device, we

may collect information from that device about your browser type, location, and IP address, as well as the pages you visit.

So, thanks in part to cookie technology, Facebook is basically recording and collecting everything we do online. And they're just one site of the hundreds or thousands that you visit that are doing this. Put all that data together and the fine-grained detail and behavioral profiling that can occur is unprecedented.

Some people are beginning to be a bit freaked out by the level of information being collected on them and how ads for shoes (see Helft & Vega, 2010) and such can follow them around. But others point to how attitudes toward privacy are changing. Mark

> "People want things now. But the harms from privacy are defuse and they are later. So people will tend to discount things that happen later in favor of things that happen now." –Aleecia M. McDon- ald (2010), Online Privacy Researcher

Zuckerberg (2010), the CEO and founder of Facebook, in an interview noted that "People have really gotten comfortable not only sharing more information and different kinds but more openly with more people. That social norm is just something that's just evolved over time. We [at Facebook] view it as our role in the system to constantly be innovating and be updating what our system is to reflect what the current social norm is." Yet researchers have shown that people do still care about privacy (Kerr, Steeves, & Lucock, 2009; Lenhart & Madden, 2007; McKee & Porter, 2009). It's just that when presented with the immediate use of a site—wanting to join Facebook to communicate with friends and family—versus the threats to privacy, people will choose the immediate gratification. This manufacturing of consent is one of the real dangers I see to the future of the Web. In exchange for goods and services—to be able to play a particular game or use a particular file sharing site—people will simply hand over—and already are handing over—all sorts of private information to corporations.

Stuart Selber (2004) argued that it's essential to help students understand and see the power moves associated with technological regularization, including the power move of deflection where "The technology provides compensatory goods or services to people in an attempt to deflect attention away from what is really going on" (p. 102). Comparing the language in statements directed at users of sites and the language in statements directed at potential marketers is a fascinating space to see this deflection at work. For example, Facebook's directions to users about Basic Directory Information (as of September, 2010) are "To help real world friends find you, some basic information is open to everyone. We also suggest setting basics like hometown and interests to everyone so friends can use those to connect with you." This sure makes it seem that Facebook is all about friends finding friends, right? Well, not quite. At its site for developers who seek to use Facebook's Platform service or its Social Plug-ins, Facebook states: "At Facebook's core is the social graph—people and the connections they have to everything they care about. Facebook platform is the set of APIs and tools which enable you to integrate with the social graph to drive registration, personalization, and traffic—whether through applications on Facebook.com or external websites and devices" (FacebookDevelopers, 2010).

No wonder Facebook, as of January 2011, is valued at 50 billion (Craig & Sorkin, 2011)—what a treasure trove for marketers, to have at their disposable 500 million "people and the connections they have to everything they care about."

Okay, I realize I've dwelled a long time in the present when this is supposed to be an article about the future, but I think it's important to understand what's happening now in order to work to change it. Unless we aim to take students and ourselves offline entirely or operate exclusively within open-source, not-for-profit sites (which may lessen, but not eliminate the problem)[7] , we face a future where everything we write and do online will be open for data mining. Certainly there are steps we can take at our institutions and in our classrooms toward education, but there are also national policy decisions that will impact our Internet futures as well. Specifically, the current approaches by the FTC are not sufficient for regulating and protecting privacy of people online. Companies' privacy policies are too complex and time-consuming to read, having to opt-out is even more complex and time-consuming, and the mass collection of data by corporations and data mining companies, such as eXelate or Rapleaf, make it nearly impossible for an online user to know what information is being collected, by whom, and for what purposes. In an effort to address these problems, on December 1, 2010, the FTC released a 122-page preliminary staff report on "Protecting Consumer Privacy in an Era of Rapid Change." Some of the recommendations in this report are to create simpler, easier to read policy statements and to create a browser-based "Do Not Track" option that Internet users could select, thus disallowing companies from collecting data on their Web searching and browsing. If these recommendations are approved and enacted, then these would be important steps in at least reducing corporate data mining.[8] I'm not sure we can ever eliminate corporate surveillance, but we can aim to make ourselves and our students more critically aware of the data mining that is occurring and may occur in the future with the goal, perhaps, of making it harder for corporations to manufacture consent. If Michele Sidler's (2004) predictions about biotechnologies come true (and it seems we're heading that way), then if we're not careful we may end up with advertisers sending electronic signals directly into our brains. Let's try to prevent that now if we can.

But at least with corporate data mining there is some semblance of notification and consent, even if it's manufactured and illusionary. With government surveillance of online communications, there is no consent or notification needed. Big Brother (and all of his agents) are most certainly watching us.

3. Living in a panopticon: Government and institutional Web surveillance

I don't know about you, but most of the writing students and I do online probably doesn't garner much attention from law enforcement or Homeland Security. But the fact that government officials could, if they wish, be reading, viewing, listening, and collecting our communications (often without a warrant) still deeply troubles me. In a sense, the Internet serves as a panopticon.[9] Rather than bringing greater freedom as heralded in the first decades of the Internet, the Internet also potentially brings greater constraints. Like Bentham's prisoners in our cells (although we get to interact with each other rather than exist in total isolation), we go about our online lives with some level of awareness that our digital data could be collected and monitored. But the mechanisms and persons doing that collection are not—at least to the average Internet user—visible. As Michel Foucault (1995) explained "The Panopticon is a machine for dissociating the see/being seen dyad: in the peripheric ring, one is totally seen, without ever seeing; in the central tower, one sees everything without ever being seen" (pp. 201-202). But just because we can't see the agents who may be observing us, doesn't mean that they are not there.[10]

I'm not fully sure about the effects of this surveillance on writing and the teaching of writing or what the implications for this are in the future, but it's easy to get paranoid and imagine far-right (or far-left, but more likely right) regimes coming to power in this country where suddenly it could be illegal to write about certain issues, express certain views, or teach some topics. In fact, efforts like that are already well underway. In May 2011, the Tennessee State Senate passed a bill mandating that in grades K-8 public school teachers and students (and any organizations or groups doing presentations in schools) can only discuss "natural reproductive science" by which they mean heterosexuality (as was clear in the first version of the bill). The text of the revised bill is frightening and its implications and effects if it passes the Tennessee House and is signed into law (as is predicted to be likely in 2012) are even more frightening—teachers and other school personnel fired for answering students' questions about LGBTQ issues and LGBTQ parents forbidden (it would seem) from participating in any school events and their child's classroom activities (Tennessee General Assembly, 2011). Although the bill does not address digital technologies, I suspect that any sort of official school communication, including e-mails and texts between teachers and students, would be scrutinized for violation of this policy. Unless efforts are made now to rein in restrictions on academic freedom, the rights of free speech, and, key to this article, the power of law enforcement and other government agencies to search and seize electronic communications, we may very well face a future of Web surveillance even more problematic than the current situation.

And our current situation is not good. Telephone calls, print communications, and digital files created and stored on individuals' computers are protected from warrantless searches because of the Wiretap Act and the Fourth Amendment to the U.S. *Constitution*. But electronic com- munications and documents uploaded to the Web are not, generally, afforded that same level of protection. For example, all online commu- nications such as e-mails that exist on a company's remote server unread for more than 180 days may be searched and seized by the government, no warrant needed. The moment they're opened they may be searched right away.[11] Been uploading photos and videos to sites such as Facebook and WordPress lately? According to current law any document uploaded to a remote server is considered immediately available for law enforcement to view. Again, no warrant needed.

Why is this the case? Well, surprisingly, don't blame the USA Patriot Act (2001) (at least not entirely, although it has certainly contributed). Instead we have a law that predates the Web to thank: The

Electronic Communications Privacy Act (ECPA), first passed in 1986 and only modified slightly since then. The ECPA is one of the primary laws governing what law enforcement officials may and may not do with digital communications. When it was first passed, as Senator Patrick Leahy (2010) explained at a Senate Judiciary Hearing, it was a "cutting-edge piece of legislation" that "provided vital tools to law enforcement to investigate crime and to keep us safe, while at the same time protecting individual privacy online" by "protect[ing] electronic communication from real-time monitoring or interception by the Government, as e-mails were being delivered and from searches when these communications were stored electronically." But, as Leahy bluntly put it, "times have changed, and so ECPA must be updated to keep up with the times."

> "The right of the people to be secure in their persons, houses, papers, and effects, against unreasonable searches and seizures, shall not be violated, and no Warrants shall issue, but upon probable cause..."—Fourth Amendment to the United States Constitution

In a detailed statement to Senator Leahy and other members of the Senate Committee on the Judiciary, James X. Dempsey (2010), the Vice President for Public Policy at the Center for Democracy & Technology, detailed the problems with ECPA in relation to digital communications. Drawing on the work of the Digital Due Process (DDP) coalition (http://www.digitaldueprocess.org), he argued that electronic communications should be afforded the same protections as print and telephone communications with the government needing to demonstrate to a judge probable cause before a warrant is issued. Another recommendation was that the government should have to obtain a search warrant before obtaining specific geographic location information about users gathered from their computers, phones, and other digital devices. The DDP coalition also seeks that the government no longer be allowed to issue blanket subpoenas where they ask companies such as Google for all e-mails sent or all search queries made on certain dates. Currently this blanket subpoena practice means that many people who are not actually under investigation have their private queries and communications collected and analyzed. Another recommendation was to curtail what transactional data the government may obtain in real time. In 2001 when the USA Patriot Act passed, it revised the ECPA to allow for the collection of "electronic communication transactional records" which may include when and with whom an individual sends e-mails, IMs, social networking exchanges etc. and the specific IP addresses of the Internet sites individuals visit. This level of detail far exceeds the transactional records accessed with traditional telecommunications when the law was written.

Layered into this matrix of surveillance laws is the Communications Assistance for Law Enforcement Act (CALEA), originally passed in 1994 to cover telecommunications but then extended in 2001 (as part of the sweeping legal changes in the USA Patriot Act) to include online communications. Because of CALEA, Internet-service providers must ensure their network technologies are structured in such a way that law enforcement can easily eavesdrop on electronic communications. Despite objections from the educational community (EDUCAUSE Coalition, 2005), in 2005 the FCC required all Internet-service providers to revise their networks if they were not up to certain standards. In 2006 the American Council on Education challenged the applicability of the law to colleges and universities, but they lost in federal court (American Council on Education, 2006; American Council on Education v. Federal Communications Commission, 2006).

Currently, President Obama's administration plans to submit leg- islation to Congress that would require "all online services that enable communications to be technically equipped to comply with a wire- tap order. That would include providers of encrypted e-mail, such as BlackBerry, networking sites like Facebook and direct communi- cation services like Skype" (Homeland Security Newswire, 2010). According to Christopher Calabrese (2010), ACLU Legislative Counsel, "Under the guise of a technical fix, the gov- ernment looks to be taking one more step toward conducting easy dragnet collection of Americans' most private communications. Mandating that all communications software be accessible to the government is a huge privacy invasion."

> "Congress must reject the Obama administration's proposal to make the Internet wiretap ready."—Christopher Calabrese (2010), ACLU Legislative Counsel

What does this all mean for teachers and students? Basically that at this moment anything we say or do online may be viewed by the government and be part of a law enforcement or Homeland Security investigation. I realize this isn't, probably new news to the computers and writing crowd—of course, every thing we say and do online is subject to seizure! of course, the anonymity and pseudonymity possible online is illusionary!—but amid the file sharing, uploading, friending, tweeting and texting it may be possible to lose sight of that and for students and less-tech savvy colleagues it may be something they never have known. Does your institution's student handbook or faculty policy manual have a section on possible government interception and surveillance of Web communications on its networks? If so, have you read it? Have your students?

As with net neutrality and data mining by corporations, knowledge is, of course, the first step. It's hard to advocate for changing (or upholding) a particularly policy and regulation if you don't know what they are or what the impact of various alternatives might be. But beyond education, there are actions we can take, individually and collectively with colleagues at our own institutions and within professional organizations.

4. It's not too late: Pathways to action

Possible actions for addressing issues of net neutrality, data mining, and Web surveillance can be categorized into three interrelated areas: educating ourselves, educating others, and promoting advocacy.

4.1. Educating ourselves

Because of the current open structure of the Internet, we can access extensive information about these issues—from the videos and texts of government hearings and judicial rulings to real-time reactions to changing legislation or corporate policy. Organizations such as the American Civil Liberties Union, the Digital Due Process coalition, Free Press, the Electronic Privacy Information Center, the Electronic Frontier Foundation, Public Knowledge, and the OpenNet Initiative, to name but a few, are excellent resources for teachers, students, and citizen activists to learn not only the background and contexts of the issues, but also current legislative, executive, and judicial developments in terms of policies and regulations.

As with any public issue, getting informed isn't a one-time event either because, of course, circumstances and policies will change. Perhaps by the time this article goes to press, the FCC may have, for example, acted to reclassify the Internet as a common carrier (doubtful but one can always hope!), or the regulations proposed by the FTC may have been adopted, or the ECPA will have been amended. But corporations continually strive to peel back regulations and law enforcement and other government agencies will always be calling for more and easier surveillance. So regardless of what specifically the state of policy is now or in 2020, the point remains—we will need to be informed about the issues and vigilant to how policy matters impact the Web and our possible uses of the Web.

In relation to privacy online, we will also need to be informed about how we might change our settings and practices at the online sites we visit, with the applications we use, and with the digital devices (and who knows what those will look like by 2020) with which we interact. For example, as Lory Hawkes (2007) advocated in her discussion of the dangers of surveillance and data mining for researchers, there are specific actions, albeit small, that we can take to aim for more privacy online. We can change the settings on the software and hardware on our computers and mobile devices (e.g, blocking cookies, turning off location services). We can learn about the specific privacy policies of various sites we use and take action to change our privacy settings. We can find out from some corporations what our behavioral profile is, and we can choose to opt-out of targeted, personalized advertising, either on a site-by-site and company basis or, if the do-not-track option becomes available, then more widely across all the sites we visit. We can choose not to use some sites that have more egregious records of privacy violations. And we can learn more about and use more open-source, non-commercial sites and applications, either those online or ones to be downloaded and hosted on local servers. For example, the open-source Facebook alternative, Diaspora, may develop into a truly viable option, although as of this writing this privacy-oriented social networking site is still in the alpha stage and may not have the resources to compete. As one writer at Ars Technica reflected, "Online privacy remains a hot-button issue, but Facebook's popularity may be hard to overcome with a do-it-yourself solution as long as the company does enough with privacy issues to keep the general public content" (Foresman, 2010). Without word-of-mouth it can be hard to compete with industry behemoths, so informing ourselves (and students) to possible alternatives to corporate sites is important.

To become more informed we need to read more research and to conduct more research on these various issues. Research resources such as The Pew Internet and American Life surveys are excellent for finding out about how Americans use and access the Internet and what their expectations are for privacy. Reading research on topics such as surveillance in other disciplines provide frameworks for understanding the potential impacts of surveillance on online writers and the teaching of writing (e.g., Best, 2010; Dennis, 2008; Kerr et al., 2009). How have, for example, students' writing practices changed because of the potential surveillance online? Or how have their research practices changed with the advent of mobile devices, and how might their research practices change if paid prioritization and other such measures become adopted? And what of Internet access? How is the increasing reliance on mobile devices affecting student learning, and how might the lack of net neutrality impact that learning? These questions are just the start of a rich area of research opened by examining the intersections of national policy about the Internet and writing and the teaching of writing.

4.2. Educating others

As we integrate in ever more complex ways Web technologies in our classes, as we develop digitally-focused writing programs, writing majors, and graduate degrees, we can aim to build in—as workshops, as activities or units of some courses, as a course unto itself—explicit discussion of policies that shape and will shape the Internet now and in the future. As Selber (2004) persuasively showed, technological literacy is comprised of (at least) three intertwined literacies: functional, rhetorical, and critical. In order to know how to use a particular software or online application in rhetorically effective ways, we (students and instructors alike) need to know how to use it and we need to be able to interrogate the assumptions and biases built into the interfaces (and into the language developers use to frame their sites) in order to be able to resist technological regularization (see Selber, 2004, pp. 99-106 for a clear and student-accessible description of this). Users of online sites need the skills and the theoretical lenses to analyze the power relations and imbalances that exist in all technological interfaces (e.g., Selfe & Selfe, 1994; Wysocki & Jasken, 2004). We don't necessarily need to restructure our entire curricula to integrate discussion of these issues either. Instead we can layer in these discussions amid the course goals we have. In a first-year writing course studying rhetoric, we might ask students to analyze, and compare online sites' privacy policies or to study the arguments made by various stakeholders in the debates over revising electronic communication privacy laws. The primary learning outcomes are to learn rhetoric, but secondary outcomes for increasing critical awareness of the writing technologies we use would also be met. In a 200-level research writing course aimed at teaching the integration of primary and secondary research, we may, as I did, ask students to design and administer a survey about privacy and the Internet. In this case, not only did the process of creating the survey teach students a lot about research and not only did the results garner excellent primary data for students to work with, but also the survey served to help raise the issue of online privacy with the 800 Miami students who took the survey. In an upper division multimodal composing course whose primary goals are learning effective multimodal rhetoric, we might ask students to make public service announcements arguing various sides of the net neutrality issue seeking to raise awareness among different audiences. In graduate seminars we might focus the policy discussion on its workplace and professional implications, looking at how technical communicators, Web developers, and academics (to name but a few) are advocating for, challenging, or just coping with various regulations and laws or the lack thereof.

We can seek to educate colleagues at our local institutions and in our professional organizations about policy issues affecting writers, writing, and research online. And we can aim to "go public" (Mortensen, 1998) with our research too so as to reach broader audiences as well. It's hard for anyone to advocate for the importance of net neutrality, for example, if they don't know what it is or that it's threatened.

4.3. Promoting advocacy

Becoming informed and educating others are all actions too, of course, but there are also a number of more specific, direct actions we can take to advocate for changes (or retentions) to specific regulations and policies (including issues I haven't discussed here such as copyright regulations and broadband access). One is to join, volunteer for, and support organizations whose types of advocacy we wish to foster. Organizations such the ACLU, EFF, FreePress, and Public Knowledge are often up against multi-billion dollar corporations who have armies of lawyers, lobbyists and publicists to aid their cause. Hard to imagine what a 25 dollar donation might do in that scheme of things but if enough individuals contribute it may be possible for those organizations to get non-corporate perspectives heard. Communicating matters is not just up to the non-profits and their lobbyists. Your one e-mail or letter to your legislative representatives may not make a difference, but 100,000 (or more) letters from individuals might. I'm sure the staff of my Congressional Representative, House Speaker John Boehner (R), delete my e-mails as soon as they verify that I'm a registered Democrat, but what if he received 50,000 e-mails all advocating for a particular policy? As individual consumers we also have power through collective action. The Facebook user uprising over Beacon—including many people closing their accounts—got the attention of Zuckerberg and other Facebook executives because of the irrefutable formula of users' profits. No users for most of these sites means no money, so there is power in boycotts, even it's just a one-day, don't-use-X-site protest.

We also have the collective voice and power of profession-al organizations to mobilize. We might, for example, work with the membership of 7Cs to draft a position statement about a particular policy issue and its impact on the teaching of writ- ing for presentation to the CCCC membership and

> "NOT NEUTRALITY: The FCC caved to pressure from AT&T and passed a fake Net Neutrality rule. Join more than 2 million people in our pledge to keep fighting un-til we get real Net Neutrality."— Save the Internet (2010) <http://www.savetheinternet.com/>.

then the Executive Board, perhaps one affirming the importance of net neutrality. The research we conduct on the impact of particular policies on student learning and writing we can share not only within our organizations, but also with legislatures and other government of-ficials. An excellent model for this is the work the CCCC IP Caucus has done in relation to challenging provisions of the Digital Mille-nium Copyright Act (DMCA). In addition to keeping a detailed site for CCCC membership about DMCA developments, (see http://www.ncte.org/cccc/committees/ip), members of the IP caucus have written letters to the United States Intellectual Property Enforcement Coordi-nator and testified at government hearings, as Martine Rife Courant did in 2009 at a hearing about DMCA (CCCC IP Caucus, 2009). This level of advocacy is important and effective. We can also ask NCTE leadership to work with NCTE's Director of the Washington D.C. office (in 2010, Barbara Cambridge) to meet with government officials and to lobby for specific regulatory and policy changes.

But as college instructors faced with never-ending streams of digi-tal projects to grade, classes to prepare (not to mention teach), students to advise, committees to serve on, and research and writing of our own to conduct (not to mention personal lives to lead) finding the time to learn about and take action on such issues as net neutrality, data mining, and Web surveillance can seem, perhaps, overwhelming. Yet we absolutely must get informed and get involved in trying to check the Web surveillance, data mining, and corporate control of our online information. The future of the Internet—and all of our potential uses of the Internet—depend on it.

WORKS CITED

Aaron, Craig. (2010). Google-Verizon pact: It gets worse. *The Huffington Post,*. Retrieved from http://www.huffingtonpost.com

American Council on Education. (2006, June 9). Appeals court splits on CALEA suit.

American Council on Education v. Federal Communications Commission. No. 05-1404. (Court of Appeals, D.C. District).

Anderson, Daniel. (2003). Prosumer approaches to new media composition: Consumption and production in continuum. *Kairos*, 8(1).

Baker, Meredith Attwell. (2010, December 23). Dissenting statement of Commissioner Meredith Attwell Baker.

Banks, Adam. (2006). *Race, rhetoric, and technology: Searching for higher ground.* Urbana: NCTE.

Bruns, Axel. (2008). *Blogs, Wikipedia, Second Life, and beyond: From production to produsage.* New York: Peter Lang.

Calabrese, Christopher. (2010). Administration seeks easy access to Americans private online communications. American Civil Liberties Union.

Chirgwin, Richard. (2011, August 11). LinkedIn pulls Facebook-style stunt. *The Register.*

CCCC IP Caucus. (2009). CCCC's IP Caucus member, Martine Courant Rife of Lansing Community College, testifies at the DMCA hearings at the Library of Congress.

Claburn, Thomas. (2009). Google granted floating data center patent. *Information Week.*

Clyburn, Mignon L. (2010, December 23). Approving in part, concurring in part: Statement of Commissioner Mignon L. Clyburn.

Communications Assistance for Law Enforcement Act. (1994). 108 Stat. 4279. Public Law No. 103-4-4.

Copps, Michael J. (2010, December 23). Concurring statement of Commissioner Michael J. Copps.

Craig, Susanne, & Sorkin, Andrew Ross. (2011, January 2). Goldman offering clients a chance to invest in Facebook. *New York Times* Dealbook.

Dempsey, James X. (2010, September 22). Statement to the Senate Committee on the Judiciary at the Hearing on The Electronic Commu- nications Privacy Act: Promoting Security and Protecting Privacy in the Digital Age.

Dennis, Kingsley. (2008). Keeping a close watch—the rise of self surveillance and the thread of digital exposure. *The Sociological Review*, 56, 347–357.

DeVoss, Dànielle Nicole, Rife, Martine Courant., & Slattery, Shaun. Eds. (2011). *Copy(write):Intellectual property in the writing classroom.* Parlor Press.

EDUCAUSE Coalition. (2005). Statement submitted to the Federal Communications Commission. Retrieved from

Electronic Communications Privacy Act (ECPA). (1986). 100 Stat. 1848. Public Law 99-508.

Electronic Privacy Information Center. (2010). Social networking privacy.

Facebook. (2010, April 22). Privacy policy.

FacebookDevelopers. (2010, September 30). Documentation.

Federal Communications Commission (FCC). (2005, August 5). FCC 05-151 *Policy Statement*.

Federal Communications Commission (FCC). (2008, August 1). Commission orders Comcast to end discriminatory network management practices.

Federal Communications Commission (FCC). (2010, December 21). FCC 10-201 *Preserving the Open Internet*.

Federal Trade Commission (FTC). (2010, December 1). Protecting consumer privacy in an era of rapid change: A proposed framework for businesses and policy makers. Preliminary FTC staff report.

Fiveash, Kelly. (2011, August 12). LinkedIn u-turns to appease peeved users. *The Register*.

Foucault, Michel. (1995). *Discipline and punish: The birth of the prison*. New York: Random House.

Franken, Al. (2010, August 19). Net neutrality FCC hearing. Minneapolis, Minnesota.

Genachowski, Julius. (2009, September 21). Improving broadband and mobile communications. Speech to the Brookings Institute.

Genachowski, Julius. (2010, December 23). Statement of Commissioner Julius Genachowski.

Grabill, Jeffrey T. (2003). On divides and interfaces: Access, class, and computers. *Computers and Composition*, 20, 455–472.

Gross, Ralph, & Acquisti, Alessandro. (2005). Information revelation and privacy in online social networks (The Facebook case). ACM workshop on Privacy in the Electronic Society.

Hawkes, Lori. (2007). Impact of invasive web technologies on digital research. In A. McKee Heidi, & Nicole Devoss Dànielle (Eds.), *Digital writing research: Technologies, methodologies, and ethical issues*. Creskill: Hampton.

Helft, Miguel, & Vega, Tanzina. (2010, August 29). Retargeting ads follow users to other sites. *New York Times*.

Homeland Security Newswire. (2010). U.S. to make Internet wiretaps easier. Kang, Cecilia. (2011, April 12). Kerry, McCain offer bill to protect Web users' privacy rights. *Washington Post*.

Karr, Tim. (2010). AT&T's latest tactic to rewrite history. *Save the Internet*.

Kelsey, Joel. (2010). Free Press urges policymakers to reject Google-Verizon pact.

Kerr, Ian, Steeves, Valerie, & Lucock, Carole (Eds.). (2009). *Lessons from the identity trail: Anonymity, privacy, and identity in a networked society*. New York: Oxford University Press.

Leahy, Patrick. (2010, September 22). Chairman Statement to the Senate Committee on the Judiciary at the Hearing on The Electronic Communications Privacy Act: Promoting Security and Protecting Privacy in the Digital Age.

Leibowitz, Jon D. (2010, July 27). Statement at the Consumer Online Privacy Hearing held by the Committee on Commerce, Science, and Transportation.

Lenhart, Amanda, & Madden, Mary. (2007). Teens, privacy and online social networks. Pew Internet and American Life Project.

McCullagh, Declan. (2010, April 6). Court: FCC has no power to regulate net neutrality. CNet News.

McDonald, Aleecia M. (2009, September 17). Online privacy: Industry self-regulation in practice. Google Talk.

McDowell, Robert M. (2010, December 23). Dissenting statement of Commissioner Robert M. McDowell.

McKee, Heidi A. & Porter, James E. (2009). *The ethics of internet research: A rhetorical, case-based approach.* New York: Peter Lang.

McNealy, Scott. (1999). Sun on privacy: 'Get over it'. *Wired.*

Millar, Jason. (2009). Core privacy: A problem for predictive data mining. In Kerr Ian, Steeves Valerie, & Lucock Carole (Eds.), *Lessons from the identity trail: Anonymity, privacy, and identity in a networked society* (pp. 103–119). New York: Oxford University Press.

Moran, Charles. (1999). Access: The a-word in technology studies. In E. Hawisher Gail, & L. Selfe Cynthia (Eds.), *Passions, pedagogies, and 21st century technologies.* Logan: Utah State University Press.

Mortensen, Peter. (1998). Going public. *College Composition and Communication,* 50, 182–205.

Obama, Barack. (2007, November 14). On net neutrality. Speech given at Mountain View, California.

Open Internet Coalition. (2010). Why an open Internet.

Opsahl, Kurt., (2010). Facebook's eroding privacy policy: A timeline. Electronic Frontier Foundation.

Rife, Martine Courant, Westbrook, Steve, DeVoss, Dànielle Nicole, & Logie, John. (Eds.) (2010). Special issue: Copyright, culture, creativity, and the commons. *Computers and Composition,* 27.

Rockefeller, John D. (2010, July 27). Majority Statement. Consumer online privacy Hearing held by the U.S. Senate Committee on Commerce, Science, and Transportation.

Roslansky, Ryan. (2011, June 23). Ads enhanced by the power of your network. *LinkedIn Blog.*

Selfe, Cynthia L. (1999). Technology and literacy in the twenty-first century: The importance of paying attention. Carbondale: Southern Illinois University Press.

Selfe, Cynthia L. & Selfe, Richard J. (1994). The politics of the interface: Power and its exercise in electronic contact zones. *College Composition and Communication,* 45, 480–503.

Selber, Stuart A. (2004). *Multiliteracies for a digital age.* Carbondale: Southern Illinois University Press.

Sidler, Michelle. (2004). The not-so-distant future: Composition studies in the culture of biotechnology. *Computers and Composition,* 21, 129–145.

Smith, Aaron. (2010, June 7). *Mobile access 2010.* Pew Internet and American Life Project.

Strickland, Jonathan. (2010). How Web 3.0 will work. How Stuff Works.

Tennessee General Assembly. (2011). Bill information for SB0049.

Turner, S. Derek. (2010). AT&T misleads FCC about 'paid prioritization' on the Internet.

Twitter. (2009, September 18). Terms of Service. Retrieved from http://twitter.com/tos

USA Patriot Act. (2001). 115 Stat. 272. Public Law 107-56.

Verizon & Google. (2010, August 9). Verizon-Google legislative framework proposal.

Waters, Maxine. (2010). FCC net neutrality rules don't go far enough, could harm many American consumers of color.

Weinberg, Michael, & Bergmayer, John. (2010). Public Knowledge explains the Comcast-Bittorrent decision.

Westin, Alan F. (1967). *Privacy and freedom.* Atheneum.

Westin, Alan F. (Ed.). (1971). *Information technology in a democracy.* Cambridge: Harvard University Press.

Westin, Alan F. & Baker, Michael A. (1972). *Databanks in a free society: Computers, record-keeping, and privacy.* Times Books.

Wysocki, Anne F. & Jasken, Julia I. (2004). What should be an unforgettable face. *Computers and Composition*, 21, 29–48.

Zuckerberg, Mark. (2010, January 8). Mike Arrington interrogates Mark Zuckerberg. Upstream.

Notes

1. Net neutrality is a policy issue about access and control of information and technologies. For more detailed discussions of access and/or policy issues surrounding access see (Banks, 2006; Grabill, 2003; Moran, 1999). Important policy issues I will not be discussing in this article include issues of copyright and intellectual property (for recent discussions of copyright, see DeVoss, Rife, & Slattery, 2011; Rife et al., 2010).

2. Verizon refused in September 2007 to allow NARAL Pro-choice America to send text messages to subscribers over its network. As one of the two largest phone companies in the U.S., this refusal affected millions of potential subscribers to NARAL's text-messenging system. Because public outcry was so vocal, Verizon reversed its decision one week later without any legal or government action necessary.

3. I strongly recommend reading the five FCC commissioners' statements about their votes on "Preserving the Open Internet Broadband Industry Practices" (FCC, 2010). It's fascinating reading. With the exception of Genachowski (2010), none of the other commissioners, even the two who voted for it, are positive about the order. The two Republican members, Meredith Attwell Baker (2010) and Robert McDowell (2010), blast the regulations as government interference and take-over of a free market enterprise in their statements of dissent. The two Democratic members, Mignon Clyburn (2010) and Michael Copps

(2010), begrudgingly support it while noting many of the serious problems with the regulations. Rather than "approve" they just "approve in part, concur in part" and "concur" respectively.

4. Despite the fact that these new FCC regulations are basically a capitulation to industry, Verizon, less than one month after the release of the regulations, filed a lawsuit in the same federal court in D.C. that had ruled in favor of Comcast earlier. Verizon argued that the FCC had no authority to regulated fixed broadband providers either because the Internet is not a common carrier. The lawsuit was later thrown out on a technicality because Verizon filed before the regulations had been published in the Federal Register. But, if Republicans in the House of Representatives are successful, no lawsuits may be needed. They have twice passed legislation to ban the FCC from regulating the Internet; however, the legislation currently has no chance to pass in the Senate with a Democrat majority.

5. This definition of privacy focuses on control of information. For more detailed discussions of privacy and concepts of privacy in relation to online communications, see Kerr, Steeves, & Lucock, 2009, a collection that includes extensive references to other privacy sources.

6. In a more recent example in the summer of 2011, the social networking site LinkedIn changed its privacy policy to allow the use of users' photos in advertising—what it called "social advertising" (Roslansky, 2011). That is, photos of users would be embedded among advertising—not just advertising for LinkedIn, but third-party advertising too. Upon full roll-out in early August, all users were automatically enrolled in this, meaning that anyone's photo could be used in advertising. Users were outraged and one day after the feature was discussed in the online technology journal The Register (Chirgwin, 2011), LinkedIn changed its policy to discontinue the feature (Fiveash, 2011).

7. As one reviewer of this article noted, however, simply moving to open source applications and sites may lessen but will not eliminate the possible corporate data mining of online communications (and it certainly doesn't solve the problem of government surveillance).

8. In April 2011, Senators John Kerry and John McCain introduced an Internet privacy bill that adopted many of the recommendations in the FTC's report. If this bill becomes law, it would be easier for people to opt-out of data collection and companies would need to inform people of what data they collect. However, the bill would not do anything about how long companies are allowed to keep the data for and how they might use the information they collect (Kang, 2011).

9. I focus here on surveillance by government and law enforcement agents but the Internet has also led to what Kingsley Dennis (2008) called the "participatory panopticon" where "bottom-up surveillance" also affects people's actions—what they write, do, and say online.

10. In two widely-acclaimed books Access Denied and Access Controlled (available for free at http://opennet.net), the OpenNet Initiative (ONI) tracks and reports on Internet censorship and surveillance worldwide.

11. In an appendix to a prepared statement for a Congressional Hearing, James X. Dempsey (2010), the Vice President for Public Policy at the Center for Democracy & Technology provides an interesting explanation of how one e-mail may have multiple legal standards applied to it. For example, all e-mails during transmission—from the time the sender clicks send and the message appears in the receiver's inbox—are protected by the Wiretap Act, which requires a warrant to intercept communications in transit. For up to 180 days, if the e-mail is not opened and read, the government needs a warrant to be able to access it. But from the moment the e-mail is read or after 180 days of being stored unopened, the e-mail then, as Dempsey explained, "loses warrant protection and can be obtained from the service provider with a mere subpoena."

ENCULTURATION

Enculturation is on the Web at http://www.enculturation.net/

Enculturation was started in 1996 by two graduate students. In its 17 years it has never had institutional support beyond web space provided by a university and has never been affiliated with a press or organization. Currently it is hosted on an individual's server and supported with one RA through the University of South Carolina. All of the managerial, editorial, and production work has been done by young faculty and graduate students in the field of rhetoric and composition. The mission of the journal has generally been to publish broader ranging interdisciplinary work related to rhetoric and composition that is more theoretical or media-oriented.

Re-Reading Marshall McLuhan: Hectic Zen, Rhetoric, and Composition

"Re-reading Marshall McLuhan" was published in our special issue on Marshall McLuhan. The essay pulls together academic writing, poetry, and Veeder's own visual art to offer a counter-history of the field—not a linear history of the connections and sequences of rhetoric and the work of McLuhan, but a "compositional jazz riff" that combines movements inspired by McLuhan, rhetorical practice, and scholarship in composition and media ecology. The essay itself also has a unique history. It was republished on another (established) site without the author's consent or Acknowledgment of prior publication in *Enculturation*. Since *Enculturation* has a Creative Commons license that allows author's to republish as along as prior publication in *Enculturation* is acknowledged, the editors contacted Veeder who then contacted the site. He decided to allow the site to republish the essay with an attribution to *Enculturation*. Such an event speaks to some of the challenges facing independent scholarly publishing as more of our field turns to online and digital forums for our scholarship. We selected Veeder's essay because it is an excellent example of mutli-genre scholarship and of the reach of online scholarship in general and Veeder's essay in particular.

5 Re-reading Marshall McLuhan: Hectic Zen, Rhetoric, and Composition

Rex Veeder

Figure 1: All art unless otherwise indicated by Rex Veeder.

Marshall McLuhan deserves to be re-evaluated as a rhetorician be-cause he has described and demonstrated a perspective on rhetoric that remains significant. That perspective involves aesthetic, social, and cultural elements that gravitate around a mythos of (w)holistic understanding: an auditory experience, which is the evolutionary result of electronic media. McLuhan's explorations, not explanations, are in harmony with rhetorical studies, and he is a sophist. His work resonates with Kenneth Burke's. *Counter Statement* and *Counter Blast* are manifestos for a revolution by evolution through the artistic creation necessary to resist "Mechanization."

Those who recognize the vitality of counter rhetoric offer us access to them. For example, Jeff Rice's *The Rhetoric of Cool* describes a rhetoric resonating with the patterns offered a composer, whether writer or reader, in the hectic environment of juxtaposition, nonlinearity, and imagery—the environment of the mosaic. Byron Hawk's *A Counter History of Composition* acknowledges three motives for composition that apply to this environment: oppositional, investigative, and complex. In both cases, the environment and work site for composition becomes a rhetorical space where what is complex is massaged into meaning through the recognition of patterns (relationships) so that the complexity is revealed as more than chance. The mind of a composer in this situation becomes a Zen mind, dedicated to grasping and articulating the whole in moments of discovery amid the clamor of seemingly contradictory information.

Yet, we do not often practice our scholarly work with these things in mind, and depend instead upon the forms and structures of linear composition. What follows is an essay not an explanation, an exploration with argument growing from discoveries along the way. It is a compositional jazz riff, and offers the mosaic as a genre or form appropriate to the auditory universe McLuhan describes. The mosaic, in both visual and literary form, has a long history and is cross-cultural. The essay explores some of that history. Electronic rhetoric can be multi-modal and multi-genred. McLuhan's interest in counter cultures, the beats and others, offers a warrant for working with art and poetry as one of the ways of exploring the topic.

A Hectic Zen Meditation

Sit in a dark room with one hundred mosquitoes
and listen to the news
play a blues baseline
as if each note were a coupon

for what we want to know

after time withers
grind black ink from pine
burned for weeks in the mountains

find white paper
this is when Burke's dream
the grammar
and McLuhan's space raider
drag you through a vanishing point

long for something missing
don't be afraid
something is always missing

dance with the attraction

perform the longing
before the paper —
before paper turns to sand
paint on the sand
whateverwhen

Allatonce—buzzing

listen in the fuzzing
for what you want to say

hey!

this is Burke's invitation to rhetoric
McLuhan's hectic pattern dancing.
Therefore,
        do the dance.

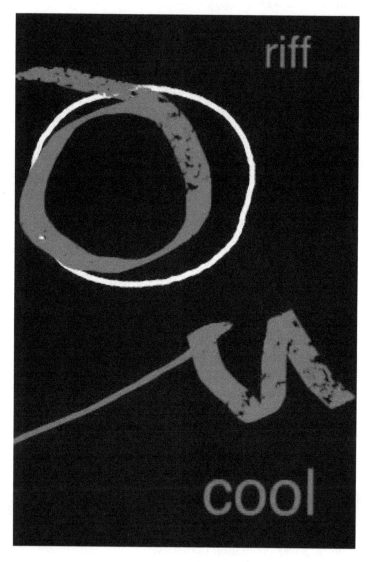

Figure 2

THE SCENE

As a student of rhetoric, I was introduced to McLuhan in one or two classes during the 60s and 70s but the introduction was brief – more like having a family member introduce you to an uncle from Canada who, although he was family, some how didn't fit in. He was inappropriate. Perhaps he would have one too many drinks and start to talk about family secrets or tell some jokes that would spoil the mood. I distrusted him, even though I was familiar with the political and cultural revolutions of the time. He was, I know now, something of a Timothy Leary in the eyes of my teachers. Someone who dealt out the drug of altered consciousness. My fundamental conclusion about McLuhan, however, was that he was also a gift giver.

McLuhan's first gift is a gift of an altered perception that harmonizes us with the spirit of the age. His second gift is the recognition that media awareness and critique can afford us moments of response in the electronic hurricane. When we deliberately practice this repose, we are not awash anymore. When we make something of the fragmented information rather that wait for a message from it, we are massaged, and, perhaps for a moment, comforted. Like books, our analytical habits are not going to go away but will be transformed to this end by the instruments of the age.

Those instruments are a third gift to us, and I want to be conscious of those instruments. The jacket of *Counter Blast* has it that "We have passed beyond the plodding word by word along the straight and narrow path of Linotype, eyes glued to the track, the reward of Meaning awaiting us at the end." Book lovers are expert at walking the path and understand the need for books, but if nothing else McLuhan has challenged us to address the current and future ocean of kinesthesia and simultaneous sensations in the holistic environment of his auditory experience.

HECTIC ZEN AND COMPOSITION

I imagine a moment when someone asks Marshall McLuhan if his interest in the East meant that he would be interested in Zen. In my imaginary conversation his answer is: "Never mind." I believe such a response would be in keeping with the kind of rhetoric McLuhan suggests to us. One perfectly clear note in Zen is once you have the idea you have lost the Zen. Or, having ideas is a preparation for the realization Zen practice offers. One of the best works on Zen and haiku is Robert Aitken's *A Zen Wave*. Aitken quotes Yamada Roshi: "When your consciousness has become ripe in true zazen – pure like clear water, like a serene maintain lake, not moved by any wind – then anything may serve as a medium for realization"(3-4). Zen is the practice of preparing the mind for a moment of realization, and Zen practice encourages constant inquiry in preparation for a realization about a question or a problem rather than an answer. This is exploring rather than explaining and meaning making rather than answering. As Aitken says, "The entire teaching of Zen is framed by questions"(4). And, the art of Zen practice has to do with the performance of contemplating the questions that created the frame – or the background against which the drama of questioning is performed.

Aiken offers haiku as an analogy for this act of realization. Exploring the form and content of a traditional haiku, one that has three hundred years of exposition and contemplation on record, he describes the acts of the mind in practicing either writing in the form or in reading it.

> Old pond!
> Frog jumps in
> water's sound.

First, as W.S. Merwin points out in his introduction, the haiku is not just a single poem but has relationships with all other haikus. Reading a collection of haiku, for example, violates a sense of unity for the Western reader who might be expecting more means of development than the poem allows. The short poems, like fragments, jar the Western mind. One reader said that the experience was like "being pecked to death my doves" (xiii). But what seems to be fragments are not. The form of the haiku comes from poets writing poems together, each contributing a haiku and then passing the poem on. There was a communal act of creation and meaning making as poets contemplated the series of poems and then contributed something that completed the form at the moment. It was an act, I believe, of unifying a mosaic – Hectic Zen.

McLuhan's work focuses on the hectic but acts in the spirit and formal space of Zen. His description of the electronic age, the auditory universe, reveals its frantic nature; there's an assault on the mind and senses from fragments of experiences in images, sounds, words, thoughts, and immediacy of the global village, which is in itself a metaphor for a state of mind in need of unifying legislation. The term *hectic* echoes this cacophony and jangle but suggests the street version of the term, which partakes of being cool in the midst of chaos – and enjoying it. Thus, an intellectual haiku for Hectic Zen might be:

> Frantic is to street
> what cool is to beat!
> in the ringing stillness extremes meet.

Again, the purpose of Zen is not answering questions but contemplating them. So, writing in a Zen space is always writing away from understanding—exploring rather than explaining, waiting for the plop of a frog in a pond of the mind. This is rhetoric in the acoustic—a rhetoric in a new key. I am grateful to Cynthia Selfe, Michael Spooner, Kathleen Yancey, Victor Vitanza, and Gail Hawisher. I like "composition in a new key," and I imagine rhetoric in a new key is much the same since all rhetoric is about composition after all (see Yancey 791).

New technologies have become a new strange attractor in rhetoric and composition studies. Usually, the revitalization of rhetoric emerges through the study of rhetorical history and theory with composition studies echoing. Perhaps the McLuhan universe changes the ratios of influence in the relationship. It may be that rhetoric needs to focus on the acts of rhetoric and their products as composition more than ever before.

Figure 3: Dance after the plop in the pond

In *The Rhetoric of Cool*, Jeff Rice introduces a philosophy of electronic composition, and finds in the beats an example of a composition for a new consciousness. Rice works with Burroughs to draw from literature a process for *composing* as distinguished in emphasis from writing. The rip, mix, burn, and remix of the Flash presentation offers a composing process related to, perhaps, but distinguishable from writing processes as it has been taught. Writers and teachers, such as Selfe and those I mentioned earlier are organizing the environment for us. However, as Rice says, "Overall, the mix reveals this type of composing in most twentieth-and twenty-first-century new media writings. The one place the mix as appropriative rhetoric is missing is in writing pedagogy" (65). It is into this pedagogical gap that a concept and process, based on Hectic Zen can work to our advantage. The idea that we are working with a pedagogy of composing with writing as <u>only</u> one component among many is a powerful idea in itself.

Hectic Zen is the result of the fusion of electronic media with Zen practice. For McLuhan, the acoustic environment is the experience of *allatonceness*. It is a Hectic-Zen experience where enlightenment is possible, perhaps even as in the silence of deep meditation.

Participating in McLuhan's consciousness is an exploratory venture. In a situation where knowledge making is more important than knowledge explaining, exploration is essential, exploration in keeping with the McLuhan universe, which is the universe of the new physics where Strange Attractors make more sense than conventional organizational models. There is a mathematical definition of strange attractors, basically that, and I'll go with a *Wikipedea* definition here, "an attractor is a set towards which a dynamical system evolves over time." I am using the attractor as an analogy for centering in an electronic universe. For composition, attraction is pattern creation with the recognition of resonance. The pattern happens when a force gathers in a spot that attracts unexpected but perfectly aligned elements and they form up in a once-in-a-life-time shape. If our compositional design depended on strange attractors they would resemble Zen gardens.

McLuhan recognized that the East's orientation toward space offered a corrective or counter blast to Western perception. In *Through the Vanishing Point*, (a gesture to Alice's looking glass) he includes a passage from of *The Book of Tea*: "The usefulness of a water pitcher dwelt in the emptiness where water might be put, not in the form of the pitcher or the material of which it was made. Vacuum is all potent because all containing. In vacuum alone motion becomes possible" (265). He also recognized the resonance of the new physics with art and Eastern perceptions, as in:

Figure 4: A strange attractor without math

The more that one says about acoustic space the more one realizes that it's the thing that mathematicians and physicists of the past fifty years have been calling space-time, relativity, and non-Euclidean systems of geometry. And it was into this acoustic world that the poets and painters began to thrust in the mid-19th century. Like Coleridge's Mariner, they were the first that ever burst into that silent sea. (*Counter Blast* 114)

Whether Western Physics or Eastern Aesthetics, the emphasis for McLuhan is on the shift of perception away from the carefully fenced mind.

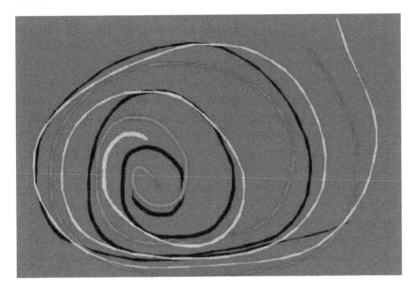

Figure 5: A question looking for a way out of the frame

The mythology of the well-made and orderly universe and the clock maker is clearly an idea McLuhan identifies as bankrupt. That mythology is countered by the mythology of the new physics, where all elements of the universe are subject to change through relationships with everything else. It is a mythology of "Wow" and "Oh. Oh." Surprise, delight, and devastation are wrapped in the same package and the frail, emotional and psychological worlds of human beings must learn to account for this disruptive and volatile universe. Our universe is either fragmented or a mosaic.

McLuhan recognized the significance of art as a way to create a mosaic from the fragments of perception and society. In Through the Vanishing Point, he says: "Any artistic endeavor includes the preparing of an environment for human attention. A poem or a painting is in every sense a teaching machine for the training of perception and judgment" (238) By extension, the artistic act of unifying fragments becomes the human act of unifying cultures and nations.

Rhetoricians are well aware of the mosaic of human kind and its implications. Michael Halloran, for example, says in "Further Thoughts on the End of Rhetoric":

What "O.E.R." ["On the End of Rhetoric"] ignored was the possibility that we live in multiple and fragmentary worlds, worlds that overlap, compete, and transform themselves continuously, worlds provided by family, ethnic community, neighborhood, profession, political affiliation, and so on. A more accurate portrayal of the modern condition, and perhaps of the postmodern and premodern conditions as well, would have emphasized the way identity is shaped by the voices of these multiple worlds in which we live, each of us an unstable, occasionally harmonious but often cacophonous chorus of these voices or—to return to spatial metaphor—a mosaic or quilt, made up of bits and pieces of past identities that were themselves assemblages of fragments. (114)

With Halloran, I've made an obvious gesture to rhetoric's historians. It is not necessary to reconcile McLuhan to rhetorical history and theory. His motives resonate with rhetoricians. Reading the *Gutenberg Galaxy*, we at some point recognize a history of rhetoric as heard through the timber and inflection of its technologies and epistemologies.

In addition, McLuhan addresses two areas of rhetoric relevant to both historians and theorists of rhetoric: aesthetics and epistemology. The aesthetic dimensions of his work are obvious and plentiful. His books and presentations, such as *Through the Vanishing Point*, are examples of art and dedicated to transforming consciousness (a way of making knowledge)—something he shared with the Beat generation, its Jazz and drugs and with Timothy Leary in regard to . . . well, consciousness and drugs.

The aesthetic experience in the counter and sub-cultures of the 50s through the 70s challenged not only the aesthetic sensibilities of the dominant culture but the epistemological and political dimensions as well. In McLuhan's universe, poets and artist are explorers and on the edge. He says in *Counter Blast*:

The external landscape technique of the Romantic poets and painters were pushed to the extreme point where they suddenly become internal and musical with Rimbaud and the symbolists. Instead of using a single external space to evoke and control mental states, it was suddenly discovered that many spaces could be included in a single poem or picture. The newspaper contributed directly to this new art form. And no sooner had this occurred than artists were enabled to see that all language and experience was, and had always been, this simultaneous and many-layered thing. (83)

This is the acoustic universe recognized in art before the electronic universe became pervasive. In such a space, where seemingly discordant elements exist together, we either make meaning through a mosaic or live with fragments and alienation.

POETS, RHETORICIANS, SOPHISTS – BURKE'S VAGABONDS

In *Culture is Our Business*, McLuhan writes, "Poets and artists live on frontiers. They have no feedback, only feedforward. They have no identities. They are probes" (44). Always an artist, McLuhan's revolution is a consciousness evolution. All his work is a mosaic, requiring our interpretation. What information he offers tempts us to reconsider, redesign, and to create our own knowledge. In his mosaic, time and space as we know them are moot and in the Zen sensibility evanescent. Among the implications of this mosaic is a particularly interesting and rhetorical one: the mosaic is suited to invention and the rhetorical practice of copia, which are both an attitude and a technique familiar to rhetorical conventions.

To understand the context of McLuhan's (w)holistic or auditory rhetoric, I want to create a space wherein McLuhan's *Counter Blast* and Kenneth Burke's *Counter Statement* resonate. For example, McLuhan, carried on Burke's "program," pretty much as Burke describes it. I am not suggesting that McLuhan's reading of Burke shaped his approaches but that McLuhan's motives and Burke's *resonate*.

In the practice of Hectic-Zen composition, resonating and making replace the practice of matching information. One of the maddening things about research as it is currently practiced is the assumption that without a physical or temporal connection no connection exists. *Copia* and *resonance* are key terms for Hectic-Zen research, which is (w)holistic and auditory and suggests that to insist on proximity as a criteria is a kind of empirical babble.

In this mode of research, we are influenced; we tingle together through our systems of interest. Thus, we tend to look for patterns of agreement in ways other than chronological or proximity scholarship. It is our shared systems of interest and alliances with like thinkers, as well as strangers who contradict us, that encourage us to sound out the interesting possibilities found in a community of thought. For example, Gloria Anzaldua's *Boarderlands* is one of the most reverberating examples of mosaic rhetoric and resistance to the machine Kenneth Burke opposes in *Counter Statement*. If not for resonance, getting Anzaldua and Burke together for a dinner conversation would be impossible. Proximity scholarship denies familial and tribal sharing, whereas (w)holistic and auditory scholarship encourages it.

Another example, Richard Enos in his *Greek Rhetoric Before Aristotle* presents a history of Greek rhetoric influenced by Homeric traditions *simpatico* with Anzalua's modality. The relationship of dialogue, rhetoric, and poetics is dynamic. If I might summarize Enos's assertions, the assent and dominance of Aristotle and Plato's rhetoric constitutes a major epistemological as well as cultural omission.

Aristotle's intolerance for sophistic rhetoric and the popularity of his *Rhetoric* consigned the sophists and the epistemology of Homeric rhetoric to the back room closet of academics and public life and law. The *Rhetoric*, which separated mythos and poetics from the appeals and the epistemological foundations of western civilization, "produced a theory of rhetoric so constricted that later attempts to trace its development allocated commonly associated elements of rational discourse such as thought, conceptualization and expression to distinct disciplines (philosophy and rhetoric) rather than viewing a unified progression of cognitive processes" (89).

The reintegration of Sophistic and poetics with rhetoric are counter blasts to Aristotle's dominance. This, too, is McLuhan's message: "The poet dislocates language into meaning. The artist smashes open the doors of perception" (*Culture is Our Business* 44).

Let there be no mistake, this is a political act recognized by McLuhan, Burke, and the echoing voices in rhetoric's history. Burke and McLuhan, both sensed and explored the reverberations of the poetic, the rhetorical stepchild, and recognized the social implications of the way we compose. For both of them the consciousness evolution requires the active participation of the artist.

K.B.'s program in *Counter Statement* is a testimony to the social involvement of an artist, literary critic, and dedicated "vagabond." Burke's blatant advertisements for his fiction and poetry at the beginning and end of the book are neither accidental nor offered with apology. I remember the first time I met Kenneth Burke. He was giving a talk to an academic audience in Normal Illinois. We were all waiting for a rendition of Dramatism. He cracked his journals and read us his poetry. Very Zen in Normal.

Figure 6: Kenneth Burke's Frog

If the key to Burke's rhetorical motives is identification, and it is, then Burke identifies with the artist as counter puncher in a fight for nothing less than humanity. His adversary is the efficient and productive culture that makes a religious duty of the practical, efficient, material possessions, and increased consumption along with "higher standards of living" and the "ubiquitous optimism" as well as "evangelizing" that characterizes the "practical-aesthetic" (110-111). Against the practical aesthetic, he posits the "Bohemian-aesthetic" in order to provide a corrective to the machine of efficiency and its pervasive culture. His *exordium*: "Let us attempt to bring to the fore such "Bohemian" qualities as destroy great practical enterprise" (119).

If you are following the ragged map I'm making and seeing the access roads that run along side, there is a philosophic resonance between Burke and McLuhan. The resonance may or may not be supported by scholarly documents and their own critiques of one another. In *Language as Symbolic Action*, Burke criticizes McLuhan for focusing on Media while neglecting language but then acknowledges that some messages are best suited to certain media. However, if we look at their shared questions about society, McLuhan and Burke share an artistic, complex, and holistic form of exploration, writing, and thinking.

McLuhan, for example, would contend that the challenge of rhetoric is to "first restore, and then to understand in a connubium, the unity of all the elements which men have abstracted by their codes from the primordial matrix" (*Counter Blast*, 62). There is resonance, here, with Burkes understanding of rhetoric's transforming and transcending role in the *Rhetoric of Motives* since rhetoric is "concerned with the state of Babel after the fall" (23) and seeks the final identification in "its ultimate expression in mysticism, the identification of the infinitesimally frail with the infinitely powerful" (326). Dealing with Babel and McLuhan's primordial matrix requires both the adaptation of multiple vocabularies and multiple composition modes – practiced as a Hectic Zen meditation/contemplation in the mosaic genre.

To compose with the mosaic, as composers, we have to suspend our point of view for a moment in an act of faith. We will want to plight our troth to the other, the strange, the anti-environment—not as tourists in a quest for exotic titillation or colonization but as thoughtful guests and vagabonds who recognize we are always as strange to ourselves as we are to others and they to us. The practice of this faithful and hectic composition is not idiosyncratic or rare.

MEDLEY WITH FOUR COMPOSERS AND MOSAIC

Figure 7: Zen Moon, Hectic Tree

Consider, what do we get when Burke, McLuhan, Gloria Anzaldua, and Ann E. Berthoff say the similar things in different modalities that create a shared effect and message? It's research in the auditory mode, where what "proofs" are available are not dependent upon chronology or proximity.

We should, for a moment, think back to Jeff Rice's assertion that "The one place the mix as appropriate rhetoric is missing is in writing pedagogy" (*Rhetoric of Cool* 65). The mosaic, and the satire, as a modes of composing in McLuhan's electronic age offer an opportunity to see how disparate ideas and information may resonate and offer us a sense of process as we negotiate the electronic universe. In the mosaic, the writer engages the topics and issues from a variety of positions and tonalities and, sometimes, mixes the visual with the phonetic. There is a sense in which the mosaic is musically inspired, drawing on the repetition of themes amid a number of variations on those themes. Finally, the mosaic is a form of satire.

It's a common place that McLuhan practiced Menippean satire with a mix of Joyce and Symbolist poets. Satire's etymology includes its Latin roots, which is a dish of mixed fruits offered to the gods, a "medley" or "mishmash." Our habitual understanding of satire includes irony, attacks on vices, and exaggeration. However, as a mode of composition, we also must recognize the kaleidoscopic formats and modualities of the satiric genre in poetry, novels, drama, and essays. The satire is a mosaic art, and when the irony and satirical intent is either toned down or dismissed, the mosaic remains. To say that McLuhan's work is satirical is to acknowledge the mosaic as much as to acknowledge his wit and temperament.

McLuhan's satire, his multi-modal and multi-genre explorations are foregrounded to the point that his books are performances. His poetic juxtaposition of words and images seldom settle anything for a reader but lead from the hint of an explanation to explore the scene in an act of interpretation and, like Burke, sense the resonance in seemingly dissociated thoughts. The typography in *Counter Blast* is an example of mosaic style, as if the words themselves were (as they truly are) susceptible to any configuration at any moment. Harley Parker performs McLuhan's idea of the auditory through visual manipulations and the oral dimension of language is suggested in the shifts in typeface and point as well as juxtaposition of words that appear to be leaping from the page with standard type. McLuhan's commitment to the mosaic is total, closely allied with his belief in the purpose of the book in the age of the mosaic. The book, he says, suggesting the whole of print culture as well, "HAS ACQUIRED NEW INTEREST AS A TOOL IN THE TRAINING OF PERCEPTION" (99).

In Burke, always the composer, the mosaic tendency as a habitual mode of composition is most obvious in his controlled associative approach to topics, and we read Burke best I think when we read him impromptu, choosing random sections to compare to other sections of his writing and sensing a resonance in his seemingly dissociated thoughts— a jazz tribute to linguistic riffing. With Burke, we are challenged to make meaning as he explains himself through exploring the interesting possibilities of a topic, where he comes to a position and abandons it with a concerned but satirical attitude, the attitude of a vagabond of thought.

The place where Burke and McLuhan meet is in the need for pattern recognition in McLuhan's description and Burke's focus on form. Burke recognizes that form is a matter of finding repose, or peace, in "a mutually adjusted set of terms" where "conflicting terms 'cooperate' in the building of an overall form" (*Rhetoric of Motives* 23). Thus, even the neurotic finds repose in form. McLuhan contends that our only response our neurotic environment of information overload is pattern recognition (*Medium* 132), the pattern being a fair analogy for the sense of form in Burke.

Gloria Anzaldua's Borderlands/*La Frontera* is an example of mosaic and multi-genred composition. She writes as she reflects on writing *Borderlands* that, "In looking at this book . . . I see a mosaic pattern (Aztec-like) emerging, a weaving pattern, thin here, thick there"(88). *La Frontera* is also, in the terms of this discussion, a satire in keeping with McLuhan's electronic universe. Her resonance of form and intention is a performance of McLuhan's auditory rhetoric, Hectic Zen, although Anzaldua is naturally practicing composing from her position as an indigenous writer.

Defined as a *Mestiza* by society and by self-definition, Anzaldua accepts the mosaic of her culture and composes from that position. The cacophony of languages and genres in *Borderlands* is a harmonious composition of competing languages, personalities, and genres. Resistance, art, and rhetoric are blended, and Borderlands is intensely personal while intensely public. Azaludua's poetry is an essential part of her argument and she chooses poetry, the use of line and image, to punctuate and deepen her message. Her final exordium, "Don't Give In, Chicanita," is a poem in both Spanish and English, and the last stanza nails her petition to the door:

> Yes, in a few years or centuries
> la Raza will rise up, tongue in tact
> carrying the best of all the cultures.
> that sleeping serpent,
> rebellion-(r)evolution, will spring up.
> Like old skin will fall the slave ways of
> obedience, acceptance, silence.
> Like serpent lightning we'll move, little women.
> You'll see. (225)

On the one hand, Anzaldua writes about history, culture and race. On the other, she reflects on the processes of composition and the *mestiza* consciousness, passages in her chapter "Tlilli, Tlapalli/The Path of the Red and Black," offer us an analogy for writing in an ambiguous and complex environment. In a segment entitled "A Tolerance For Ambiguity," (a title Ann Berthoff would applaud) Anzaldua writes:

La mestiza constantly has to shift out of habitual formations; from convergent thinking, analytical reasoning that tends to use rationality to move toward a single goal (a Western mode), to divergent thinking, characterized by movement away from set patterns and goals toward a more whole perspective, one that includes rather than excludes. (101)

The *mestiza* stands, "where phenomena tend to collide. It is where the possibility of uniting all that is separate occurs." (101)

Interest in indigenous rhetorics, as demonstrated in the most recent *CCC's Indigenous and Ethnic Rhetorics*, indicates our recognition of counter and resistive rhetoric. The shift in emphasis in our profession from considering such rhetorics as necessary rather than exotic is welcomed. If anyone wants to understand the scope and significance of Mestiz@ rhetoric, they should read Damian Baca's *Mestiz@ Scripts, Digital Migrations, and the Territories of Writing*. Baca engages Anzaldua's rhetoric as a strange attractor for a rhetoric of resistance and (r) evolution. He finds in the traditions:

performances of indigenous people of meaning-making that provide arguments for and against certain things, namely, the dominant narratives of assimilation. Moreover, both Mestiz@ ritual dance and paintings/writings embody a process of interactions whereby certain meanings and social realities specific to the Americas are shaped, destroyed, and sustained through official, resistant, and ritualistic use of rhetoric. (3)

Anzaldua's artful rhetoric is the performance Baca describes, a performance that suggests how we might compose in the auditory environment McLuhan's extended definition.

Ann E. Berthoff is a teacher, a philosopher of language and rhetoric, and composition theorist who raised composition theory above the empirical ocean and some considerable formulaic nonsense of modern traditional rhetoric. For her, Hectic Zen is a matter of responding to ambiguity, not in the sense of a dualistic perspective but in a multifaceted response where she follows I.A Richard's lead in exploring the deliberate disciplines of the mind necessary to working with complexity and ambiguity as "the hinges of thought" (*Making of Meaning* 70-71). She writes that, "chaos is scary: the meanings that can emerge from it, which can be discerned taking shape within it, can be discovered only if the students who are learning to write can learn to tolerate ambiguity" (71). The disciplines of thinking and philosophy such as "Extremes meet, compare to learn, and abstract to unify, are offered as the means for working with complexity, the chaos she says is necessary for writing and that McLuhan argues is a permanent component of our lives.

Berthoff's medium of choice is the mosaic. Like Burke's, her writings are generally collages of language and topics framed by a directive idea. *Forming, Thinking, Writing: The Composing Imagination* is one of the most clear examples of mosaic composition, where "There are some enterprises in which a careful disorderliness is the true method" (Melville qtd. in Berthoff 49). She practices satire in the definition of satire as mosaic, being multi-genred and multifaceted and blending contrasting ideas into harmony. She says: "Satire offers what Kenneth Burke, a learned and witty rhetorician calls "perspectives by incongruity." Things that don't belong together can, in juxtaposition, give us new insights, help us form concepts. Transforming is at the heart of Burke's theory of rhetoric" (138).

Such transformation can take us through the vanishing point McLuhan alludes to toward a place where we are making whatever we discover. In McLuhan's words: "The method of our time is to use not a single but multiple models of exploration—the technique of the suspended judgment is the discovery of the twentieth century as the technique of invention was the discovery of the nineteenth" (*Medium* 89).

The mosaic seems an ironic choice to represent a holistic perspective. That is not, in fact, the function of the mosaic. Its function is the creation of perspectives that come from the contemplation of the whole as experienced in fragments, the complexity from which we create a perspective – Hectic Zen. Since the mosaic as a form breaks up a single point of view and compounds relationships and implications, it is an instrument allowing suspended judgment. The mosaic is a way of contemplation or (waiting for a Strange Attractor) that empties our singular perspective and our new understanding comes from the hollow of this absence.

Hectic Zen and the Art of Mosaic
Maintenance: Be an Artist or Die

McLuhan's embedded message is that the singular point-of-view no longer stands as the one way for the West. His bell sounding for the East and its aesthetic echoes throughout his works. Hectic Zen is practiced in the space between things. It is the means for connection among the many languages, voices, images, and civilizations that are now present to us through media and the inter-connectedness implied by the dance of electrons and tweets.

In that space a realizing intuition, some one thing, be it image or term, starts us moving toward a unified conception of the mosaic. This is pattern recognition and when it happens we have a Zen moment, an *Ah Ha* experience. Having the patience and discipline to suspend judgment and believe in such a moment is to practice Hectic Zen.

To practice Hectic Zen is to enter the spaces among things rather than the things themselves, much in the same way that one could practice trying to see the spaces among objects rather than the objects themselves. That sort of mediation is disorienting visually, as the practice of contemplating or resonating with the space between cultures and ideas is disorienting. Thus, disorient. Accept "perspective by incongruity." What is predictable is meaningful to the degree the prediction is confounded. In a universe of information overload accepting disorientation is necessary, as well as gaining the repose in order to recognize relationships among the fragments. For McLuhan, Hectic Zen was a necessary instrument for survival. He writes:

FACED WITH
INFORMATION OVERLOAD,
WE HAVE NO ALTERNATIVE
BUT
PATTERN-RECOGNITION. (*Medium*132)

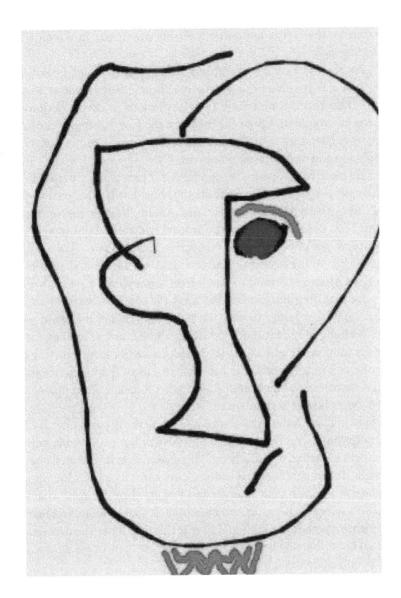

Figure 8

A more emphatic statement, one that McLuhan might make, is: "Be an artist or die." Like Burke, McLuhan sees the artist as providing a counter statement or counter blast to the dominant society. He also sees the artist as someone who demonstrates the activity of Hectic Zen, the discovery of patterns among complex relationships. McLuhan's understanding of the artist reverberates with the Balinese indigenous perspective that art is doing life well. He points out in *Through the Vanishing Point*:

Like the Balinese . . . Electronic Man approaches the condition in which it is possible to deal with the entire environment as a work of art. This presents no solution to the previous problems of decorating the environment. Quite the contrary, the new possibility demands total understanding of artistic function of society. It will no longer be possible to add art to the environment. (7)

The most basic pattern recognition is "formal" in a more (w)holistic sense—some would say aesthetics, but that is a western way of describing the sensation and not passing on through the vanishing point. K.B. describes form as the arousal and fulfillment of expectations, and the opposite is also attractive and resonates with pattern recognition. In the electronic universe, as in art, the arousal and denial of expectations are central to moving on since what is next is always a surprise requiring integration. We need the spark of "bang," "ahhh," ahha," ohoh," or "zing" to keep our compositions and the world moving. Without this, education and living are reduced to looking for an answer to someone else's questions, which like linear form is fine but not the end of it (or even the beginning). Hectic Zen realization is a sensation seeking whatever language makes it mean. We compose and move on, seeking the moment of "zing."

Hectic Zen troubles those who want something particular. In Zen composition, if you want something you will not get it; what you do get might be better. What is hectic? If you don't get **it**, you aren't hectic enough. Incompatible-juxtaposition, pun and metaphor, diremption, Russian *ostramenie*. Be a stranger and you are there. You see what it is that you were enveloped in and breathing. It's a break out and tearing up with a moment of making. To say it this way is not the experience, but saying it this way reminds me of it. We get there or we do not. We get it, or we do not.

In Hectic Zen composition, the composer, as an artist, becomes sophistic, becomes Homeric, becomes indiginous the composing, perhaps in harmony with Anzalua's sense of complexity or McLuhan's claim that we have "evoked a super-civilized sub-pimitive" being (*Counter Blast*). This is not in the sense of anyone "going native," but in the reality of the social environment described by McLuhan. Also, an artistic rhetorician joins in a perspective Anzaldua describes for

the writer as "shape changer, is a nahual, a shaman" (*Borderlands* 88).
McLuhan writes:

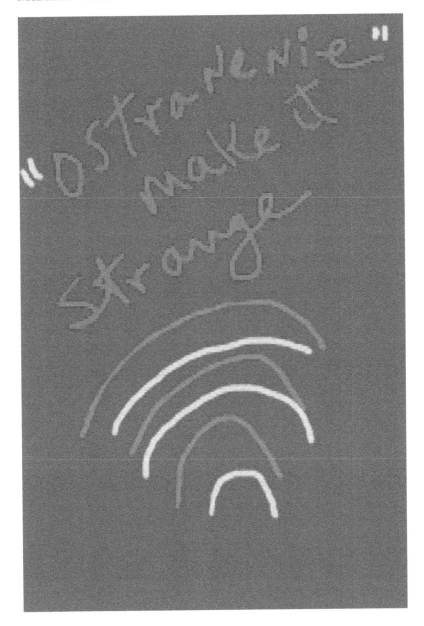

Figure 9

The artist is a person who is especially aware of the challenge and dangers of new environments presented to human sensibility. Whereas the ordinary person seeks security by numbing his perceptions against the impact of new experience, the artist studies the distortion of sensory life produced by new environmental programming and tends to create artistic situations that correct the sensory bias and derangement brought about by the new form. In social terms the artist can be regarded as a navigator who gives adequate compass bearings in spite of magnetic deflection of the needle by the changing play of forces. So understood the artist is not a peddler of ideals or lofty experiences. He is rather the indispensable aid to action and reflection alike. (238)

The emphasis on rhetoric and society has always been on civic engagement and political action. Since Aristotle, however, poetics have been secondary considerations in social action and the most artistic division of rhetoric, the epideictic, given less attention. This doesn't mean that in the 20th and 21st centuries rhetorician and compositionists have neglected art and epideictic but that we should continue to explore ways of including them. I take it this is one of McLuhan's primary points of exploration. He, by demonstration, mixed scholarly, artistic, and popular topics and modes of composition, demonstrating that the form and protocol of the scholarly article need not reflect the Newtonian universe or doggedly upholding the linear modes and models of composition.

The braiding of our threads of rhetorical studies since the 60s has included rhetoric(s) of resistance to our mediums and our message. Feminist, sophistic, ethnic, resistive, counter, and electric rhetoric(s) have been foregrounded in our discipline and yet the approach of scholarly discourse continues, in the main and under sail power, to plow through the sea of a traditional model. As Leonard Cohan puts it in a blues song, "Everybody knows the boat is leaking; everybody knows the Captain lied." We are no longer able to be in the exact same boat, but have to find room on the sea of discourse for boats that we may share from time to time, and this may be one of the only ways to understand the Global Village or to live in it. Or, as the radrhetor Victor Vitanza has it in his afterword to *Writing Histories of Rhetoric*, *"Preparing to Meet the Faces That 'We' will Have Met"*:

My *Program* is to a/void a progrom and thereby is to discover systemic (accountable) and nonsystemic (nonaccountable) places for all of us. In *language* we are all intermittently a (scape)goat. Language is/has a *double effect*, if not also a *triple effect*. It is not, then, a necessity any longer – as Puritans did in their sermons – of simply separating *sheep* from *goats*, or simply separating *sheep* from *goats* and *dancing satyrs*. So as to make the way for *The* (One True, and Catholic) History of Rhetorik. (247).

This passage is a demonstration of his earlier statement on writing; "When I write, I try to maintain a sense of 'discovery,' of being on the joyful Road to Serrendip; or to maintain a sophistic sense of the motion of the whole" (245). Do we sense the beat in this, the dealing with fragmentation in parallel comparisons, the resistance to a conclusion, and a playful (witty) engagement in a language seeking some unifying moment of repose in the complexity? Finding languages and structures to encounter and engage complexity, because complexity is not only our necessary environment but also because it can help us on a joyful road to realizing our world together, is the practice of Hectic Zen and the compositional compass for finding directions as we pass through the vanishing point into McLuhan's universe.

Dear Ann Berthoff,

To construe is to construct and
how we construe is how we construct,
and to construct is to construe.
What messages we MEAN are
more than seen and Strange
Attractions.
We feel what we think
and believe,
meaning (as well as understanding)
is a suspended-judgment bridge
and we are all poetry
crossing
an act of poetic faith
to be present to one another,
for a moment,
testifying to a system of interests
system sing
blue-green light on/in a web of light
zinging
BELIEVE me,

if you live this, the world is yours;
if you do not, it belongs to another.
As Marshall McLhuan says,
Nothing is inevitable, preordered, (ordained)!
if there is a
willingness
to contemplate.

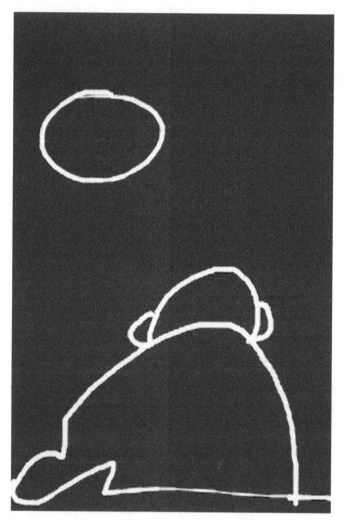

Figure 10: A moment of repose

AFTERWARD

I am grateful to the readers and editors who have gone along with me on this exploration of Marshall McLuhan's modes of composition. For one thing, I began with the notion of a parataxic approach that brings together starkly dissimilar ideas in parallel. This approach, one that McLuhan discusses in *Through The Vanishing Point* as contributing to the end of the "'story line' as a means of organizing verbal structures," (26) turns the composing process into an intellectual haiku, a mode of composing that McLuhan used throughout his work and that he saw important to negotiating the electronic or auditory environment. McLuhan uses this approach to comment on works of art and literature in *Vanishing Point,* as in his first comment on William Blake's "The Tyger": "Resonating acoustic space. A vast echo chamber for reader participation"(139).

Parataxis is particularly difficult to manage in a scholarly article since it abandons sublimation of phrases and clauses and the establishment of syntactical relationships in favor of leaving things parallel in order for the reader to make her or his own discoveries and connections. It happens on a structural and formal level more than with sentence construction. In order to manage the distance between the parataxic approach and the hypotaxic approach, which specifies relations, some wrangling is necessary. This is, of course, the challenge of composing scholarship in the mosaic genre, a challenge McLuhan managed to meet.

Once a writer (composer) shifts from parataxic to hypotaxic, the story line or history and reasoning are foregrounded, thus any article, such as this one, that attempts to shift from one to the other is difficult for a reader expecting a scholarly argument, much in the same way a haiku is difficult for Western readers. We, I think, have more practice with haiku that with parataxic form in scholarly writing. The editors and readers suffered with me through this back and forth transformation, and Kevin Brooks helped me fish out the argument that went with first my intellectual haiku and then my story line. He recognized that what the story line was attempting to do was "emphasize that this sort of auditory rhetoric and mosaic composition has been practiced for quite some time (Burke and McLuhan), has been practiced (or at least noticed) by people more closely associated with composition and rhetoric (Enos and Berthoff), and is practiced outside the discipline

(Anzaldua and Mestiz@), emphasizing the long history of auditory rhetoric and mosaic composition." I could hardly say it better.

Works Cited

Aitken, Robert. *A Zen Wave: Basho's Haiku and Zen.* Washington D. C.: Shoemaker & Hoard, 1978.

Anzaldúa, Gloria. *Borderlands: The New Mestiza.* San Francisco: Aunt Lute Books 1999.

Baca, Damian. *Mestiz@ scripts, Digital Migrations and the Territories of Writing.* New York: Palgrave Macmilan, 2008.

Berthoff, Ann E. *Forming, Thinking, Writing: The Composing Mind.* Hayden Book Company, Inc., Rechelle Park, New Jersey, 1978.

—. *The Making of Meaning: Metaphors, Models, and Maxims for Writing Teachers* Upper Montclair, NJ: Boynton/Cook Publishers, Inc, 1981.

—. *The Mysterious Barricades: Language and its Limits.* Toronto: University of Toronto Press, Scholarly Publishing Division, 1999.

Burke, Kenneth. *Counter-Statement.* Berkeley: U of California P, 1968.

—. *Language as Symbolic Action: Essays on Life, Literature, and Method.* Berkeley: U of California P, 1966.

Enos, Richard L. *Greek Rhetoric Before Aristotle.* Prospect Heights, IL: Waveland, 1993.

Halloran, S., Michael. "Further Thought on the End of Rhetoric." Ed. Theresa Enos & Stuart. Brown, *Defining the New Rhetorics.* SAGE Series in Written Communication. Newbury Park, CA: SAGE, 1993. 109-119.

Hawk, Byron. *A Counter-History of Composition: Toward Methodologies of Complexity.* Pittsburgh Series in Composition, Literacy, and Culture. David Bartholomae and Jean Ferguson Carr, Editors. U of Pittsburgh P., 2007.

McLuhan, Marshall. *Counter Blast.* New York: Harcourt, 1969.

—. *Culture is our Business.* New York: McGraw-Hill, 1970.

—. *The Gutenberg Galaxy: The Making of Typographic Man.* Toronto: U of Toronto P. 1962.

McLuhan, Marshall & Quentin Fiore. *The Medium is the Message.* New York: Bantam, 1967.

McLuhan, Marshall & Harley Parker. *Through the Vanishing Point: Space in Poetry and Painting.* New York: Harper, 1968.

Rice, Jeff. *The Rhetoric of Cool: Composition Studies and the New Media.* Southern Illinois UP, 2007.

Selfe, Cynthia L., Editor. *Multimodal Composition: Resources for Teachers.* New Dimensions in Computers and Composition Series, Gail E. Hawisher and Cynthia Selfe, Eds. Cresskill, NJ: Hampton Press, Inc., 2007.

Vitanza, Victor, ed. *Writing Histories of Rhetoric*. Carbondale: Southern Illinois P, 1994.

Yancey, Kathleen Blake, ed. College *Composition and Communication*. Special Issue: Indiginous and Ethnic Rhetorics. Vol 63.1, September 2011.

Yancey, Kathleen. "Made not only in words: Composition in a new key." *Cross-Talk in Comp Theory*. Ed. Victor Villanueva and Kristin L. Arola. Urbana: NCTE, 2011. 791-826.

JOURNAL OF BASIC WRITING

Journal of Basic Writing is
on the web at http://wac.
colostate.edu/jbw/

Journal of Basic Writing was founded in 1975 by Mina Shaughnessy, who served
as the journal's first editor. Basic wriing, a contested term since its initial use
by Shaughnessy in the 1970s, refers to the field concerned with teaching writing
to students not yet deemed ready for first-year composition. Originally, these
students were part of the wave of open admissions students who poured into
universities as a result of the social unrest of the 1960s and the resulting reforms.
Though social and political realities have changed dramatically since then, the
presence of "basic writers' in colleges and universities--and the debates over how
best to serve them--persists. JBW articles take on the social, political, and pedagogical questions related to educational access and equity at the core of open
admissions.

Reflecting on the Liberal Reflex: Rhetoric and the Politics of Acknowledgment in Basic Writing

Matthew Pavesich's article offers a close look at basic writing's fraught history
of access and its relationship to democracy. Pavesich tackles the uncomfortable conflict between the liberal tradition and educational justice, confronting
liberalism's "injustice of assimilation." In response to the problem he identifies,
Pavesich advances a "renewed politics of basic writing," informed by political
theory, particularly Patchen Markell's "politics of Acknowledgment." Pavesich
grounds his political vision in the story of one basic writing program's radical reform to advocate "contextualized rhetorical action in constant need of revision."

6 Reflecting on the Liberal Reflex: Rhetoric and the Politics of Acknowledgment in Basic Writing

Matthew Pavesich

ABSTRACT: *In the 1990s, leading rhetoric and composition scholars criticized basic writing programs for their "liberalism." Basic writing had its defenders, however, and the ensuing debate exposed deep rifts in the field. This article argues that neither side in this formative debate nor the more recent alternative models of teaching basic writing manage to escape liberal hegemony. By combining political theory with rhetoric/composition scholarship, and relying on examples from recent changes to the basic writing program at Roosevelt University, I propose an approach to basic writing that combines rhetorical pedagogy with a new politics of Acknowledgment in order to simultaneously concede and resist the university's inevitable liberalism.*

> *"[Any] mode of government . . . both enables and constrains the possibilities for political action" (Cruikshank 2).*

Basic writing's recent history tells a story of the long-running tension between the liberal tradition of equal treatment and democratic justice. This tension came to a head in the 1990s, and basic writing programs found themselves under attack from outsiders like journalists and legislators but also from compositionists within the field (Otte and Williams Mlynarczyk 11). Up to this point, many basic writing programs were influenced to some degree by Mina Shaughnessy's influential work in 1977's *Errors and Expectations*, in which Shaughnessy encouraged teachers to assume basic writers' potential for success and to teach accordingly—a change heralded as a victory for pedagogical justice. Administratively, however, basic writing continued to operate nationally on a testing and tracking model, which the 1990s critics said prevented pedagogical change from truly making just the basic writing enterprise. Testing and tracking, from this perspective, represented a liberal system of exclusion and/or assimilation, regardless of pedagogical approach. Unable to reconcile such a fundamental tension, George Otte and Rebecca Williams Mlynarczyk tell us, basic writing then splintered into a mostly disconnected collection of programs occupied primarily with their own modest goals and local strategies, which they call the "generational shift" (12).

Critics of basic writing's liberalism echoed a growing dissatisfaction with liberalism in political theory. Scholars in both fields agreed, in principle, that while liberalism's supporters equate with justice its commitment to the equal treatment of all people, clear-eyed accounts tell us something different: that for many liberalism offers only the injustice of assimilation or exclusion. Some took this opportunity to call for the "abolition" of basic writing, while others vehemently defended it, insisting instead that to abolish basic writing would be dangerously liberal. Each side in this debate accused the other side of relying on liberal logic and practice, while claiming for itself the achievement of justice.

Relying on contemporary political theory, I will argue, however, that both sides in this conversation work within the liberal paradigm. As Patricia Mann notes of liberalism: "It required several hundred years for liberal economic and political structures to develop . . . and our notions of agency remain deeply embedded in their practices . . ." (qtd. in Grego and Thompson "Repositioning" 82). Mann's description resonates with David Bartholomae's characterization of liberalism as a *reflex*, paraphrased in my title. Liberalism is so entrenched, that is, it has become reflexive. We re-enact it in our opinions, arguments, and decisions, sometimes even without intending to. Since we enact liberalism reflexively, it would be more productive to think about the opportunities it creates in basic writing, as in my epigraph, rather than identifying the (inevitable) liberalism of our institutions as the rationale for doing away with them or defending them, as we saw in the 1990s crisis. Further, if basic writing sits at a crossroads in need of a new political vision, as Mike Rose has recently claimed, any such effort must come to terms with the 90s crisis and what has happened since.

This paper steps toward that goal in two ways. First, I create room for a renewed politics of basic writing with a political theory-driven critique of the accepted crisis narrative. Second, I describe the formation of a new basic writing program at Roosevelt University, known in Chicago and nationally for its social justice mission and history of welcoming into higher education those historically excluded from it. In the fall of 2009, when I was hired as part of a four-person composition faculty team, we were charged with the reconstruction of the basic writing program, among other curricular and administrative projects. When we began our work, we turned to the basic writing literature for the most recent programmatic and pedagogical innovations, and we found a wealth of practices and strategies, many of which we adopted for a pilot program in 2011-2012, that matched a rhetorical pedagogy with a Stretch-style program.[1] Our work drew on basic writing research for both a program proposal and the pilot curriculum, which I describe in detail. Frankly the program is too new to deem either a success or a failure. Yet, in writing about these experiences, I look back through the lens of political theory because I believe that this lens can help to interpret the work we did and the political possibilities it indicates. By moving between basic writing scholarship, political theory, and an account of our work at Roosevelt, I propose that a rhetorical teaching practice based on Patchen Markell's *politics of Acknowledgment* can help us to politically re-imagine basic writing pedagogy, while also promising a new way to think about the administration of basic writing within our inevitably liberal colleges and universities.

ON LIBERALISM

Even though the term "liberal" popularly connotes progressiveness in American political culture, liberal political philosophy represents the opposite of what many people would think of as progressive. Hardly radical, it provides the bedrock of the American political landscape, the enduring *doxa* of our political life. As we all know, one of the earliest and most familiar liberal principles is the separation of church and state. In his formative account of religious toleration, John Locke separates the private sphere, a metaphorical space symbolized by one's home in which people conduct the vast majority of their lives as they see fit, from the public sphere, the narrow space left for matters to be governmentally adjudicated. Over time, American courts and our legislative bodies have solidified our reliance on neutral procedures to determine what belongs to each sphere and the management of the public. By "neutral procedures," I mean the state's governance of public life according to laws and values that stand independent of any group's particular view of the world, religious or otherwise. Who you are and what you believe, in traditional liberalism, are not supposed to matter when it comes to the rule of law, which derives its neutrality from the fact that its most important work occurs behind a "veil of ignorance." John Rawls, in his contemporary re-articulation of procedural liberalism, devises this metaphor to emphasize the irrelevance of any one person's cultural affiliations regarding the proper operation of liberalism. Famously capturing the individualist spirit of American liberalism, Thomas Jefferson colloquially noted, "It does me no injury for my neighbor to say that there are twenty gods or no God; it neither picks my pocket nor breaks my leg." The history of American liberalism represents the evolution of a once-controversial method for governing ideologically diverse populations into a contemporary article of common sense: that the equal treatment of every *one* means justice for *all*.

While these foundational liberal principles have become so accepted in everyday discourses as to be nearly invisible, and self-evident when visible, they have nonetheless drawn a good deal of critique in political philosophy. Though the particular critiques of liberalism would not crescendo until the 1980s and 1990s, Chaim Perelman in 1967's *Justice* questions liberalism on grounds that anticipate arguments in both political philosophy and basic writing in the 1990s. Opposing Rawls by name, Perelman claims that the equal treatment of "non-identical beings," the beating heart of liberalism, is fundamentally unjust (21-22). In his words, "equity is sometimes opposed to the uniform and mechanical application of a given rule . . ." (26). By inserting our non-identical natures into the liberal political calculus, Perelman calls into question what I described above as the very bedrock of American politics, the justice of equal treatment. Furthermore, he proceeds to re-introduce practical reason into the philosophical pursuit of equality, fairness, and justice, and in so doing, also raises the concerns of deliberative rhetorics, the importance of what we do and say in the presence of others amidst the particulars of everyday life. Thus, Perelman anticipated an important shift in political theory in which political philosophers would begin to think about the particulars of individual identity and their sources in cultural affiliations.

In the 1980s and '90s, we find prominent political philosophers, including Stanley Hauerwas, Michael Sandel, Charles Taylor, and Iris Marion Young, intensifying the criticism of liberalism along the same lines. This group, among others, cast doubt on value-neutral procedures, in principle and in practice. Once this ground becomes unsteady, liberalism begins to look less like a fair system that favors no single group over any other, and more like a subtle force reflective of one dominant group. In "The Politics of Recognition," Taylor insists that because identity is dialogically formed, individuals, qua individuals who are simultaneously members of identifiable social groups,[2] can "suffer real damage" at the hands of this subtle force—damage that he dubs "misrecognition" (25). In this account, even as most people describe, think of, and resort to liberalism for its neutral fairness, in practice it operationalizes a pressure that is at once assimilatory, regulatory, and disciplinary. Taylor concludes that liberal institutions must account for difference in substantive ways, an approach he calls the "politics of recognition."

As an example of the knot in which liberalism ties minority groups, Kwame Appiah points, in the *Ethics of Identity*, to Canada's universal motorcycle helmet law. When this law was passed, Canadian Sikhs, who wear *pagri* (turbans), protested that requiring helmet use meant something different for them than for others. That is, any Sikh who wanted to ride a motorcycle, a right of all properly licensed Canadians, would have to make a difficult religious choice, one that amounted to either assimilation or self-exclusion. Furthermore, not all Canadian motorcyclists were forced to make the same choice. Sikhs argued that such a law disproportionately affected them, and further that the law amounted to their exclusion from equal citizenship (Appiah 94-95, 160). The point here is that laws, regardless of universalizing logic or language, impact people of different cultures differently. Canada eventually began to make exceptions in such cases, referred to as "reasonable accommodations"—an example of Taylor's politics of recognition in action. Canadians recognized Sikhs' freedom as being disproportionately impeded upon by the helmet law, and they did something about it. This accommodation required recognizing that equality does not necessarily equal fairness, the essence of Perelman's position. This argument has come to be known as the communitarian critique ("communitarian" because it recovers the identity/community connection so long ignored by liberalism), and it grew into an entire subfield of liberal political philosophy, including work such as James Tully's *Strange Multiplicity* and Will Kymlicka's *Multicultural Citizenship*. Clearly, liberal philosophers have struggled over the tension between liberal individualism and cultural affiliation; this struggle, in very similar form, sparked the basic writing crisis.

BASIC WRITING'S LIBERAL CRISIS

Within a few years of each other, both David Bartholomae and Sharon Crowley identified the problem of basic writing as its fundamentally liberal nature. Bartholomae writes that basic writing marginalizes students by placing them according to their "skill" and only allowing them to advance in accordance with their ability to demonstrate increased merit. As a communitarian might argue that a helmet law excludes or assimilates a Sikh motorcyclist, Bartholomae worries that universal composition requirements exclude and/or assimilate an increasingly diverse student population within a narrow and supposedly neutral account of what constitutes good writing, hence his claim that basic writing is produced by the "grand narrative of . . . liberal reform" (18). Bartholomae eventually identifies what he calls the "liberal reflex": programs that implicitly insist, "that beneath the surface we are all the same person . . ." (18). He elaborates:

> I find myself characterizing basic writing as a reiteration of the liberal project of the late 60s early 70s, where in the name of sympathy and empowerment, we have once again produced the 'other' who is the incomplete version of ourselves, confirming existing patterns of power and authority, reproducing the hierarchies we had meant to question and overthrow way back then in the 1970s. We have constructed a course to teach and enact a rhetoric of exclusion and made it the center of a curriculum designed to hide or erase cultural difference. . . . (18)

Bartholomae echoes the communitarian critique: that one-size-fits-all writing instruction reflects the hegemonic group and the remedial mechanism unjustly assimilates, disciplines, and regulates everyone else. It might be more just, he concludes, since basic writing is so thoroughly liberal, to do away with it altogether.

In her more radical assessment, Sharon Crowley agrees with Bartholomae's characterization but goes one step further, arguing that not just basic writing but the first-year writing requirement altogether must be abolished (241). Crowley especially attacks writing programs' mobilization of "the language of democracy and freedom" insofar as they "subject students to a battery of standardized tests, which, in the name of individualization, simply placed them on one or another predefined rung of the educational ladder" (186). Further, Crowley's following zinger resonates with the account of liberalism as a my-way-or-the-highway system that parades as neutral procedure: "It takes considerable rhetorical chutzpah to tout a universal requirement as a liberatory practice" (186). To put it in communitarian terms, this would be like saying that forcing a Sikh to remove his turban for a helmet makes him freer. Crowley's comment here resonates with Taylor's characterization of liberalism, that it is equipped only to advocate for the purported universal good, which really only benefits the historically dominant group. Basic writing, that is, has continually mistaken its *equal* procedures, like the universal requirement and placement testing, for *fair* procedures and, based on that mistake, forces thousands of increasingly diverse students to assimilate to normative language standards or be relegated to a kind of purgatory in higher education. Social justice for Crowley and Bartholomae demands the de-liberalization of basic writing or, if that can't be managed, its abolition.

Predictably, many practitioners of basic writing resisted these attacks, especially defending it as substantively empowering and hence equating it with social justice rather than liberalism. In particular, Karen Greenberg and Ed White stand out among basic writing's defenders in the 1990s. Greenberg argues that tracking enables student success in higher education, rather than marginalizing or assimilating them. She scoffs at the accusation of oppression, insisting rather that basic writing elevates the "right to succeed" over the "right to fail" (70). To abolish basic writing would secure students only the "right to fail," she says, suggesting the absence of basic writing amounts to the real danger. Struggling writers would have no recourse, no aid; they would be left to sink or swim, like marginalized citizens in a free market economy without socioeconomic safety nets. Greenberg echoes both the communitarian rejection of procedural "justice" and the hope for something more substantive, in the sense that her "right to succeed" rationale interprets tracking as a form of recognition. Basic writing, that is, recognizes the need for extra instruction and provides it. As such, she takes the abolition position and inverts it. Ed White makes a similar argument in his defense of basic writing. Like Greenberg, he uses the same binary of the critics (justice versus liberal oppression). And like Greenberg, White relies on "rights rhetoric" to achieve the inversion, stating that, "American education is subject to two contrasting underlying motifs: egalitarianism, the argument that everyone should have opportunities for success, and elitism, the restriction of opportunities to the most 'deserving"—which often means to those from a relatively privileged home" (75). For White, the abolition argument signifies a rising elitism, a willingness to abandon the university's new diversity and to deny minority students all the privilege higher education can bring. The critique *and* the defense of basic writing work in the same rhetorical mode; they uncover the buried liberalism of the others' position. And here's the kicker: from where I'm looking, both sides are right.

First-year composition (and basic writing by extension) has always been liberal; it would perhaps be absurd to expect it to be anything else. In fact, it seems ironic that while liberal-style procedures have always been the university's response to recurrent literacy "crises" over the last one hundred plus years, it was liberalism itself that caused the crisis about which I write. Many histories of composition have told the much-chronicled story of Harvard's composition course, the response made by late 19th Century faculty to what they saw as inadequate writing by unprepared students (Russell 7; Crowley 4). Built into the very fiber of composition, and its *raison d'être*, is the notion of remedial normalization as crisis response. Said one student, "In an endeavor (and a not very successful one) to conform to certain rules, I have lost all originality,—everything has a sort of labored rehashing, which makes whatever I have to say, dull and uninteresting" (qtd. in Crowley 75). Though this sentiment might have been expressed by a student in a basic writing class in the years 2007, 1993, or 1979, it was in fact expressed by a Harvard student in 1901. Composition courses have been assimilating students for a very long time indeed. The explosion of diversity in higher education did not create a new situation so much as make an old situation more visible and less comfortable. As critics noted, basic writing exerts a liberal pressure on the minority group to conform to normative language standards, but no one has yet observed that the abolition of this requirement amounts to a rough version of liberalism too, in the sense that one-size-fits-all writing instruction invokes the commonsense equivalence of equal treatment with justice.

Neither side in the 90s debate escapes the liberal paradigm; the abolition option activates one-size-fits-all liberalism, while remediation activates assimilatory mechanisms. As long as scholars and practitioners share the assumption that social justice requires the absence of liberalism, basic writing will remain in a political holding pattern, whether or not the field has seen a generational shift. At this point, I believe ceding liberalism's reflexiveness affords the greatest potential for political change. To ground these issues, I turn to the circumstances at Roosevelt University, an urban university with a social justice mission and a significant basic writing population, which I hope will illuminate how complexly the logics and rhetorics of liberalism and social justice can intermingle.

PROBLEMS FOR BASIC WRITING AT ROOSEVELT, 2009-2011

Neither an historically black institution nor a women's college, Roosevelt University (RU) nonetheless commits itself to those who have been traditionally excluded from higher education. In 1945, Edward Sparling, then-president of Chicago's YMCA College, feared that his board of trustees would require an accounting of the school's demographics so as to institute quotas on racial minorities, women, and immigrants. Even though such policies were common for the time, Sparling envisioned a more inclusive institution. Rather than comply with the board's request, he resigned, taking sixty-eight faculty members with him to form what became Thomas Jefferson College, later re-named for the recently deceased Franklin D. Roosevelt ("Our History"). For sixty-five years and counting, RU has remained committed to redressing the historical exclusivity of American higher education with progressive admission policies and curricula, a spirit that informs the school's mission for social justice.

Sparling's story echoes in the halls of Roosevelt. Tenured faculty tell it to new faculty; student orientation leaders tell it to prospective students and their parents; the university president tells some version of it in most of his convocation and commencement addresses. *Roosevelt exists because Sparling rejected injustices common to his time; we must continue to resist those of ours.* This commonplace constitutes a significant element of what we might call the discursive fabric of RU, a self-reflective account of ethos. It says, "This is who we are," in a way that both represents the past and shapes the present and future. This story also lines the halls of Roosevelt, literally. Hanging on almost every floor, photos of early Roosevelt students, young women and men of color, constantly remind present-day students, faculty, and staff of RU's commitment to social justice. Today, this commitment manifests in a variety of ways, foremost perhaps in the many student organizations dedicated to identity groups and social justice issues, from the group for Roosevelt's lesbian, gay, bisexual, transgender, queer students and their allies, *RU Proud*, to a chapter of the National Association of Black Accountants. RU's current president, Charles Middleton, was the first publicly gay man to head a university, and he participates in a small national consortium of gay and lesbian university presidents. This ethos informs volunteer service days, which pepper the calendar all year long, as well as the influential Mansfield Institute for Social Justice and Transformation, which organizes both service learning courses and programming for the university and the public. Roosevelt's curriculum even requires for graduation a third writing class, a rarity in higher education, focused on writing about social justice issues.

The basic writing classes, however, present a more complicated picture. While basic writing must be examined closely at all institutions, especially those with significant populations of minority students (who tend to be overrepresented in basic writing), Roosevelt's foundational commitment to social justice demands an even closer look. More specifically, while the discourse within and about RU suggests an enlightened politics, RU basic writing policy and its consequences on the ground suggest a much more typical institutional culture. At the same time, the social justice mission and Roosevelt's culture provide perhaps greater potential for change.

I would characterize basic writing in the 2000s at RU as exemplifying a collision between its social justice ethos and typically liberal basic writing policies, such as placement testing, remedial tracking, and a focus on normative error correction. While this collision happens at other institutions, it might not be going too far to say that RU's very identity is at stake in its management of basic writers. Basic writing at Roosevelt, until 2010-2011, consisted only of English 100, a remedial, skills-based writing class. Because the department employed only one full-time writing faculty member/administrator, virtually no composition *program* existed. What documentation was once provided for the many adjuncts teaching English 100 took the form of a long expository text articulating an account of basic writing very much in the style of Shaughnessy; it encouraged focus on writers' potential for success, not their errors. Even though the program expressed its commitment to writing as a process, the pass/fail class culminated in a timed essay written in response to an article and prompt. Students, therefore, received a profoundly mixed message. Their classes were exercises in process pedagogy, but they were assessed with a method that valued product only.

In the view of Bartholomae and Crowley, furthermore, RU's tracking policy remained its most significant fact. English 100 represented liberal management, leaving many students to struggle to assimilate to normative language standards or to remain in English 100 forever. The strict liberalism of testing and tracking, however, did not entirely define basic writing administration at Roosevelt. RU offered a free retake of English 100 for any student who failed the class. This policy represented an impressive financial commitment to students who very often could barely afford to take English 100 the first time, but it could be argued that RU created the need for such compensation in the first place.

Another complicated situation arose involving transfer students. Transfers who tested into English 100 were lumped together with first-year students, whether or not they had completed their writing requirements at their prior school. This would be hardly worth mentioning but for the fact that Roosevelt participated in the Illinois Articulation Initiative. This agreement stipulated that Roosevelt would not require incoming transfers to take courses whose requirements they already had fulfilled at their prior institution, a decision often described on campus as one that illustrated our respect for students' credentials and the quality of higher education across the state. In this particular instance, Roosevelt claimed to honor transfers' prior work, but then reverted to the liberal management of their writing with a one-size-fits-all placement test, general basic writing class, and timed final exam. To put it bluntly, RU's basic writing policies strained its commitment to social justice.

If all this weren't complicated enough, it became clear in 2009 that retention and persistence to graduation numbers indicated troubling trends at Roosevelt, especially when it came to basic writers. For example, of all first-time RU students in the fall of 2008, only 51.9% returned in the fall of 2009.[3] The scene was worse for students of color, as it so often is. We discovered that students of color at Roosevelt, mostly African-Americans and Latinos, simply were not making it to graduation in six years or less. Only 34% of Latino students in the Fall 2003 cohort had graduated by 2009 and only 19% of African-American students had done so. When we dug into the retention numbers regarding basic writers, it turned out that for the cohorts from 2006-2009, that percentage dipped significantly below 50% in three out of four years, meaning basic writers came back the following fall at even lower rates than our already unacceptable fall-to-fall numbers for the whole student population.[4] Something needed to be done.

RECOGNITION MEETS ACKNOWLEDGMENT: AND (MORE) JUSTICE FOR ALL

The new composition faculty and program director took as our first project the re-construction of basic writing. We turned, of course, to the large body of scholarship on basic writing for strategies and models, and we found that much like Canada's reasonable accommodations for cultural diversity in a liberal framework, basic writing scholars and teachers have looked for creative work-arounds to the issues raised in the 1990s crisis. Like Taylor's politics of recognition, these alternatives turn away from one-size-fits-all answers.

Innovation since the 1990s has come in many forms, both programmatic and pedagogical (which is not to say that there is always a tidy division between the two). Most new models have shared a powerful refusal to abolish basic writing coupled with an effort to blunt liberalism's sharp edge. At their most successful, these models represent smart and inventive options that address the worst aspects of liberalism's influence on the administration of basic writing; collectively, they strive to set new paths around the earth scorched by the heated debate of the crisis years. Given the above arguments, it is no wonder that the 90s crisis created a generational shift in which the field turned to local contexts, needs, and solutions. Indeed, this shift in basic writing and the communitarian critique in political theory share a similar direction, a turn toward practical reason away from universalizing solutions. Hewing to Roosevelt's history and mission, we too were looking for ways to teach basic writing that neither marginalize students nor ignore their needs, while developing a program that we faculty felt equally comfortable describing and defending to students *and* administrators (what I have come to think of as a social justice litmus test).

Administrative Alternatives

William Lalicker has described the most important post-crisis models for administering basic writing, which he calls the "alternative models." Of these, we eventually adopted Gregory Glau's popular "Stretch" model. Stretch replaces remedial instruction (often ungraded and without college credit) with a "stretched" college-level course. Students take a two-semester version of "regular" English 101, with 150% of the work and the same faculty and peers both semesters, on the theory that what they need is more time to do college-level work, not remedial instruction. Both semesters are graded and credit-bearing, and this two-semester system offers time to build community among a population that tends to be an institution's most vulnerable by various measures (Glau "The 'Stretch Program'"). While we settled on Stretch, all five alternative models provide more nuanced procedural alternatives to the mainstreaming/segregation binary of the basic writing crisis in the sense that they seek variously articulated middle spaces between mainstreaming and marginalizing.

To call these models alternatives, however, is to imply that they are alternatives to the liberal programs attacked in the crisis. For that to be accurate, however, they would have to depart from the mainstreaming/tracking binary, and, to put it simply, they do not. Stretch, for example, still segregates writers from the larger population. Studio and Enrichment models, conversely, try to mainstream and segregate at the same time by requiring basic writers to attend both a "regular" writing class and a separate basic writing lab. One can also make the opposite claim, that Stretch mainstreams insofar as it relies on the same curriculum as "regular" 101, and the Studio and Enrichment models still track in the sense that only part of the population is required to attend Studio. In other words, these models make liberalism less visible or re-locate it. Directed self-placement, in which programs recommend a writing placement but students make the final decision, offers a more complicated example, in that it recognizes student choice over liberal management of their writing track. I would still suggest, however, that it mobilizes liberalism in the sense described by Barbara Cruikshank, in *The Will to Empower*, when she argues that empowerment discourses often rely on self-regulation along liberalism's lines, what Foucault described as the "conduct of conduct," or the "conduct of the self." In the case of directed self-placement this would look like the student who, through exposure to liberal education policies, has come to self-identify as a remedial writer and chooses the basic writing class regardless of placement, arguing that she "needs it" in a replication of the liberal logic of normalization. While the alternative models, like recognition, revise traditional liberalism, they are still liberal. The era of the alternative models, then, does not offer alternatives to liberalism, no matter what we call them, as much as a temporary truce in the unresolved hostilities of the 90s.

Pedagogical Alternatives

Similarly, in some of the writing pedagogies devised since the crisis we see other connections with the politics of recognition. Basic writing scholars and practitioners responded to the 90s crisis perhaps even more ardently with pedagogical models (Pepinster Greene and McAlexander 12). Some of these pedagogical innovations seem, to me, very much to mirror the politics of recognition. Min-Zhan Lu, Matthew McCurrie, and Angelique Davi, for example, have offered sophisticated new models of basic writing pedagogy, all of which I would identify as mobilizing a politics of recognition. As one of the earliest to take basic writing in this direction, Lu seeks to avoid the problem of assimilation, insisting that one of basic writing's foundational goals must be "to conceive and practice teaching methods which invite a multicultural approach to style" (442). Interpreting students' writing differences as styles rather than difficiencies offers a form of recognition. Likewise, Matthew McCurrie, in the context of summer bridge programs, encourages teachers and administrators to engage students' "demographics" as a way to fight the assimilation model of traditional liberalism (31-32). Similarly, Angelique Davi's insistence on the relevance of race, class, and gender to higher education and "intellectual growth" recognizes students (73). Davi echoes Taylor's claim that misrecognition not only disempowers but causes real damage when she writes: "for students who have been perceived as weak writers and thinkers and, in many cases, have internalized these perceptions, the service-learning component allow[s] them to occupy a new and empowering position" (91). Lu, McCurrie, and Davi all very much manifest the spirit of the politics of recognition when they resist assimilatory educational models.

The Problem with Recognition

And yet, the politics of recognition might not be all it is cracked up to be, suggests Patchen Markell in *Bound by Recognition*. The act of recognition, Markell argues, finds itself stuck in a kind of identity cul-de-sac, a circular politics implicitly reliant on an *a priori* account of identity. More specifically, Markell insists that recognition mistakes the necessary fragility of political and social life for something that can be overcome. And if Taylor believes recognition can overcome this fragility, Markell argues, he must also understand identity as preceding recognition. If so, recognition relies on the possibility of mutual transparency, a social and linguistic impossibility. We see a similar critique in composition in the argument that certain forms of reflective and expressive writing ask students to peer into an identity that was always already there (Feldman 112).

Markell's alternative, the politics of Acknowledgment, emphasizes ongoing action in the presence of others, an argument I see as fundamentally rhetorical. The politics of Acknowledgment "demands that each of us bear our share of the burden and risk involved in the uncertain, open-ended sometimes maddeningly and sometimes joyously surprising activity of living and interacting with other people" (7). Acknowledgment emphasizes identity as the result of action over time, requiring ongoing insight into oneself and the other. In other words, the politics of Acknowledgment demands engagement in a continual *rhetorical* negotiation for justice in the spirit of practical reason, as opposed to the implied finality and totality of recognition.

Recognition in a writing class can easily veer away from the need for rhetorical action. Based in the mutual transparency of one's *a priori* identity, recognition seeks what Markell calls the elusive "pleasure of sovereignty" (188). Markell sounds as if he might have an alternate career in basic writing when he insists that the goal rather should be to engage others by using, "serviceable forms of meaning [which] emerge out of local, contingent patterns of language use, [whose] operation does not depend upon the illusion of certainty" (184). As opposed to the politics of recognition, then, the politics of Acknowledgment offers "the less grand and more tentative pleasure of potency" (188), a worthy, and politically defensible goal for basic writing, and one that emphasizes the importance of rhetorically-oriented writing instruction.

But what has this meant for the students at Roosevelt, and our programmatic proposal and new course design? In what follows, I describe both our formal proposal to pilot a new stretched basic writing class and the common syllabus for that pilot through Markell's lens.

Proposing Change at Roosevelt: Stretching Rhetoric

At RU, writing faculty decided upon two angles of action for 2010-2011, writing a proposal for a Stretch-style pilot program in 2011-2012, and the design of a common syllabus for the pilot. Our goals were twofold: 1) to write a proposal that utilized liberal logic and language in order to win money to run the pilot and 2) to write a common syllabus that would move the program toward teaching writing rhetorically and away from teaching it as an elementary and transparent technology. We believed both Stretch and a rhetoric-focused course design enhanced the social justice elements of the program without overestimating our power to alter the University's liberalism.

In the proposal, we appealed to both economic arguments and arguments for social justice. By emphasizing how much money was being lost with our poor retention numbers, we hoped to make the case for how much we could save (and even earn) the university with a revamped basic writing program, a compelling argument at a tuition-driven university like RU. Glau's follow-up report on Stretch's effects on retention at Arizona State proved crucial in this regard ("'Stretch' at Ten"). In short, we were able to say that even if we were only half as successful as Glau's program, we could have saved RU $1.3 million dollars over the last four student cohorts. Our social justice argument entailed comparing the persistence to graduation rates of basic writers and students of color at RU to our peer institutions in Illinois by various measures. Our numbers looked even worse by comparison than they did alone. If RU was as committed to social justice and those historically underserved by higher education, we said, approve our proposal.

This document worked within liberalism in that it made the economic argument first, in spite of the fact that most of us were much more concerned with the social justice implications of the status quo. Secondly, when we began to discuss our plans, upper administrators seemed willing to simply allow us to put in place just about whatever we wanted. We, our new director especially, insisted on writing a proposal, starting with limited pilot sections of the new program, and only later moving toward full implementation if our data supported doing so. We *wanted* to solidify our own efforts within the institution, to work in ways recognized by the bureaucratic liberal structure. Even the choice of Stretch was an effort to negotiate embedded liberalism. Though we were not using the political theory language I use here, there was discussion about whether we wanted to use a model that continued to segregate basic writers from other writing students as Stretch does or to use a more mainstreaming model like Studio. One reason we went with Stretch was that its continued segregation of basic writers would be familiar, given the liberal reflexes of administrators in charge of whether our proposal went ahead. Though still liberal, Stretch emphasizes a less marginalizing experience for students in its use of the same curriculum as "regular" English 101 and its graded, for-credit status. In the end, we were lucky; we received $20,000 for a one-year pilot in a bad economy, winning the stamp of approval for both the Stretch-style pilot and a rhetorical curriculum and pedagogy.

Potency without Certainty

Rhetoric, as I intend it here, does not adhere to the classical persuasive strategies of the virtuous man speaking well, nor to the "modes" lionized in scores of textbooks throughout the 20th century. For our purposes, rhetoric referred broadly to any communicative action taken in response to a particular situation. Rhetoric, so defined, connects the language of students' everyday lives to academic and other discourses by emphasizing each as the product of strategic choices negotiated within complicated social situations (Swales). A growing number of first-year writing programs, including basic writing classes, work from a fundamentally rhetorical perspective on writing (Lu, Grego and Thompson, Davi, Pine, Berlin, Bawarshi, Feldman, Miller). In general terms, what this has meant for college composition is a seismic shift away from teaching writing as though it were a universal and universally recognizable skill towards writing as a specifically social act occurring within highly complicated and particular contexts—a shift that begins to explain its confluence with the politics of Acknowledgment. Basic writing, however, still needs to intensify its commitment to rhetorical instruction and to more thoroughly consider the political implications of this commitment.

I believe we achieved something like the politics of Acknowledgment in rhetorically-oriented writing classes by asking students to write in a way that is conscious of and reaches out to the other, with critical awareness of situation, audience, purpose, and genre. Students choose some of their own purposes, audiences, and genres for writing, and because they write analyses of their choices and the possible consequences of them in the public sphere, we acknowledge the student and her interests, offering what Markell calls the "tentative pleasure of potency" without the "illusion of certainty." Rhetoric and its effects are unpredictable, to put it mildly. The key is to value differences among students, as in the politics of recognition, while also mobilizing Acknowledgment by setting students into certain types of rhetorical motion.

The new curriculum at RU exemplifies what I came to think of, in hindsight, as features of Acknowledgment, which I can describe in two categories: the overall course design and process-oriented mechanisms.

Acknowledgment as Course Design

Overall, the course begins where students are and then takes an outward turn, following an ever more public trajectory. More specifically, the class first encourages students to recognize what rhetorical savvy they already possess. In discussion and low-stakes writing, students consider when they are most aware of their own language use, what sorts of circumstances cause this heightened awareness, and what this change does to their efforts of self-representation and persuasion. Doing so acknowledges students' pre-existing and unique rhetorical savvy in some contexts and provides an intellectual path to the thresholds that we want them to cross, the belief that all writing is rhetorically motivated and situated, and the skills to analyze and utilize broadly rhetorical factors like situation, genre and language choice.[5]

Continuing its outward turn, the class next considers others' uses of rhetoric and how rhetoric operates at the community level, along with increasingly public writing assignments. Accordingly, writing for the teacher gives way to blogging and other online writing. Students explore and write about discourse communities—ones they belong to, first, and then ones they do not, including conducting interviews with members of those communities. The course ends with a writing project in which the students join an ongoing, public discourse, or what Jenny Edbauer and others call a rhetorical ecology.[6] The outward turn of the course, then, is embedded in the sequence of assignments and the scaffolding that leads to each of them. We begin by recognizing each student's rhetorical expertise in one situation or another, then acknowledge them by *asking them to acknowledge others* through their writing, to examine, that is, their own rhetorical positions and the community's discourses they wish to join and tailoring their writing accordingly.[7]

Process as Politics

Here, I follow Joseph Harris in doubting that the process approach constitutes a pedagogy *per se* (55). In our pilot, process amounts to a political commitment in that we understand peer review, meta-cognitive analysis, and the format of final assessment as all part of the rhetorical model of Acknowledgment. Like Mark Hall, in *The Politics of Peer Response*, we re-imagine peer review as a democratic process in which students collaboratively construct peer review guidelines and even grading rubrics. This primarily takes place in the form of open classroom discussion. Doing so constructs students as part of a community enterprise demanding self-awareness, awareness of others (including peers, faculty, and institutional context), and ongoing deliberative negotiation *about writing*. In other words, it emphasizes the message that writing and its evaluation constitute dialogical processes, precisely in line with the participatory emphasis of Acknowledgment.

Simultaneously, every major project includes what we call meta-writing. Meta-textual analysis plays an important role by requiring students to analyze their rhetorical choices in light of audience, genre, and possible outcomes. Meta-writing asks students to perform a deep reflexivity, and politically acknowledges student-writers' intentions as significant. It also asks students to write in another relatively high stakes situation. They write to their teacher explicitly instead of implicitly, as in all the traditional classroom genres where students are instructed to write for the "general academic audience." Assigning meta-texts asks students to raise their level of self- and other-consciousness and to consider the ways they have interacted with those others, and the kinds of outcomes those choices create, a way to emphasize potency without certainty.

Lastly, we replaced timed writing with a portfolio of student work in the final assessment, an uncontroversial move at this point. Accordingly, I spend little time explaining or defending it, except to note that Pepinster Greene and McAlexander cite portfolio assessment as one of the most widely embraced elements of the process approach. Portfolio assessment acknowledges students in that it, "allows the student to be a participant. . .rather than simply an object of assessment" (13). Again, we can see Acknowledgment's emphasis on self- and other-directed action.

While our proposal worked self-consciously to grasp opportunities within a liberal value system, I believe that the pedagogical approach of our pilot course, wedding rhetoric and the politics of Acknowledgment, resisted traditionally liberal composition. Rhetorical education represents a significant re-boot for basic writing, a change that has been happening here and there across the field, but our model begins to realize more fully the deeply political implications of this shift.

AGONISTIC ACKNOWLEDGMENT

We know from the work of Mary Soliday and Barbara Gleason ("From Remediation to Enrichment") and Gleason alone ("Evaluating Writing Programs in Real Time"), that pedagogical change cannot generate on its own a new politics. As I have noted, our changes at Roosevelt matched a rhetorical pedagogy with a Stretch-style program, creating the overall effect of a politics of Acknowledgment. While Patchen Markell himself cautions us against hoping that the politics of Acknowledgment can, "settle political controversies or prescribe courses of action" (178), he hopes for "other, subtler effects" (178). He believes Acknowledgment, "can change our view of the nature of the problems we confront; it can alter our sense of what courses of action are open to us in the first place" (178). I must ask, therefore, what sorts of institutional negotiation are "open to us" in basic writing once we've ceded liberalism's reflexiveness?

Chantal Mouffe's concept of *agonistic pluralism* suggests an answer. Mouffe both acknowledges liberalism's hegemony and advocates the generation of productive pressure (*agon*) within that paradigm. I do not propose this last section as an unearthed solution to the 90s political crisis—as an eureka! moment—but as a way to re-consider and re-organize our relation to the liberal reflex.

In *The Democratic Paradox*, Mouffe approaches the same set of problems addressed by Perelman and Taylor, the tension between the liberal tradition and the pursuit of democratic justice. Like them, she takes on John Rawls, among others. Unlike Perelman and Taylor, Mouffe does not argue that Rawls has incorrectly solved the problem of liberalism and democracy. She argues, instead, that *there is no solution*. More specifically, Mouffe identifies the source of liberal democratic political tension as, "[resulting] from the articulation of two logics which are incompatible" (5). These two logics do not fit and never really have: "On one side we have the liberal tradition constituted by the rule of law, the defence of human rights and the respect of individual liberty; on the other the democratic tradition whose main ideas are those of equality, identity between governing and governed and popular sovereignty. There is no necessary relation between those two distinct traditions but only a contingent historical articulation" (2-3). Like Markell's claim that recognition seeks the unattainable, Mouffe characterizes as fraught the very grammar of liberal democracy, concluding that there is no resolution to such a tension. We can only aim for "temporary stability through pragmatic negotiations" (5). Rejecting consensus as a political goal, Mouffe calls for a process of temporary stabilization she calls *agonistic pluralism*. Her theory focuses on active negotiation toward always-temporary, imperfect agreement, and thereby forwards a permanently dialogical account of politics (15). Mouffe calls political agents "friendly enemies" who share common symbolic space but have different organizing goals for that space (13). Rhetorical practice within liberalism, in this model, operates like a complex ecology, rather than according to the more strictly persuasive definition, which operated like a train that stayed on the tracks and arrived at its destination (consensus) or didn't. Mouffe's approach suggests a productive mindset for basic writing administrators, who constantly negotiate the shifting terms of upper administration anyway.

Rather than seeking solutions to the political tensions that fractured basic writing, we can craft dialogues that maintain an agonistic space, even as they require constant revision. The seeds of this kind of thinking exist in much of the literature I have already cited. Perelman, for example, argues that legislation is creative work, requiring a kind of public, discursive synergy (67). Similarly, Markell claims that time constitutes part of the difference between Acknowledgment and recognition; Acknowledgment is a perpetual dialogical process, rather than the end point of a teleology (15). In pedagogical circles, Grego and Thompson, in *Teaching/Writing in Thirdspaces*, evoke something like agonistic pluralism when they claim that Studio seeks not solutions, but "lateral interactions across previously existing institutional hierarchies or boundaries" (50). Practicing acknowledgment in our classes and in our larger institutional contexts, with the goal of maintaining agonistic space rather than foreclosing it, generates productive forms of pressure on traditional liberal practices.

I have argued that the crisis over liberalism in basic writing in the 90s overestimated anyone's ability to operate outside of liberalism. Furthermore, I have advocated for the combination of 1) a rhetorical writing approach crafted in the image of the politics of Acknowledgment with 2) a rhetorical effort to maintain agonistic space within liberal institutions. Students benefit, yes, but the combination of the two provides a model for how to realistically manage administrative relationships, too. We practice what we teach: contextualized rhetorical action in constant need of revision.

Postscript, on Roosevelt

I left Roosevelt and the Stretch Coordinator position the summer before the pilot began, in order to take a job in the city my partner had already lived for two years. I'm still in touch with friends and colleagues at Roosevelt, and they tell me the pilot has gone well, reporting anecdotally that students have embraced the rhetorical pedagogy, and seem to feel less marginalized than did their counterparts in English 100. We will know more once final portfolios are evaluated and programmatic assessment is conducted over the summer.

Programmatically speaking, there has been an interesting conversation in the last year that I think nicely illustrates agonistic pluralism. Earlier, I described the problematic practice at Roosevelt of placing transfer students in basic writing in spite of our articulation agreement that assured them that we would honor their prior completion of any school's writing requirement. Many of us in the writing program had repeatedly argued that forcing transfers into a first-year basic writing course was unjust, in light of the articulation agreement. But now, if Stretch entirely replaces English 100, RU cannot continue to require transfers with incoming 101-credit to take the class because Stretch utilizes the same curriculum as "regular" 101 and is thus coded as a 101-level class in the catalogue. Our new program closed this particular liberal loophole. For a period of time, it looked like transfers would simply not be required to take any writing classes, a possible outcome about which many felt ambivalence. It was not long, however, before university administrators began to insist that many transfers would still need formalized basic writing in some form and that the old English 100 would serve this purpose nicely. It should be no surprise, I suppose, that in the face of change the liberal reflex kicks in, and that is precisely why my former colleagues at Roosevelt must continually mobilize their own rhetorical practice aimed at maintaining a space for agonism. If English 100 is indeed maintained, now exclusively for transfers, it would continue to exert a blunt assimilatory pressure on students of the very sort that sparked the basic writing crisis in the first place.

At this point, however, RU writing faculty are engaged in a more complex conversation about basic writing than had existed at Roosevelt for some time. Indeed, the conversation continues. I'm happy to report that the writing program has been negotiating with upper administrators to adopt a Studio-style option for transfers, perhaps driven by directed self-placement. Such an outcome would signify, I believe, the successful adaptation of the politics of Acknowledgment in maintaining agonistic pluralism at Roosevelt. The replacement of RU's former program with a rhetorically-oriented Stretch program for freshmen *and* a Studio for transfers, it seems to me, represents a significant improvement—for now. And "for now" is the best any of us can do, when our re-orientation to institutional liberalism is driven by the creative effort for a practical and socially just approach to basic writing.

ACKNOWLEDGMENTS

For their contributions to the Stretch Program at Roosevelt, I thank my fellow lecturers, Amanda Wornhoff, E. Mairin Barney, and Ji-Hyae Park; Writing Center Director, Carrie Brecke; and Director of the Composition Program, Sheldon Walcher. For her insightful comments on this text, I thank Hope Parisi, as well as the *JBW* reviewers. For just about everything else, I thank Kirsten.

Notes

1. I write about this experience from a distance, both geographically and chronologically, as I am no longer at Roosevelt and most of the events I describe occurred in 2010-2011, during the planning of our program proposal and pilot classes.

2. I borrow the term "social groups" from Iris Marion Young's chapter "The Five Faces of Oppression" in *Justice and the Politics of Difference*, a term she defines as neither an association nor an aggregate, but a group that is publicly identifiable in Heidegger's sense of "thrownness" (39-65).

3. All retention numbers came from the Common Data Set from RU's Office of Institutional Research.

4. Data on retention and persistence on students of color who began as basic writers was not available.

5. While "starting where they are" is close to an old chestnut in rhetoric and composition (see anyone from Shaughnessy to Graff), it also constitutes an important element of Acknowledgment insofar as it goes beyond recognition of communicative differences.

6. See Rivers and Weber for a detailed example of this sort of assignment.

7. Nancy Pine's model of service learning in basic writing achieves something similar to our pilot's outward turn, especially in her ethnography assignment and in the way she connects this to academic writing. I would argue, however, that her model sometimes settles for recognition over Acknowledgment, especially when Pine's assignment leans toward what Thomas Deans calls "writing-about" rather than "writing-for" a community agency.

Works Cited

Appiah, Kwame Anthony. *The Ethics of Identity*. Princeton, NJ: Princeton UP, 2005. Print.

Bartholomae, David. "The Tidy House: Basic Writing in the American Curriculum." *Journal of Basic Writing*. 12.1 (1993): 4-21. Print.

Bawarshi, Anis. *Genre & The Invention of the Writer: Reconsidering the Place of Invention in Composition*. Logan, UT: Utah State UP, 2003. Print.

Berlin, James. *Rhetoric and Reality: Writing Instruction in American Colleges, 1900-1985*. Carbondale, IL: Southern Illinois UP, 1987. Print.

Crowley, Sharon. *Composition in the University: Historical and Polemical Essays*. Pittsburgh, PA: U of Pittsburgh P, 1998. Print.

Cruikshank, Barbara. *The Will to Empower: Democratic Citizens and Other Subjects*. Ithaca, NY: Cornell UP, 1999. Print.

Davi, Angelique. "In the Service of Writing and Race." *Journal of Basic Writing* 25.1 (2006): 73-95. Print.

Deans, Thomas. *Writing Partnerships: Service-Learning in Composition.* Urbana, IL: National Council of Teachers of English Press, 2000. Print.

Edbauer, Jenny. "Unframing Models of Public Distribution: From Rhetorical Situation to Rhetorical Ecologies." *Rhetoric Society Quarterly* 35.4 (2005): 5-24. Print.

Feldman, Ann Merle. *Making Writing Matter: Composition in the Engaged University.* Albany, NY: SUNY Press, 2008. Print.

Glau, Gregory. "The 'Stretch Program': Arizona State University's New Model of University-Level Basic Writing Instruction." *WPA: Writing Program Administration* 20.1-2 (1996): 79-91. Print.

Glau, Gregory. "'Stretch' at 10: A Progress Report on Arizona State University's 'Stretch Program.'" *Journal of Basic Writing* 26.2 (2007): 32-50. Print.

Gleason, Barbara. "Evaluating Writing Programs in Real Time: The Politics of Remediation." *College Composition and Communication* 51.4 (2000): 560-588. Print.

Graff, Gerald. *Clueless in Academe: How Schooling Obscures the Life of the Mind.* New Haven: Yale UP, 2003. Print.

Greenberg, Karen L. "The Politics of Basic Writing." *Journal of Basic Writing* 12.1 (1993): 64-71. Print.

Grego, Rhonda and Nancy Thompson. *Teaching/Writing in Thirdspaces: The Studio Approach.* Carbondale, IL: Southern Illinois UP, 2008. Print.

Grego, Rhonda and Nancy Thompson. "Repositioning Remediation: Renegotiating Composition's Work in the Academy." *College Composition and Communication* 47.1 (1996): 62-84. Print.

Hall, Mark. "The Politics of Peer Response." *The Writing Instructor* (July 2009). n. pag. Web. 7 August 2009.

Harris, Joseph. *A Teaching Subject: Composition Since 1966.* Upper Saddle River, NJ: Prentice Hall, 1996. Print.

Kymlicka, Will. *Multicultural Citizenship: A Liberal Theory of Minority Rights.* Oxford: Oxford UP, 1995. Print.

Lalicker, William. "A Basic Introduction to Basic Writing Program Structures: A Baseline and Five Alternatives." *BWe: Basic Writing e-Journal* 1.2 (1999): n. pag. Web. 7 January 2011.

Locke, John. *Two Treatises of Government and A Letter Concerning Toleration.* Ed. Ian Shapiro. New Haven, CT: Yale UP, 2003. Print.

Lu, Min-Zhan. "Professing Multiculturalism: The Politics of Style in the Contact Zone." *College Composition and Communication* 45.4 (1994): 442-458. Print.

Markell, Patchen. *Bound by Recognition.* Princeton, NJ: Princeton UP, 2003. Print.

McCurrie, Matthew Kilian. "Measuring Success in Summer Bridge Programs: Retention Efforts and Basic Writing." *Journal of Basic Writing* 28.2 (2009): 28-49. Print.

Miller, Carolyn. "Genre as Social Action." *Quarterly Journal of Speech* 70 (1984): 151-67. Print.

Mouffe, Chantal. *The Democratic Paradox*. London: Verso Press, 2000. Print.

Otte, George and Rebecca Williams Mlynarczyk. "The Future of Basic Writing." *Journal of Basic Writing* 29.1 (2010): 5-32. Print.

"Our History." *Roosevelt University Web site*. n.d. Web. 30 April 2012.

Pepinster Greene, Nicole and Patricia J. McAlexander. *Basic Writing in America: The History of Nine College Programs*. Cresskill, NJ: Hampton Press, 2008. Print.

Perelman, Chaim. *Justice*. New York: Random House, 1967. Print.

Pine, Nancy. "Service Learning in a Basic Writing Class: A Best Case Scenario." *Journal of Basic Writing* 27.2 (2008): 29-55. Print.

Rawls, John. *Political Liberalism*. 2nd Ed. New York: Columbia UP, 1996. Print.

Rivers, Nathaniel A. and Ryan P. Weber. "Ecological, Pedagogical, Public Rhetoric." *College College Composition and Communication* 63.2 (2011): 187-218. Print.

Rose, Mike. "Remediation at a Crossroads." *Inside Higher Ed* (21 April 2011), n.pag. Web. 15 May 2011.

Royer, Daniel and Roger Gilles. *Directed Self-Placement: Principles and Practices*. Cresskill, NJ: Hampton Press, 2003. Print.

Russell, David R. *Writing in the Academic Disciplines: A Curricular History*. 2nd Ed. Carbondale, IL: Southern Illinois UP, 2002. Print.

Shaughnessy, Mina. *Errors and Expectations: A Guide for the Teacher of Basic Writing*. New York: Oxford UP, 1977. Print.

Soliday, Mary. "From the Margins to the Mainstream: Reconceiving Remediation." *College Composition and Communication* 47.1 (1996): 85-100. Print.

Soliday, Mary and Barbara Gleason. "From Remediation to Enrichment: Evaluating a Mainstreaming Project." *Journal of Basic Writing* 16.1 (1997): 64-78. Print.

Swales, John M. *Genre Analysis: English in Academic and Research Settings*. Cambridge: Cambridge UP, 1990. Print.

Taylor, Charles. "The Politics of Recognition." *Multiculturalism and "The Politics of Recognition."* Ed. Amy Gutmann. Princeton, NJ: Princeton UP, 1992. Print.

Tully, James. *Strange Multiplicity: Constitutionalism in an Age of Diversity*. Cambridge: Cambridge UP, 1995. Print.

White, Edward M. "The Importance of Placement and Basic Studies: Helping Students Succeed Under the New Elitism." *Journal of Basic Writing* 14.2 (1995): 75-84. Print.

Young, Iris Marion. *Justice and the Politics of Difference*. Princeton, NJ: Princeton UP, 1990. Print.

JOURNAL OF TEACHING WRITING

The Journal of Teaching Writing is on the Web at http://journals.iupui.edu/index.php/teachingwriting/

The Journal of Teaching Writing publishes articles of interest to teachers at all grade levels, from preschool to university, that address the practices and theories which bear on our knowledge of how people learn and communicate through writing. Articles may range in length from short descriptions (10-15 pages) of principles and practices that offer helpful insights to longer pieces (16-20 pages) that explore topics in greater detail. All articles should have a clear philosophical or theoretical basis.

Positioning the Textbook as Contestable Intellectual Space

Kelly S. Bradbury's "Positioning the Textbook as Contestable Intellectual Space" models the kind of article that our readers find stimulating, informative, and practical. Arguing that textbooks "can counter classroom practices designed to promote critical thinking and intellectual exploration," Bradbury takes a part of every teacher's experience—the textbook—and flips it, putting students in charge of their learning through researching, selecting, and "interrogating" the course readings. Her observations and reflections on her teaching "experiment" are detailed, probing, and thought provoking. In addition, she provides the teaching artifacts to guide readers if they should choose to replicate such a classroom experience for their students. It's the story of a well-conceived experiment, and Bradbury tells it masterfully.

7 Positioning the Textbook as Contestable Intellectual Space

Kelly S. Bradbury

> *As teachers and scholars in composition and rhetoric continue to reread and reinvent our discipline, we cannot afford to neglect the dynamic role textbooks play in conserving, challenging, and transforming the academic culture, the discipline, and the tradition of teaching writing.*
>
> –Xin Liu Gale and Fredric G. Gale, (Re)Visioning Composition Textbooks, 12-13

Compositionists have long recognized the ideological nature of the composition classroom and the significant role textbooks play in the politicization of education. In *Fragments of Rationality*, Lester Faigley argued that textbooks are "embedded in a long history of institutional practices and discourses that, as Foucault has demonstrated, are themselves mechanisms of power working quietly across social hierarchies and traditional political categories" (133). In 1996, Mona Scheuermann fueled the debate about the role of textbooks in the writing classroom by claiming teachers intentionally use readers to indoctrinate students with their personal political beliefs (77-78). Extending compositionists' skepticism toward textbooks are their concerns about whether textbooks work against our discipline's goals of fostering students' inquisitiveness and intellectual development. In her 1987 groundbreaking *CCC* article, Kathleen Welch argued the "textbook-bound classroom as it now often exists . . . promotes passivity" because of an emphasis on rule-based "technical rhetoric" (279). Additionally, Kurt Spellmeyer contended that though textbooks are theoretically intended to incite inquiry, in practice they "help suppress questioning" because they detach knowledge from where it originated and present it to students as something that "comes from somewhere else–and from someone else" (45-47). Unfortunately, while many scholars work to make textbooks challenging and stimulating, they are produced within a profit-driven context that privileges sale-ability and accessibility over educational benefits (Olson; Otte; Garnes et. al).

Despite writing teachers' awareness of the ideological and intellectual boundaries created by textbooks, for many students textbooks constitute a tacit discourse in the classroom and define what knowledge is deemed valuable and uncontestable. Even when teachers encourage students to read critically the other texts they assign, textbooks themselves are rarely presented as intellectual spaces that students help create and to which they contribute. Consequently, textbooks in the writing classroom can counter classroom practices designed to promote critical thinking and intellectual exploration. Recognizing these challenges, I sought to reposition the course textbook in my classroom as a space for students to collaboratively discover and contest knowledge.

This article reports the results of my attempt to combat the boundaries textbooks create by replacing the commercially-published readers I had previously used in my writing courses with a "textbook" the students would create by researching and selecting the course readings. My hope was that by positioning the course content itself as flexible and contestable knowledge, students would become more critical readers, writers, and researchers. I also hoped giving students the power to select the course readings would engage them in their own learning and encourage them to see knowledge as accessible and contestable–as something they could seek out and critique as individuals and collaborators.

Positioning the textbook as a collaboratively-composed and contestable intellectual space is a teaching practice informed by the liberatory, student-centered pedagogies valued by our discipline. It enacts James Berlin's argument for teaching students to critique and resist the discourses working to influence them (52). It adds to the list of pedagogical practices responding to Ira Shor's call to empower students by not treating knowledge as a commodity to impose on students, but rather as something to be investigated and debated (11-16). And it helps students become, in Mike Rose's words, "agents in their own development" (416). Further, this practice embodies the "pedagogy of possibility" advocated by Kay Halasek because it is "student-generated" and not just "student-centered," situating students as "co-authors" of classroom pedagogy (180-184). More importantly, this pedagogical practice helps us reexamine the relationship among our teaching methods, the location of boundaries and contestable spaces in our classrooms, and the goals of our discipline.

In what follows, I outline the design, execution, and results of my experiment with teaching students to research, select, and interrogate the course readings in my English Honors 151 class. I share the successes and challenges of this practice, drawing on both my own observations and reflections and on those of my students.

Constructing and Contesting the Textbook

On the first day of class, I told my first-year composition students that because the primary objectives of this course (the second of a required three-course sequence) were to help students further develop their critical reading skills, their analytical writing skills, and their academic research skills, they would indeed read and write several college-level essays that critiqued, integrated, and documented research. I also told them that the course textbook was "up for debate"–literally. Part of their work this semester, I explained, would be 1) to collectively create the course "textbook" by researching and selecting our course readings, and 2) to collaboratively evaluate and question those readings by composing and presenting a series of thought-provoking discussion questions along with contextual information about the author and text. Based on their reactions that first day, the students seemed a bit surprised, but interested.

Because students likely were not used to selecting their course readings, I prepared them to research and select the readings by assigning in the first two weeks a few model articles they could use as a kind of benchmark or starting point. Having chosen "Reading Popular Culture" as our course theme, I assigned the following essays: Mark Miller's "Getting Dirty," a perspicacious and playful essay analyzing a 1980s Shield soap commercial; Aeon

J. Skoble's "Lisa and American Anti-intellectualism,"[5] an essay critiquing the message *The Simpsons* sends about education and intellectualism; and Dianne Williams Hayes' examination of the narrow portrayals of black college students in film, titled "Athletes, Outcasts, and Partyers."[6] I presented these texts to students not only as examples of the types of readings they should search for because they exemplified the academic reading students should be encountering at the college level, but also as models of the type of analytical writing and thinking the first writing assignment required of them (analyzing a popular culture artifact, focusing on the messages it sends about a social, cultural, political, or economic issue). These three articles were also ideal models for course readings because my former students had found them accessible, interesting, and provocative.

On Day Three of the course, a campus librarian gave students the orientation to the campus library and its services, generously tailoring the session to helping students locate scholarly readings on popular culture. To further assist students, I gave them a list of the types of publications I recommended (including academic journals and reputable magazines like *The Journal of Popular Culture*, *The Journal of American Culture*, *Harper's Magazine*, *The Nation*, *The New Yorker*, and *The Atlantic*), as well as those of the ilk I did not recommend (i.e., *People*, *Us*, *Glamour*). I asked them to think about what forms of media and what social, cultural, and political issues they were most interested in reading and writing about, and I encouraged them to think about these as possible search terms (see Appendix A for the assignment prompt). An additional resource for students was an online "Research Guide" the librarian had created just for our course. The Guide contained links to relevant journals students had access to at the college, to pertinent (and reputable) websites and internet resources, to the most useful research databases for this assignment, and to the library's specialized encyclopedias related to popular culture.

Students had one week from the library orientation to find and select one or two articles to nominate for our course "textbook." During that week, we spent time in class working on the crafts of writing summaries and citing sources. At the end of Week Three, students submitted to me a brief self-composed abstract (four-tosix sentences long) along with the citation information for the articles they were nominating. I compiled the information provided by students, distributed it to the class, and collected their votes for their top seven choices at the beginning of Week Four. The ten articles (out of the twenty-four submitted) that received the most votes became the semester's readings. Students whose article was selected by the class as a course reading were automatically assigned to co-present and lead the discussion on that reading. For those whose article was not selected, I assigned them to present on an article for which they had voted so everyone was able to present on an article in which they had expressed interest.

For the presentation assignment, I asked students, in pairs, to research and share with the class background information on the article's author(s) and the publication source. The purpose, as I explained to the students, was to provide the class pertinent contextual information that could assist us in reading the text critically. Kathleen Welch criticizes composition readers for presenting readings out of context, sending the message to students that writing occurs absent context (273). This assignment, however, repositions the text in its original context. As we discussed in class, knowing the authors' educational background, job history, publication record, race, gender, and political leanings and the publication's date, reputation, editors, and political affiliations could enrich our readings of the texts by shedding light on the author's motivation, audience, and purpose.

For the second part of the presentation assignment, students collaboratively composed a handout that contained an original one-to-two-paragraph summary of the piece (essentially an expanded version of the abstract submitted by the nominator), the background information they gathered on the author(s) and publication, and five-to-seven questions they generated to facilitate and guide our class discussion of the piece. To aid students in creating thoughtful questions, I encouraged them to compose questions that would assist the class in doing the following: interrogate the quality of the article's argument, organization, support, and style; consider the contemporary application of the article's argument; connect the argument to other media forms; put the piece in conversation with any of the other course readings; or connect it to a current (or past) political, social, or economic issue. I provided them a handout with sample discussion questions for each category (see Appendix C), and I modeled this activity by generating the discussion questions for the first three articles I assigned. We also practiced these cognitive skills (interrogating and connecting texts) as a class throughout the semester.

From my perspective, the various steps of these complementary assignments would exercise students' reading, writing, and research skills. More specifically, they would provide practice conducting and reading scholarly research, summarizing others' ideas, citing sources, researching contextual information, and questioning texts—skills central to the primary objectives of the course as defined by the college and to the outcomes of first-year composition sought by the Council of Writing Program Administrators ("WPA Outcomes Statement").

From the outset, I had only two concerns. First, I knew that teaching the articles students selected would be more time consuming for me than teaching articles with which I was already familiar or had already taught. Second, and more importantly, I was concerned that giving up control of the course "textbook" could have unpredictable–perhaps negative–consequences. What if all the students picked poorly-written and poorly-researched articles? What if they picked poor articles but thought they were good? What if I didn't like the articles they selected? What if they all picked articles on the same subject or from the same magazine? Would I really just go with the choices they made, or would I "take control" if the selection and voting process went poorly?

Because of these concerns, I initially considered not giving students complete control, but rather giving them *some* power. For example, I could let them select from several readings I had picked ahead of time, or allow them to select only two-to-three weeks worth of readings, or have them select readings from a handful of contemporary magazines I would require them to purchase. Ultimately, however, I decided to see what students– and I–could learn by genuinely positioning the course readings as an intellectual space they would create, contemplate, and question.

Lessons Learned

Despite my initial concerns about students' choices, students did select a variety of texts, both in terms of the content and in terms of the purpose, audience, organization, writing style, and overall quality of the texts. Some authors supported their claims at length and by citing scholarly research while other pieces were under-developed and under-supported. Some were written in a traditional academic voice while others employed a more conversational style. The authors included scholars, journalists, cultural critics, and a graduate student, and the publications varied from academic journals like *Policy Review* and *Journal of Popular Film and Television*, to magazines like *Newsweek* and *The New York Times Magazine*, to general web articles. The readings covered topics as varied as violence in video games and

music, class issues in the Harry Potter series, body image and advertising, TV's influence on intelligence, and the relationship between
American superheroes and politics (see Appendix B).

In an end-of-the-semester survey asking students to reflect on their
experiences researching, selecting, and evaluating the course content,
several students mentioned this diversity in articles as beneficial for
their critical reading skills. One student wrote,

> We read a large variety of articles with respect to length, qual-
> ity, topic, source, type, etc. . . . . Having articles that varied so
> widely. . . allowed me, as a student, to become more trained
> in criticizing articles in many different forms. For example,
> looking at title/body 'agreement,' evidence of claims, sources
> of research, or biases.

Additionally, as I observed in class, after reading a few of the more
well-written and well-developed pieces, students seemed to notice and
compare to these stronger essays the effects of other authors' different
writing styles, vocabulary, organization, and use of sources and support. In one case, on the day we discussed "Violent Video Games:
Myths, Facts, and Unanswered Questions," students pointed out that
while the author cited several sources in his bibliography, they were all
authored by him or a collaborator of his, a quality they thought weak-
ened his credibility in comparison to the stronger articles that cited
several reputable sources by other authors. Students were also critical
of the way he organized his essay, which led to unnecessary repetition.
Overall, they commented in class, they were surprised that someone
with a Ph.D. could have published such a poorly-written article in
Psychological Science Agenda.

Students also expressed in their surveys what they learned about
writing from reading this collaboratively-selected diverse set of articles. One student commented, "I really feel that certain articles influenced my own writing style and believe it or not I think having the
occasional 'bad' article is constructive for the class to see what not to
do or to avoid in their own writing." Another student wrote, "Even
though some of the readings were a bit undeveloped or stylistically un-
intriguing, I think it actually helped by giving us examples of what not
to do and allowed us to see both sides." This was clear to me in several
of our class discussions of the articles. For example, when we analyzed
the *Newsweek* article "I'm a PC: Keep the Change," students said that

though they agreed with Daniel Lyons' argument, they thought the sarcastic tone and the lack of development of the piece hurt his case. We discussed as a class how students themselves might avoid such criticism of their own writing.

Conversely, the stronger articles became the subject of class discussions on what students could do to strengthen and improve their writing and their essays. In fact, several students tried to emulate the tone or writing style of their favorite authors or used an author's organizational structure in their own paper. Students' favorite articles ("Beauty and the Patriarchal Beast," "Eminem is Right," and "Watching TV Makes You Smarter") were the strongest of the student-selected course readings, and students encouraged me to use the essays as model articles in subsequent semesters. Notably, "Watching TV Makes You Smarter" has been included in several commercially-published composition readers, including Pearson's *Beyond Words: Cultural Texts for Reading and Writing*, Bedford/St. Martin's *Fields of Reading: Motives for Writing*, and a reader I helped create several years ago, *Reading Popular Culture: An Anthology for Writers*. An additional (and unexpected) outcome of students' selections was that these three articles served as excellent models for students as they researched and wrote their final paper–a research paper examining a "representational trend" in popular culture.   "Beauty and the Patriarchal Beast" pointed to a trend in the representation of men and women in contemporary sitcoms. The author of "Eminem is Right" investigated the trend of violence in rap and hip-hop music. And, Steven Johnson revealed a trend of narrative complexity in television dramas.

Further evidence that students became more sophisticated and reflective readers as the semester progressed is the quality of the discussion questions they generated for their presentations. As one student noted in class a few weeks before the semester's end, the lists of discussion questions were getting progressively longer as the semester went on. From my perspective, this showed students' growing investment in *and* confidence in their ability to read the course texts critically. The two sets of discussion questions below (one generated by the first group to present, and the other composed by the final group to present) demonstrate more concretely how students' ability to question and contest the texts developed over the course of the semester.

FIRST GROUP'S DISCUSSION QUESTIONS

"Beauty and the Patriarchal Beast: Gender Role Portrayals in Sitcoms Featuring Mismatched Couples" by Kimberly Walsh, et al.

1.   The authors attempt to prove their point by listing names of sitcoms. How relevant and how effective were the shows they used in proving their argument?

2.   What is the author focusing on in his [sic] analysis and comparisons?

3.   Can you think of any other shows that use Satellite and Kernel narratives to depict power struggles?

4.   Are these types of shows responsible for the "postfeminism" trap?

5.   How is this article similar to "Athletes, Outcasts and Partyers" and "Getting Dirty" in its' [sic] message?

FINAL GROUP'S DISCUSSION QUESTIONS

"The Politics of Superheroes" by Jesse Walker

1.   What are the overall strengths/weaknesses of the article?

2.   Walker talks about a lot of subtle imagery that he feels the common viewer will not notice. For example in Spider-Man 3, he compares Venom and Sandman to oil and sand, and notes how Spiderman briefly pauses before an American flag to go fight them. However these villains have been around for a very long time in comic books, long before the War on Terror. Do you think these possible metaphors were placed there on purpose, or are politicians looking for imagery that simply isn't there?

3.   With the exception of a very brief reference to comics at the beginning of the article, Walker only compares superhero movies to politics, [sic] could he have perhaps strengthened his argument by comparing other elements of pop-culture (other movie genres, video games, etc.) to politics as well? If so, which ones?

4.   Walker opens his article by talking about how some politicians were ruined by a failed political program, but the fictional su-

perheroes used in the program were not. He then goes on to speak about how politicians see political symbolism in comic book films. Does his intro lead into the main argument of his essay well? Or does it seem to have little relationship to his argument?

5.   If the films mentioned have these political metaphors and continue to be very popular movies year after year, does this in turn suggest a widespread increase in political interest among viewers?

6.   In what specific films, shows, and other forms of media do you see political aspects present? How are these examples the same or different than those mentioned in this article?

Representative of the types of questions students generated early and then late in the semester, these lists show how students' questions became more specific, more layered, and more contextualized. They also became more sophisticated in their understanding of the authors' rhetorical strategies and the effect of those strategies on readers. For example, the first group asked their peers in a simple "yes/no"-structured question if they knew of any additional shows that employed the narrative types discussed in "Beauty and the Patriarchal Beast" (Question 3). Similarly, in Question 5 they asked their classmates very generally if they could connect this article to two previous articles we'd read. The final group made a similar move with Question 6; however, they asked students for *specific* related examples and asked them *how* those examples related. Demonstrating their recognition of the benefits of comparison and of writers' choices, this group's third question asked the class to consider whether comparing other forms of popular culture to politics could have strengthened Walker's argument. Once again, they asked for *specific* examples in a follow-up question.

Questions 2, 3, and 4 in the second set of questions also reveal the students' tendency to contextualize their questions by briefly summarizing or explaining something about the article before asking the class to apply or question those ideas/examples. One weakness in this set of questions is that some of them lead the reader to a specific response or imply the composers' opinion. For instance, Question 4 seems to imply that the presenters think the introduction has little connection to the argument. What these leading questions show, I think, is students' confidence in their critical reading of the text. By the end of the semester, students instinctively read the texts critically, and, evident in our class discussions, they were better able to articulate and justify their criticisms. For this particular group, their criticisms of the text were transparent in their questions. These questions (and those generated by all groups) rival–and perhaps far exceed–the quality of the discussion questions generated for students in pre-assembled textbooks, further supporting this method of teaching. Additionally, the act of generating the discussion questions (in contrast to responding to pre-packaged questions) allows students to determine the perspectives and critical orientation that guide the class' reading of the texts.

When asked what they had learned about research from this process, several students said that finding well-written and well-researched articles that were also interesting was the most challenging part of the assignment. Ultimately disappointed by some of the readings they had selected, a number of students admitted that they hadn't read their articles closely before nominating them, and that consequently, they had learned the importance of reading texts carefully and not judging them based on a cool-sounding title and a quick skim. In their new role as "coauthors" of classroom pedagogy, a few students suggested to me that to help avoid poor choices in the future, I should show students more model articles at the beginning of the semester; some suggested I give students more time to find an article. Both of these suggestions reveal students' investment in the process and their understanding of learning by modeling. I also believe that this challenge is a good one for students to face. It is important for students to learn that though they have access to a lot of information, they must be careful, critical researchers to locate quality sources and texts.

Students' research into the background of authors and publication sources also enriched our critical examinations of the course readings because they shed light on the audience, purpose, and motivation for the pieces. During our discussion of "Beauty and the Patriarchal Beast," students' realization that all three authors were women led them to contemplate the authors' investment in arguing that, despite their portrayal of women as smarter and more attractive than their husbands, contemporary sitcoms send a patriarchal message. In addition, when we critiqued "Eminem Is Right," students took into account the information their classmates presented that *Policy Review* is a conservative journal and the author is the consulting editor of the publication. To what extent, they wondered, did Eberstadt's political beliefs and the publication's political standing play a role in her interpretation of the reasons contemporary youth appreciate violent music? Getting students to consider the importance of this contextual information can make them more sophisticated readers and can help students to reflect more critically on the context in which they write their own essays.

In their final reflections, a number of students further highlighted as successful the collaborative nature of this learning experience. One student wrote, "It made it feel more like the class was a collaboration, then [sic] you just talking at us." Others wrote about how they were more motivated to read the articles because they knew their peers had selected them. In one student's words, "It definitely made me feel more interested in the readings because I thought if one of my classmates found this interesting, maybe I will too." Students' positive reactions to the collaborative nature of these assignments accords with anthropologist Susan Blum's recent findings about contemporary college students. Based on interviews with 234 students, Blum notes that because of students' numerous and early experiences with collaborativelycreated and remixed texts like blogs, social networking sites, *YouTube* videos, etc., they are collaborative by nature and they think differently about boundaries, originality, and individuality (3-5). In fact, she states, "[t]he preference for working with and around others" is, for today's student, instinctive and inherent (68).

Related to students' recognition of the collaborative nature of this project was their sense of responsibility for the class's learning. For example, a few weeks before the end of the semester the two students in charge of presenting on and leading our discussion of the final course reading ("Batmanalyzed") expressed to me after class one day their embarrassment about the quality of the article that one of them had nominated. After reading a number of well-written, well-researched articles over the course of the semester, they seemed–in preparing to present on their reading–to recognize it as weak in substance and writing. Struck by their concern, I told the students that if they wanted to research a few other options covering the same or related topic (superheroes), I'd be happy to switch out their new selection for the previous one. The students jumped at the opportunity and later that day sent me links to two other articles they found. The class agreed to replace the original article with a different article the two presenters felt was stronger. This seemed a great educational moment for students: it showed they had learned to read the texts critically, were invested in the course content, and saw the course as collaborative because they knew their choice affected others.

I learned from this pedagogical experiment that teaching students to select the course texts not only fostered their engagement with the readings and their willingness to critique them, but also challenged them to evaluate and reconsider their choices in light of what they were learning about reading, writing, and research as the semester progressed. In my experience, my students have never expressed as much interest or investment in, nor have they been as critically reflective about, the course readings as they were when they were given the power–and responsibility–to search for, select, and contest the course content. Several students commented on their end-of-thesemester survey on the freedom and control this methodology gave them. One student wrote, "It was somewhat of a challenge and it gave a certain amount of freedom, which is not that common in college. Personally I thought it was successful overall because it gave us as students some control." Another wrote, "[I]t's engaging and fun to have a class discussion about something we've opted to read." In response to my query about whether I should use this method in the future, one student wrote, "I would definitely do this again in the future. It gets the students involved in their coursework, taught us how to research and read in a critical manner, and gave us some concrete examples of a well-written piece." In fact, all but one student encouraged me to use this method in the future.

CONCLUSIONS

My reflections and my students' reflections above tell us something about what students (and their teacher) in a first-year composition class can learn about reading, writing, research, and student engagement when we present course content as flexible and contestable. What, then, can the field of composition and rhetoric learn from making the course textbook a flexible, contestable intellectual space? What does this experiment tell us about the relationship among our teaching methods, the location of boundaries and contestable spaces in our classrooms, and the goals of our discipline?

As Xin Liu and Fredric G. Gale argue in *(Re)Visioning Composition Textbooks*, writing teachers cannot ignore the influence textbooks have on "conserving, challenging, and transforming" teaching and learning

(13). We must recognize and work to challenge the intellectual and ideological boundaries textbooks create in our classrooms, boundaries that often counter the liberatory and "student-centered" pedagogies we employ in our classrooms. As my experiment shows, positioning the course textbook as an intellectual space that students co-create and collaboratively question can help us contest the boundaries a pre-packaged textbook creates. The result was a "pedagogy of possibility" that, by granting students some authority and freedom in their learning, fostered students' inquisitiveness and intellectual growth while also achieving the more concrete course objectives of developing their critical reading skills, analytical writing skills, and academic research skills.

We can infer, further, that the improvement in students' ability to question and read critically was due not only to the practice they gained over the semester, but also to their recognition that because the teacher had not selected the course readings, the knowledge presented in these texts had not been already predetermined valuable (or uncontestable) by the teacher. Having selected the course texts themselves, my students engaged with the readings differently than my students have in the past when I assigned the readings. Gone from our discussions was the assumption that I had selected these readings because I agreed with them, because I wanted to indoctrinate students with the ideologies they promoted, or because I wanted students to reproduce their writing style. Students were left to contemplate for themselves the quality of the content and writing in these texts.

In addition, the collaborative nature of this pedagogy not only works with contemporary students' interest in collaboration, but also, as much research has shown, cultivates "metacognitive awareness" (Cockrell et al. 358), increases motivation (Williams et al. 48), and demonstrates to students the principle that knowledge is "actively derived and constructed" through "discourse and negotiations among group members" (Cockrell et al. 354). This principle is a central one in addressing compositionists' concerns about the political, academic, and intellectual consequences of their classroom texts. It is also foundational for cultivating in students an interest and confidence in their own and others' intellectual development.

NOTES

1 While this was an honors section of first-year composition, I believe this pedagogical practice could have the same outcomes with a non-honors section of composition.

2 The College of Staten Island's official catalog description of the course is "English 151 builds on English 111 to develop students' abilities to read, write, and do research. The course emphasizes close, critical reading of a variety of texts and analytical writing about these texts. Significant attention is given to the development of academic research methods and skills" (CSI Undergraduate Catalog 2011-2012).

3 The four major writing assignments for the course were 1) an analysis of a popular culture artifact, 2) a close, critical reading of one of the course readings, 3) a summary of two sources speaking to the same issue and a personal "weigh in" on that issue, and 4) a research-based paper analyzing a representational trend in popular culture.

4 Miller, Mark Crispin. "Getting Dirty." Boxed In: The Culture of TV. Evanston: Northwestern UP, 1988: 43-50. Print.

5 Skoble, Aeon J. "Lisa and American Anti-intellectualism." The Simpsons and Philosophy: The D'oh! of Homer. Eds. William Irwin, Mark T. Conrad, and Aeon J. Skoble. Chicago and La Salle: Open Court, 2001. 24-34. Print.

6 Hayes, Dianne Williams. "Athletes, Outcasts and Partyers." Black Issues in Higher Education 12.23 (1996): 26-28. Print.

7 I did not grade the "selecting the course readings" assignment because I wanted students' incentive to be their interest and investment in the course content. I also wanted to give students practice researching, writing abstracts, and citing sources without worry about a grade for that work.

8 The four questions on the end-of-semester survey were 1) What, if any, were the benefits of being able to choose the course readings?, 2) What were the challenges of this assignment?, 3) Do you think I should let students choose the course readings in my future classes? Why or why not?, and 4) Did you like the "reading popular culture" theme? If not, what other themes do you suggest I use in the future?

9. I confess here that I had intentionally scheduled our reading of some of the "stronger" pieces early on with the hopes students might do what they in fact did: use the strengths in these pieces as benchmarks for their reading of the later pieces.

10. The representational trend research paper I assigned to students is based on an assignment designed by the first-year writing program at The Ohio State University.

11. This student indicated on his or her evaluation that he or she did not like most of the readings the students selected and consequently thinks the teacher should choose the readings.

WORKS CITED

Berlin, James. *Rhetorics, Poetics, and Cultures: Refiguring College English Studies*. Urbana, IL: NCTE, 1996. Print.

Blum, Susan D. *My Word! Plagiarism and College Culture*. Ithaca: Cornell UP, 2009. Print.

Cockrell, Karen Sunday, Julie A. Hughes Caplow, and Joe F. Donaldson, "A Context for Learning: Collaborative Groups in the Problem-Based Learning Environment." *The Review of Higher Education* 23.3 (2000): 347-363. *Project Muse*. Web. 8 Dec. 2011.

Council of Writing Program Administrators. "WPA Outcomes Statement for First-Year Composition." *WPACouncil.org*. Council of Writing Program Administrators. July 2008. Web. 1 Aug. 2011.

CSI Undergraduate Catalog 2011-2012. College of Staten Island (CUNY). n.p. Web. 6 Aug. 2011.

Eberstadt, Mary. "Eminem is Right: The Primal Scream of Teenage Music." *Policy Review* 128 (2004). 19-33. *Academic Search Complete*. Web. 8 Feb. 2010.

Faigley, Lester. *Fragments of Rationality: Postmodernity and the Subject of Composition*. Pittsburgh: U of Pittsburgh P, 1992. Print.

Gale, Xin Liu, and Fredric G. Gale, eds. *(Re)Visioning Composition Textbooks: Conflicts of Culture, Ideology, and Pedagogy*. Albany: SUNY P, 1999. Print.

Gale, Xin Liu, and Fredric G. Gale. "Introduction." Gale and Gale 3-14.

Garnes, Sara, David Humphries, Vic Mortimer, Jennifer Phegley, and Kathleen R. Wallace. "Writing *Writing Lives*: The Collaborative Production of a Composition Text in a Large First-Year Writing Program." Gale and Gale 249-66.

Halasek, Kay. *A Pedagogy of Possibility: Bakhtinian Perspectives on Composition Studies*. Carbondale: Southern Illinois UP, 1999. Print.

Olson, Gary A. "Foreword." Gale and Gale ix-xi.

Otte, George. "Why Read What?: The Politics of Composition Anthologies." *JAC* 12.1 (1992): 137-49. Print.

Rose, Mike. *Possible Lives: The Promise of Public Education in America*. New York: Houghton Mifflin, 1995. Print.

Scheuermann, Mona. "Freshman Writing & Ideological Texts." *The New Criterion* 15.2 (1996): 75-80. Print.

Shor, Ira. *Empowering Education: Critical Teaching for Social Change*. Chicago: U of Chicago P, 1992. Print.

Spellmeyer, Kurt. "The Great Way: Reading and Writing in Freedom." Gale and Gale 45-68.

Walsh, Kimberly, et al. "Beauty and the Patriarchal Beast: Gender Role Portrayals in Sitcoms Featuring Mismatched Couples." *Journal of Popular Film and Television* 36.3 (Fall 2008): 123-132. *Humanities Full Text.* Web. 6 Feb. 2010.

Welch, Kathleen E. "Ideology and Freshman Textbook Production: The Place of Theory in Writing Pedagogy." *CCC* 38.3 (1987): 269-82. Print.

Williams, David L., John D. Beard, and Jone Rymer. "Team Projects: Achieving Their Full Potential." *Journal of Marketing Education* 13.2 (1991): 45-53. *Sage Premier 2011.* Web. 8 Dec. 2011.

APPENDIX A: ASSIGNMENT PROMPT FOR "SELECTING COURSE READINGS" ASSIGNMENT

In order to give you some control over the course content and give each of you experience locating information through the library system, for this assignment you will research and select 1-2 articles addressing the course theme–American popular culture–to submit as possible readings for the semester. You will learn how to use the college's library databases and locate the current holdings on the shelves to search for relevant articles.

On **Thurs., Feb. 11**[th], each of you will turn in a document citing and briefly summarizing (in your own words) the 1-2 articles you've selected as possible course readings on popular culture. The document should contain the following information: the article title, author, publication title, date of publication, volume and/or issue number, page numbers, and a brief (4-6-sentence) summary of the article. You must also state where you found the article–on the shelves at CSI or in a particular database.

On **Tues., Feb. 16**[th] the class will vote on what articles you'd like to read and discuss this semester. Those articles not selected by the class may still be used for your other papers, especially the final research paper.

Suggestions for the types of publications to search for college-level articles about popular culture: *The Journal of Popular Culture, The Journal of American Culture, Time, Harper's Magazine, The Nation, The Atlantic, Dissent, Newsweek, The New Yorker, The New York Times, The New Republic, The American Prospect.*

Avoid such popular magazines as *People, Us, Glamour*, etc., as they do not contain the caliber of articles we're looking to read and analyze for this course.

You may locate the articles through the CSI Library databases OR by perusing the hard copies of these publications on the library shelves. Be sure not to select a book review. Be sure you can find the article in full text.

Example key terms to search:

- race and movies
- homosexuality and tv shows
- eating disorders and advertisements (or ads)
- reality tv and gender (or race, or class)
- music and stereotypes
- sports and the news
- If there's a specific tv show, film, song, or musical artist you're particularly interested in, you could search the title along with an issue. For example: "Gossip Girl" and gender.

APPENDIX B: STUDENTS' SELECTIONS FOR COURSE READINGS

Anderson, Craig A. "Violent Video Games: Myths, Facts, and Unanswered Questions." *Psychological Science Agenda*. American Psychological Association, Oct 2003. Web. 8 Feb. 2010.

Dawson, C.J. "Literary Analysis: Social Class Prejudice in Harry Potter." *Helium* (Jan. 2009): n.p. Web. 7 Feb. 2010.

Derenne, Jennifer L., and Eugene V. Beresin. "Body Image, Media, and Eating Disorders." *Academic Psychiatry* 30.3 (2006). 257-261. HighWire Press. Web. 6 Feb. 2010.

Eberstadt, Mary. "Eminem is Right: The Primal Scream of Teenage Music." *Policy Review* 128 (2004). 19-33. *Academic Search Complete*. Web. 8 Feb. 2010.

Hardin, Marie, and Erin Whiteside. "Maybe It's Not A 'Generational Thing': Values and Beliefs of Aspiring Journalists About Race and Gender." *Media Report to Women* 36.2 (Spring 2008): 8-16. Web. 7 Feb. 2010.

Johnson, Steven. "Watching TV Makes You Smarter." *The New York Times Magazine*, 24 Apr 2005. 54-9. *InfoTrac Custom Newspapers*. Web. 9 Feb. 2010.

Lyons, Daniel. "I'm a PC. Keep the Change." *Newsweek,* 13 Apr. 2009. *Academic Search Complete.* Web. 6 Feb. 2010.

Poyntz, Stuart. "Homey, I Shot the Kids: Hollywood and the War on Drugs." *Emergency Librarian* 25.2 (Nov/Dec 1997): 8-13. *ERIC.* Web. 8 Feb. 2010.

Varney, Allen. "Batmanalyzed." *The Escapist Magazine,* 2 Feb. 2010. Web. 5 Feb. 2010.

Walker, Jesse. "The Politics of Superheroes." *Reason* 41.1 (May 2009). 46-50. *Academic Search Complete.* Web. 15 Apr. 2010. (Replacement article for "Batmanalyzed.")

Walsh, Kimberly, et al. "Beauty and the Patriarchal Beast: Gender Role Portrayals in Sitcoms Featuring Mismatched Couples." *Journal of Popular Film and Television* 36.3 (Fall 2008): 123-132. *Humanities Full Text.* Web. 6 Feb. 2010.

APPENDIX C: ASSIGNMENT PROMPT FOR STUDENT PRESENTATION

The aim of this assignment is to advance our collaborative readings of each text and to give you the opportunity to help guide these collaborative discussions. In pairs, you will give a short 5-10-minute presentation on one of the assigned readings and develop a list of 5-7 open-ended discussion questions that will help the class collaboratively analyze, complicate, and apply what we learn from these readings.

The Presentation

The short 5-10-minute presentation should consist of the following:

- biographical information on the author of the publication
- background information on the original source of publication (Find out what you can about the magazine, newspaper, or book the article was originally published in.)
- a short 1-2 paragraph summary of the article, highlighting the author's main points. (You should compose this summary collaboratively and not simply copy an abstract written by the author or a reviewer.)

The Discussion Questions

Generate a list of 5-7 discussion questions to hand out to the class. The following categories and sample questions should help you in generating these questions.

- **Questions that help the class critique the article.** For example, In what ways is Aeon Skoble wrong about intellectualism in American culture? Are there any weaknesses in Miller's argument about the Shield commercial? Or, What is Hayes leaving out of her argument?
- **Questions that "update" the author's argument.** For example, If Hayes were to write "Athletes, Outcasts, and Partyers" today, how might it be different? Or, Does Skoble's argument still apply?
- **Questions that connect the author's argument or main points to other media.** For example, Do modern American films use pseudofeminism in the same way Miller argues the Shield commercial does? Or, Do we see evidence of anti-intellectualism in political advertisements?
- **Questions that help us put the article in conversation with (or in comparison with) any of the other articles we've read as a class.** For example, What might Skoble say about Hayes' argument in "Athletes, Outcasts, and Partyers"? Or, Would Hayes agree with Skoble's argument?
- **Questions that ask the class to connect the author's argument or main points to a current (or past) political, social, or economic issue.** For example, How might our political views regarding intellectualism influence popular culture's representations of intellectualism? Or, Are contemporary advertising techniques reflective of the current economic crisis?
- Other types of questions you think will help spark a discussion that will ultimately help the class understand, complicate, analyze, and apply the ideas presented in the article.

The Handout

You and your partner should collaboratively create a handout for your classmates that you provide the day of your presentation. The handout should include your short 1-2paragraph summary of the article (in your own words), a bulleted list of the biographical and source information you found, and the 5-7 discussion questions you generated. Your handout should be carefully proofread.

Grading Criteria:

- ***Completion of assignment.*** Do the presenters provide some background information on the author(s) of the article and on the publication in which it was published? Do they provide a brief 1-2 paragraph summary of the article (in their own words)? Have they generated 5-7 discussion questions? Have they composed a handout containing this information?
- ***Thoughtfulness of the discussion questions.*** Do the discussion questions help the class understand, complicate, analyze, and/or apply the ideas presented in the article?
- ***Preparedness of the presenters.*** Do the presenters appear prepared and organized?
- ***Quality of the handout.*** Is the handout readable? Does it contain the required information? Is the summary written by the presenters? Is the handout carefully proofread? Do the presenters have enough copies of the handout for each member of the class and the instructor?

KAIROS

Kairos is on the web at http://kairos.technorhetoric.net

Kairos: A Journal of Rhetoric, Technology, and Pedagogy is the longest-running digital media journal in writing studies. The journal was first published in 1996 and maintains its editorial and publishing independence through virtual collaboration by staff members across 24 universities in the US With no budget, the journal runs exclusively on in-kind donations and volunteer editorial and technical labor.

The mission of *Kairos* has always been to publish scholarship that examines digital and multimodal composing practices, promoting work that enacts its scholarly argument through rhetorical and innovative uses of new media. We publish "webtexts," which are texts authored specifically for publication on the World Wide Web. Webtexts are scholarly examinations of topics related to technology in English Studies fields (e.g., rhetoric, composition, technical and professional communication, education, creative writing, language and literature) and related fields such as media studies, informatics, arts technology, and others.

Views from a Distance: A Nephological Model of the CCCC Chairs' Addresses, 1977-2011

"Views from a Distance" is a series of word clouds rendered from 35 chairs' addresses delivered at CCCC conventions from 1977 to 2011. The digital installation invites explorations of word-level patterns and anomalies within this widely recognized collection of speeches. The installation itself is underpinned with the assumption that distinctive forms of knowledge are mobilized through visualization techniques.

This text is valuable for several reasons: it's a provocative study of the field; it is in some ways a mixture of DH and comp/rhet work; and it is put together in a visually attractive way. Mueller has particularly utilized the affordances of the Web to make his argument visual, not just textual; through textual analysis (using word clouds) of CCCC Chairs' addresses, Mueller's piece allows us to look back to historical turns in the field and to see how the CCCC Chair's Address, presumably a speech that reflects current issues and concerns in rhetoric and composition, has tapped into the issues that motivate us as scholars/teachers. This article originally appeared as a webtext in Kairos 16(2), at the following URL: http://kairos.technorhetoric.net/16.2/topoi/mueller/index.html

8 Views from a Distance: A Nephological Model of the CCCC Chairs' Addresses, 1977–2011

Derek N. Mueller

Clouds were riddles, too, but dangerously simple ones. If you zoomed in on one part of a cloud and took a photograph, then enlarged the image, you would find that a cloud's edges seemed like another cloud, and those edges yet another, and so on. Every part of a cloud, in other words, reiterates the whole. Therefore each cloud might be called infinite, because its very surface is composed of other clouds, and those clouds of still other clouds, and so forth.

—Stephane Audeguy, *The Theory of Clouds* (2005)

Figure 1: *Clouds at noon*, Ernst Schutz (2002)

OPENING: MRS. PETERSON AND NETWORK SENSE

More than three decades ago, Richard Lloyd-Jones (1978) recognized the pressures that accompany an accumulating record of scholarship when he noted in the first Conference on College Composition and Communication (CCCC) address that "[k]eeping up with new work is getting harder all of the time" (p. 28). He expressed concern for challenges that come with growth and expansion in any disciplinary domain; "keeping up with new work" is a contemporary exigency facing many established disciplines (also emerging interdisciplines, fields, or subfields). In partial response to these challenges, Lloyd-Jones' address, "A View from the Center," also sought an adequate metaphor for making sense of who we are—as time-spanning audiences and as those identifying by proxy with a more or less shared domain of knowledge and practice. Lloyd-Jones deliberated on several metaphors in his address—mechanical, political, and anatomical—before settling on a network metaphor, although he never referred to it directly as network-based. The metaphor's exemplar was Mrs. Peterson, a small town telephone operator otherwise known as "central," who acted as a hub for connecting, filtering, and relaying all as a function of her work. Remaining connected and tied-in with current, accumulating conversations was the value Lloyd-Jones identified with Mrs. Peterson in response to "keeping up with new work."

The interconnected image of Mrs. Peterson may serve us well today as we continue to face challenges anticipated and described by Lloyd-Jones. There is conceptual alignment in his trope, the ideal of being centrally connected, in network-theoretic worldviews, and in abstract visual models that can provide different perspectives on changing disciplinary formations. The word clouds offered here are designed using distant reading methods to reduce and intensify patterns in one slice of a growing collection of materials: the CCCC Chairs' addresses delivered over the last 35 years. With this treatment, the addresses become visibly interconnected, an assemblage whose vocabularies fold unevenly forward through each subsequent address. Their rolling, semantic contiguities productively foreground an evolving disciplinary lexis associated with rhetoric and composition.[1] As the scholarly record grows there is an escalating value in realizing connections. This is exceedingly important for newcomers to the field who must make inroads however they can, by conversation and conventional reading and writing, of course, but also by pattern-finding, by nomadically exploring conceptual interplay across abstracts and abstractive variations, and by finding and tracing linkages among materials and ideas, new and old.

architecture **basic** buildings center
central choices chosen cultural deal
determined **disciplines** figure foundation hear
house ideas knowledge
language line
metaphor mosaic own
people petersen **political** programs
remember **skeleton** special students study talk
teachers teaching time try **view** whatever wisdom
writing

Figure 2: Richard Lloyd-Jones's 1977 CCCC address: A View from the Center, presented in Kansas City, MO.

In effect, I contend there is a value in *network sense*: an aptitude enriched by this tracing of linkages across an assortment of people, places, things, and moments. Network sense finds perspective and knowledge in actively inquiring into associative patterns among disparate resources. How we pursue network sense will vary, but abstractive instruments (e.g., models) can systematically turn our attention toward disciplinary pattern-finding and alert us to nuances and overlaps among the many subfields in rhetoric and composition. Such models can also help us grasp with improved precision how terms, figures, and schools of thought emerge and age. Similarly, network sense may illuminate or intensify pathways woven across other fields, rendering different theoretical and methodological allegiances more vividly, as well. Grasping both network topologies—one spanning shared disciplinary resources and another spanning extradisciplinary influences—will prove invaluable for junior and senior scholars alike. In fact, I would argue that network sense provides a generating principle both for graduate education and for "keeping up with new work." The tracing of lines among words, figures, affinities, and scenes—in other words, the pursuit of network sense—may be enhanced with our gazes occasionally turned toward clouds.[2]

VIEWS FROM A DISTANCE

Views from a Distance is a series of word clouds rendered from 35 chairs' addresses delivered at CCCC conventions from 1977 to 2011. The digital installation invites explorations of word-level patterns and anomalies within this widely recognized collection of speeches. The installation itself is underpinned with the assumption that distinctive forms of knowledge are mobilized through visualization techniques. Applied in this way, such visualizations enact "distant reading," a methodology advanced by literary scholar Franco Moretti (2000) to apprehend patterns in larger-scale collections of texts than readers customarily engage with at once:

> Distant reading: where distance, let me repeat it, *is a condition of knowledge*: it allows you to focus on units that are much smaller or much larger than the text: devices, themes, tropes—or genres and systems. And if, between the very small and the very large, the text itself disappears, well, it is one of those cases when one can justifiably say, Less is more. (p. 57)

Distant reading methods rely upon computational processes and data visualization to alter dramatically the scales at which readers encounter texts (Mueller, 2009). These methods assume different insights are available at non-standard (e.g., aerial) magnitudes of engagement. The series of clouds functions as a *nephological model*, a horizon-mindful (i.e., both future and past oriented) recognition of shapes, patterns, forms, and resemblances. Moretti's models include the three types indicated in the title of his well-known book, *Graphs, Maps, and Trees* (2005). I consider word clouds a promising addition to this family of model-types because they function similarly by associating the texts and showing how they drift _across_ one another, as if they are parts of a continuing collective address-ecology. About maps, Moretti wrote, "With a little luck, [they] will be more than the sum of their parts: they will possess 'emerging' qualities, which were not visible at the lower level" (p. 53). Word clouds are similar; they alight as an example of the chronotope Moretti questioned at the outset of his chapter on maps (p. 35), providing a string of word formations sized and weighted with meaningful visual cues, somewhat like a lexical heat map. Indeed, like maps, clouds are more than neutral descriptions; they are constructs with properties that deliberately bring forward selected qualities of texts while downplaying others.

attempts believe change college column
community
composition conferences designed
develop discipline doing effective english human
improving learn live measure minority
opportunity ourselves own
participation people person profession
professional program public
research responsibility student teachers
teaching test time training world
writing

Figure 3: Vivian I. Davis's 1978 CCCC address: Where Do We Grow from Here?, presented in Denver, CO.

Independent of one another, clouds may elicit wonder- or memory-encounters useful for reconsidering disciplinary narratives at scales that exceed, and therefore augment, personal and anecdotal accounts. Together, by this treatment, we can see the deepening hues in particular terms. The darker hues indicate elements of a shared vocabulary materializing over time. Lighter hues, conversely, report the opposite, a condition of recency relative to the collection of addresses. Like the literary texts Moretti analyzed, the larger collection of materials becomes interlaced. Subject to distant reading methods the addresses disappear and are replaced by substitutive, or *tropical* abstractions: *a series* of word clouds, in this case. Paradoxically, the addresses resurface in a severely abridged light as they are simultaneously remade, staged again, and resent into circulation (agitated, delivered). That the full text of a given address gets pushed aside proves temporarily necessary, precarious though this will surely appear when held up against prevailing sensibilities about alphabetic literacy and functional-normative assumptions about reading (see Schulz, 2011; Waters, 2007).

Moretti used distant reading to comment upon broader cultural patterns illuminated by the transformation of the large collection into its variously purposed reductions. Likewise, the nephological model— as distant reading—provides an account of the intellectual culture of CCCC. For example, predominant *topoi* cycle through the series, each surfacing in turn: pedagogy; students; technology and writing; culture and writing; publics, institutions, and curricula. Also, a preponderance of darker terms suggests discursive inertia operating on the genre of the address: Over time it becomes more challenging to diverge radically from the remarks made by previous chairs. The clouds present unmistakable echoes recurring across the series. And yet the echoes can be understood as discourse customs that gradually and implicitly withdraw from the unexpected, jarring, or unconventional gesture. The visibility of such patterns yields related openings for inquiry and speculation: Can we imagine a primarily light-hued cloud in years to come? Or an address to the field absent such constants as students, writing, composition, college, university, or literacy? I raise these questions cautiously aware that they may appear critical of convention; however, I am foremost interested in pointing out that heuristic openings created by the clouds are as important as the report they offer on the culture of CCCC. That is, I maintain that the model's conceptual counterpart, network sense, functions both as a perspective on the culture of the organization and a catalyst for action concerning the shape of the field to come.

THEMES, PATTERNS, TRENDS

Established studies of the CCCC chairs' addresses offer examples of how scholars have surveyed themes, patterns, and trends in this same collection. Ellen Barton (1999) located two broad classes of "evocative gestures" spanning eighteen addresses[4], from Richard Lloyd-Jones' in 1977 to Nell Ann Pickett's in 1997. First, Barton identified gestures articulating the teaching and service of composition, and, second, she found gestures articulating composition as a research field. After differentiating between these classes and grounding each type of gesture in examples selected from addresses, Barton explained that "[t]he major areas of consensus and conflict reflected in the body of CCCC

Chairs' addresses ultimately revolve around professionalism—the relationship between research, teaching, and service in an academic field" (p. 249). The addresses cumulatively reflect a synthetic, integrated view of professionalism: "work here involves research, but emphatically includes teaching and service as well" (p. 249). In his MA thesis, Rory Lee (2009) updated and extended Barton's analysis by examining eleven addresses (1998–2008) in-depth. Lee identified three patterns beyond the two in Barton's study: "(1) literacy, (2) our stake in writing, and (3) diversity" (p. 71). Although the themes are pronounced in the addresses he studied, Lee noted that they "do not receive the same amount of attention over the last eleven years" (p. 86). Nevertheless, Lee predicted that we can expect similar gestures to resurface in the future (p. 97). Lee's analysis also considered the smaller gestures in the eleven addresses he studied, which appeared as "building blocks to a larger gesture" (p. 72)—an insight that also proves useful for thinking about the implications of word clouds for pattern-tracing.

academe admissions attend class

college context course dreams

example faculty family fear friends grammar help

information interviewing jobs language learning

legacies move oral people percent read sal school

semester separate social start

students teach teachers

themselves universities usually writing

written

Figure 4: Lynn Quitman Troyka's 1981 CCCC address: Perspectives on Legacies and Literacy in the 1980s, presented in Dallas, TX.

In the introductionn to *A View from the Center*, Duane Roen (2006) adopted a similar approach by clustering themes and topics traceable across the series of addresses. Roen located and grouped by subheadings concerns for "effective teaching," "scholarly teaching," "the scholarship of teaching and learning," "giving voice to marginalized voices,"

views of CCCC as an organization, and "vexing issues." Roen's collection reached well beyond the addresses to historicize the role of the
conference chairs since the start of the CCCC organization in 1949.
Like Lee's turn to prediction, *A View from the Center* not only re-
printed the 29 addresses delivered from 1977 to 2005, it also included
with each reprint an updated reflective comment from the contributor,
which lent another layer to the evocative quality Barton emphasized
among the annual epideictic oratory at the start of each year's convention. Barton, Lee, and Roen each exceeded historical searches for patterns and oriented their findings toward the present and future.

age associate attend **book** calls class
college
community courses degree
dream education english enrolled expect graduate hinds
jean learned life major mary meeting **mississippi**
nursing offer peck program **publishing** rubin
school semester **students** sullivan teach
teachers **technical** textbook university
writing

Figure 5: Nell Ann Pickett's 1997 CCCC address: The Two-Year College as
Democracy in Action, presented in Phoenix, AZ.

Do the word clouds presented in this installation corroborate the
trends Barton, Lee, and Roen identified? To a considerable degree, yes.
At a rapid glance, terms like "teaching," "composition," "students" and
"writing" confirm frequent references to pedagogical considerations
among the addresses, while other terms, such as "CCCC," "education," "faculty," "statement," and "convention," suggest thematic variations tied to the profession. Smaller clusters of concerns, such as the
technological literacy theme Lee discussed across addresses by Selfe
(1999), Yancey (2004), and Wootten (2006) (p. 43), also appear in
the word clouds, although this pattern suggests a limitation of the
model, too. That is, the clouds alone cannot eclipse the analytical and
explanatory subtlety evident in these three studies of the addresses, but

they can powerfully corroborate these observations and complement similar theme-tracing in the future.

access american attention citizens communication composition computers continue critical cultural development economic education effects effort expand help individuals information involved issues literacy million national own pay political professional project provide responsibility schools serve social students system teachers teaching technology understanding

Figure 6: Cynthia L. Selfe's 1998 CCCC address: Technology and Literacy: A Story about the Perils of Not Paying Attention, presented in Chicago, IL.

arrangement change circulation class college communication composing composition context course create curriculum development education english genres includes invention literacy makes means medium moment move own page print process public reading school screen spaces students technology text time words writers writing

Figure 7: Kathleen Blake Yancey's 2004 CCCC address: Made Not Only in Words: Composition in a New Key, presented in San Antonio, TX.

advertising **animals** blind computer
consciousness course create **discourse**
empowered experience fence **focus** guaman
horse humans image language
learn literacy mean multimodal name
poma **read** remind renaming
students study talk teach
technology tell texts **trees universe**
users **visual** words world **writing**

Figure 8: Judith (Jay) A. Wootten's 2006 CCCC address: Riding a One-Eyed Horse: Reigning In and Fencing Out, presented in Chicago, IL.

Even though the clouds themselves do not duplicate the subtlety we find in other theme-tracing studies, they do work differently to elicit insights and evoke questions across multiple scales. Notice, for instance, how large, light-hued terms enter into the series, particularly in the mid- to late 1990s. See, for example, Ann Ruggles Gere and "extracurriculum" in 1993, Jacqueline Jones Royster and "voice" in 1995, Lester Faigley and "internet" in 1996, Cynthia Selfe and "computers" in 1998, and Victor Villanueva and "ethnicity" in 1999. Light hues indicate the moments when a potentially consequential idea was delivered broadly to the field. Although these entry points may be smaller than turns or paradigm shifts, they stand as "subsidiary gestures" (Lee, 2009, p. 72) that nevertheless mark important shifts in an evolving disciplinary vocabulary. Such gestural build-ups, micro-turns, and anomalies to the larger patterns are spotlighted in word clouds, and these secondary patterns warrant different degrees of noticing whether for long-timers, for those who attended one of these addresses, for newcomers unfamiliar with the scholarly oeuvre of any of these figures, or for future chairs of the conference.

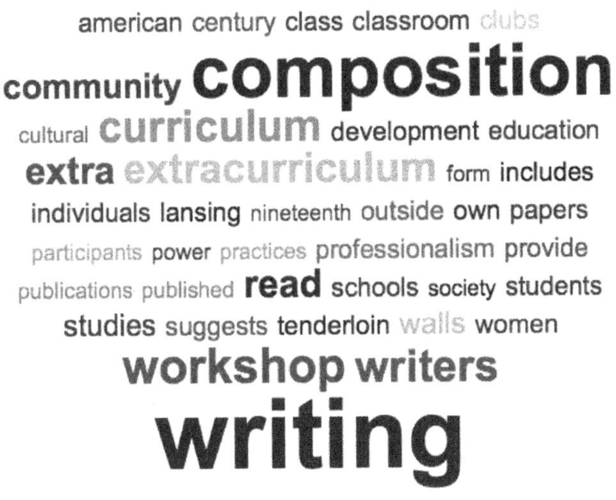

american century class classroom clubs

community **composition**

cultural **curriculum** development education

extra extracurriculum form includes

individuals lansing nineteenth outside own papers

participants power practices professionalism provide

publications published **read** schools society students

studies suggests tenderloin walls women

workshop writers

writing

Figure 9: Thursday, April 1, 1993. San Diego, Calif. Kitchen Tables and Rented Rooms: The Extracurriculum of Composition. Anne Ruggles Gere

abilities action **boundaries call**

communities compelled critical **cultural**

engage experiences heard history human

interpretations listen meaning moments negotiate

own people person **position** potential

practices question response **saying scene**

sense **speak** stories students **subject**

systems **talk** type **understanding**

value view **voice**

Figure 10: Thursday, March 23, 1995. Washington, D.C. When the First Voice You Hear Is Not Your Own. Jacqueline Jones Royster

access address change **college**
communications composition
computers connecting economic
education history
internet issues jobs life
literacy little lives major million nearly **people**
personal power public reading researchers revolution
rhetoric social **students teachers**
teaching technologies **time** united
university web world **writing**

Figure 11: Thursday, March 28, 1996. Milwaukee, Wisc. Literacy After the Revolution. Lester Faigley

african **america american**
beginning black break called class **colonial**
color concept cultural discourse
ethnicity europe france **gods** human
indians journals latinas **latinos** little matter
multiculturalism **people** peru puerto race
racism rican school silencing speaking
students teacher time university white **write**

Figure 12: Thursday, March 25, 1999. Atlanta, Ga. On the Rhetoric and Precedents of Racism. Victor Villanueva

Several more curious subtexts surface across these 35 word clouds: references to animals (e.g., Wootten's "horse" in 2006, Anoyke's "termite" and "chicken" in 2007), varying scenic orientations (e.g., classroom, convention hall, institution), and interdisciplinary inflections (e.g., D'Angelo's "arts" and "science" in 1980 and Odell's "psychology" in 1986). Thus, the clouds report more than predominant patterns (like those substantiated by Barton, 1999; Lee, 2009; and Roen, 2006); they also hint at fleeting concerns, prominent metaphors and allegories, and rotations in attention (e.g., that concerns for people, scenes, and tools take turns in the collection). In a series of clouds, there are plural exigencies for plural audiences: Looking upon them we may notice different shapes that will provoke other itinerate or exploratory searches toward an enriched network sense of the field.

activism **CCCC** chair chicken college
community COMPANY
composition **conference** corn diversity
education **farmer** fire graduate institution interviewees
invited issues learn listen membership
organization party **people** planting
profession question respondent
response rhetoric social **students**
talk teachers teaching termite time **voices**
writing

Figure 13: Thursday, March 27, 2007. New York, N.Y. Voices of the Company We Keep. Akua Duky Anoyke

Finally, amidst the subtler trends in the addresses themselves an honorific pattern has emerged in which chairs refer to the addresses of their predecessors—both by direct reference and by echoing past concerns. Such gestures have become increasingly common in recent years, which shows both through direct citation and through the deepening hues across the series of clouds. Since 2001, 8 addresses out of 11 (73%) have referred directly to an earlier address, but in the first 24 addresses, from 1977 to 2000, chairs referred to predecessors just 6 times (25%). Reminders like these beckon the opening general assembly audience to realize history as continuous, to remember as thickly interconnected and entangled with a tradition both the current address and addresses from previous years. These surveying gestures, however, will only prove more difficult to convey within the limited time available for an address. It is impossible to predict whether there will be an increased tendency to directly cite past addresses, but as the thirty-sixth address approaches, the expanding record will require that this practice become more selective. As this history extends and shared memory strains, to reiterate Lloyd-Jones' concern for "keeping up," surveying gestures cannot easily or comprehensively account for addresses delivered by predecessors, though ancillary, distant reading installations may contribute something in the way of a solution to this problem.

Figure 14: Thursday, March 13, 1980. Washington, D.C. Regaining Our Composure. Frank D'Angelo

Abstracts and Abstracting Practices

Readers of *College Composition and Communication* likely noticed that with the editorial transition from Joseph Harris to Marilyn Cooper, the journal underwent changes in size, cover design, and page layout. Cooper's first issue in February 2000 (51.3) also included article abstracts for the first time. Keith Gilyard's 2000 keynote, "Literacy, Identity, Imagination, Flight," was the first address published in *CCC* with an abstract:

> This article examines issues of literacy and identity relative to the development of a critical pedagogy and a critical democracy. An earlier version was delivered as the Chair's Address at the Fifty-first Annual CCCC Convention on April 13, 2000.

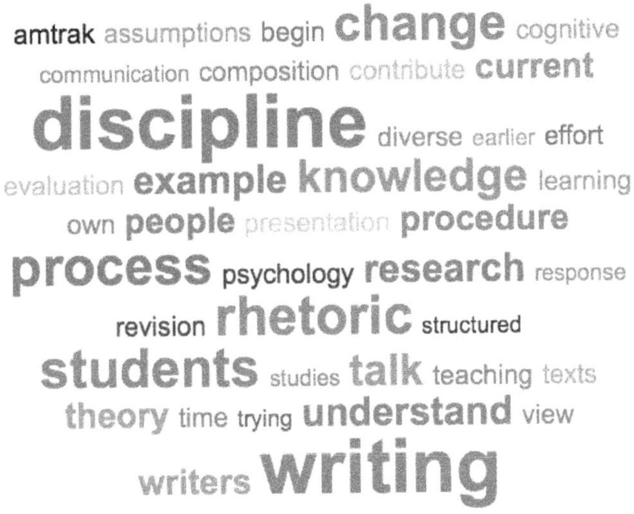

amtrak assumptions begin **change** cognitive communication composition contribute **current** **discipline** diverse earlier effort evaluation **example knowledge** learning own **people** presentation **procedure** **process** psychology **research** response revision **rhetoric** structured **students** studies **talk** teaching texts **theory** time trying **understand** view writers **writing**

Figure 15: Thursday, March 13, 1986. New Orleans, La. Diversity and Change: Toward a Maturing Discipline. Lee Odell

The cloud for Gilyard's talk accords with the published abstract considering its presentation of "students," "discourse," "value," "identity," "cultural," and "dance," among others. Three more addresses—by Wendy Bishop (2001), John Lovas (2002), and Shirley Wilson Logan (2003)—also appeared with article abstracts when each was published in the journal. Yet with the publication of Kathleen Blake Yancey's

2004 address (notably in the final issue of Cooper's editorship), abstracts no longer prefaced the published version of the annual address. Selected subsequent addresses (Wootten, 2006; Anokye, 2007; Bazerman, 2009; Valentino, 2010; and Pough, 2011) were published with an editor's note indicating the date and location of the address, but not with anything like a summative abstract. During this time, other articles published in *CCC* continued to include conventional abstracts without interruption or marked variation.

black **brown** cannon color **course** **critical** **cultural dance discourse** dunbar **flight** gilyard help ideas **identity** imagination injun **king** language line **mean money** movie orville people **play** politics question relation respect served **social students** **tao** theory **time** understandings **value** wright **writing**

Figure 16: Keith Gilyard's 2000 CCCC Address: Literacy, Identity, Imagination, Flight presented in Minneapolis, MN.

attend **community** **composition** conference continue **convention** conversion day discussion english enos **feel field** generational harris home hopkins late learned **life** listen look moment odds offered own **poem** programs read rhetoric similar **space** student studies talk **teachers** **teaching** theory **time** writing

Figure 17: Thursday, March 15, 2001. Denver, Co. Against the Odds in Composition and Rhetoric. Wendy Bishop

address american argument black books ccc

college common

community composition conference courses

day develops education **faculty** graduate ideas

institutions issue king life literacy little local mother

national pay personal professional **program**

read rev school story **students** teaching

time **university**

writing

Figure 18: Thursday, March 21, 2002. Chicago, Ill. All Good Writing Develops at the Edge of Risk. John C. Lovas

american assessment **CCCC** city college

communication **composition**

conditions development dialect **difference** diversity

education effective **english** environments faculty

graduate **language** learning matter own

past position professional **public** quality research

rhetoric rights scholars schools standards

statement

students support taught

teachers **teaching**

writing

Figure 19: Thursday, March 20, 2003. New York, N.Y. Changing Missions, Shifting Positions, and Breaking Silences. Shirley Wilson Logan

This uneven publishing practice, whatever its causes, raises questions about whether abstracts serve a vital function for published CCCC chairs' addresses. Generally, article abstracts provide a synopsis adequate for readers to remember or, when they are encountering an article for the first time, to decide whether to proceed with reading. By fitting the full article onto the head of a pin, that is by reducing it to a summative paragraph, article abstracts operate according to distant reading logics: The text itself vanishes and an effective, suggestive surrogate stands in its place. I maintain that the word clouds in this digital installation function similarly, and, as a result, that they contribute a serialized abstracting function that is not otherwise available currently. Although they are not written with the goals of coherence and summary in quite the same way as paragraph-like article abstracts are, the loosely thematic assemblage of terms drifts and billows, as a system of paratactic, rather than syntactic, address abstracts. Word clouds like these provide synoptic doubles or counterparts to conventional summary abstracts, and this is particularly useful when no other abstracts are available.[5] "Views from a Distance" is designed as a series of alternative abstracts meant to prompt memories and heuristic association and re-association within and beyond the collection.

TAGLINE INFRASTRUCTURE

As a type of distant reading, word clouds turn to data-mining processes to draw the most frequently used terms from full-text versions of the addresses. A radical reduction occurs in this meronymous amalgamation. Selected parts stand out from the thick, ecologically entangled whole. Yet this reduction is only temporary: The clouds elicit wonder or memory encounters without urging permanent annihilation of the full text. These, like all word clouds, yield a heuristic if in looking at them we find provocations to tease and shape further inquiry.

The PHP-based algorithm sifts text from the published addresses through a predetermined list of stop words, or commonplace words (see Appx: Stop Words). Next, the script stems words with common roots, assembles a list, and bunches the lists into approximate cloud-forms. A greater font size indicates a high-occurring word; smaller font sizes reflect comparably low-occurring terms, although relative to the comprehensive list, small-type words are far more common than others. Consider the cloud associated with Marilyn Valentino's 2010 address. Font sizes effectively map comparative word frequencies to reflect that *students, college, writing,* and *communication* were the most often-used words in her address.

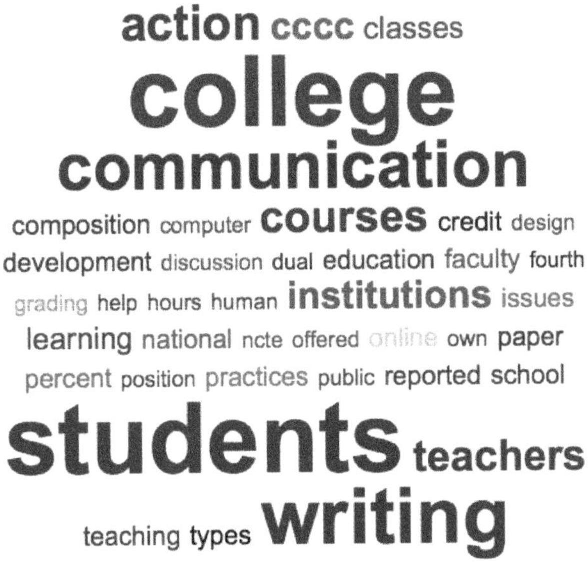

action cccc classes

college

communication

composition computer **courses** credit design development discussion dual education faculty fourth grading help hours human **institutions** issues learning national ncte offered online own paper percent position practices public reported school

students teachers

teaching types **writing**

Figure 20: March 18, 2010. Louisville, Ky. Rethinking the Fourth C: Call to Action. Marilyn J. Valentino.

Developed by programmer Chirag Mehta, the tagline infrastructure also assigns hues according to the persistence of a word in the dataset up to that point. Words with deeper hues reflect a longer persistence preceding addresses than do lighter hues. Lighter words have not been used as often in earlier addresses. This distinction grows more pronounced over time. For example, almost every term in Richard Lloyd-Jones's 1977 address appears in a similar hue; whereas, a later address, such as Kathleen Blake Yancey's 2004 keynote, reflects a comparably smaller number of newly used terms. Looking at the 2004 word cloud, terms that had not been used often in other addresses stand out in a light hue: *arrangement, circulation, genres, screen.*

   Prominent technology-related terms surface in the word clouds associated with addresses by Faigley (1997), in which "internet" appears as the leading term in large type and light hue, by Selfe (1999), in which "technology," "literacy," and "computers" are cast in large type, and by Wootten (2006), in which "multimodal" shows up in a mid-sized type and light hue. "Technology" grows darker in the decade spanning these three addresses, which suggests recurrence, but the perspectives expressed in each address are distinctive (e.g., Selfe's offered a call for attention to emerging technologies whereas Wootten expressed skepticism).

"Views from a Distance" was built with the set of PHP scripts developed by Mehta and a Javascript-based scrolling device written by Erik Arvidsson. Mehta showcased the integrated infrastructure in his 2006 installation, "US Presidential Speeches Tag Cloud." His tagline infrastructure has been adapted in a variety of projects, including Thoughtmesh (Ippolito & Dietrich, 2007), an American Studies "Visual Historiography" (Lester, 2007), and a company history of Microsoft (Bishop, 2006).[6]

academic accept access american **approach basics**
changes classrooms **college** composition develop
differences **education**
effective equal experiences functions individual
institutions instruction knowledge language
learning mean **motivations** opportunity process
programs questions required **rhetoric** skills
standards **students**
teachers **teaching** traditional universities using
writing

Figure 21: Thursday, March 18, 1982. Washington, D.C. Beyond Access to Education-Literacy and Learning in Perspective. James Lee Hill

SUMMARY, LIST, EXCESS

I have suggested similarities between the word clouds in this installation and the conventional, summary-motivated abstracts accompanying scholarly articles in *CCC*, but these two variations of distant
reading must not be understood as strict equivalents. Their abstractive
orientations are different in subtle but significant ways. Conventional
abstracts, as I have said, adhere to distant reading logics because they
reduce and select, standing in as substitutes for an article that is not
otherwise in full view. However, the descriptive acuity typically pursued in an article abstract is not nearly as binding or as disciplined
for the word cloud. I call the word cloud series a nephological model
in part to articulate an emanative quality. That is, because the clouds
operate as paratactic lists, they remain open to excess, much in the way
Umberto Eco (2009) explained in his illustrated essay, *The Infinity of
Lists*. Eco historicized a tension between lists and summaries:

> On the one hand, it seems that in the Baroque period people
> strove to find definitions by essence that were less rigid than
> those of medieval logic, but on the other hand the taste for
> the marvelous led to the transformation of every taxonomy
> into lists, every tree into a labyrinth. In reality, however, lists
> were already being used during the Renaissance to strike the
> first blows at the world order sanctioned by the great medieval
> *summae*. (p. 245)

Summary abstracts order the world in ways lists do not. Thus, if we
understand word clouds to be paratactic lists, stringing them together
in the way this installation does produces a nephological model that
advances their potential expansiveness across multiple scales. Such
models assume an unusual, resourceful ontology that is at once powerfully grounded in the published article while remaining open to poetic
recombination in contextual excess of the article (this bears resem-
blance to I.A. Richards' [1955] notion of the wandering resourcefulness of words). Each cloud billows with vaporous paralogic; its terms
inviting associations within the cloud (or within a set of clouds, as
in this case), but also beyond the cloud. Herein lies one of the most
promising properties of word clouds. They are summary-like without surrendering to a reductive logic of coherence and completeness.
Notably, this resourceful ontology typically goes unacknowledged in

much of the casual production of word and tag clouds on the Web, perhaps because it has not been sufficiently theorized or articulated in the environments supporting their creation. Yet this is why, in addition to conventional abstracts, word clouds are due for more widespread and more rigorous development and circulation. We should create more of them in the service of network sense (e.g., applicable to award-winning articles, such as the Braddock Award in *College Composition and Communication* or the James L. Kinneavy Award in *JAC*, or to entire journal archives) and, moreover, adapt them for pedagogy focally concerned with summary and source use, as well as rhetorical invention.

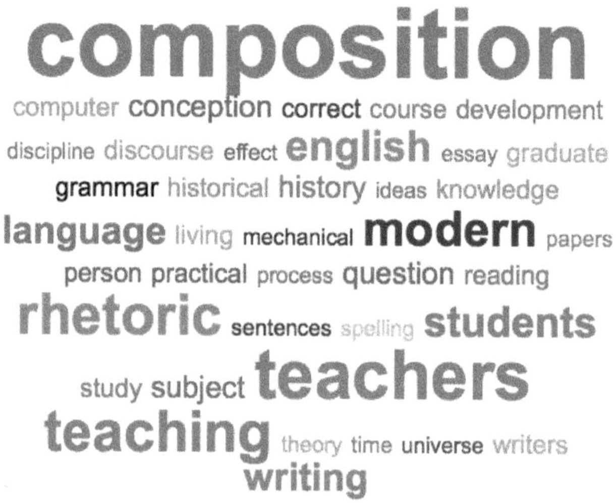

composition

computer **conception** correct course development discipline discourse effect **english** essay graduate **grammar** historical **history** ideas knowledge **language** living mechanical **modern** papers person practical process **question** reading **rhetoric** sentences spelling **students** study subject **teachers** **teaching** theory time **universe** writers **writing**

Figure 22: Thursday, March 17, 1983 Detroit, Mich. Some History Lessons for Composition Teachers. Donald C. Stewart

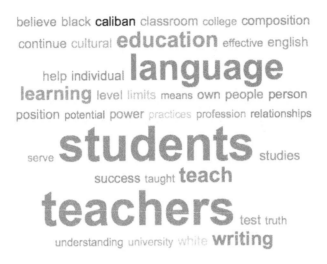

Figure 23: Thursday, March 29, 1984 New York, N.Y. Using Language to Unlock the Limits. Rosentene B. Purnell

ACKNOWLEDGMENTS

Comments from Laurie Gries and John Dunn, Jr. were invaluable to this project's early development. Adam Nannini generously assisted with troubleshooting a few key CSS snippets. I am grateful, too, for thoughtful, substantive comments from two anonymous reviewers and from *Kairos* editors who sharpened this project in many ways.

NOTES

1. Or, because naming has become so fraught, CIP 23.13, as I am increasingly accustomed to calling rhetoric and composition, is a "Classification of Instructional Programs" code assigned by the National Research Council to categorize scholarship under the heading of "Rhetoric and Composition/Writing Studies." For more, see Phelps and Ackerman (2010).

2. References to lines and tracing are influenced by Tim Ingold's *Lines* (2007), in which he distinguishes between traces and dot-to-dot connectors. As a pragmatic function of network sense, tracing in this context concerns "the trails along which [disciplinary] life is lived" (p. 81) as contrasted with

a more segmented, teleological conception of tracing. The point is that word clouds may powerfully augment the tracing practices that are tacitly understood and enacted by developing scholars. Word clouds may aid us, that is, in re-assessing how we practice and teach semantic-conceptual tracing.

3. The sunburst was created by San Francisco-based designer Arnold N. Fujita (Macrorie, 1962).

4. Addresses delivered by James Hill (1982), Donald Stewart (1983), and Rosentene Purnell (1984) were not included in Barton's study because they had not been published previously in *College Composition and Communication.*

5. Although it is not the primary focus of this project, word clouds rendered from texts (whether collections of writing or selections from readings) provide excellent support for writing summaries, abstracts, or reflections. The cloud's paratactic formation can provide just enough information about themes in readings or in one's own writing (as would be useful when reflecting on a portfolio) without offering fully formed sentences. Word clouds, in certain cases, can be put to good use as inventional heuristics for summary and reflection. To explore, visit <a href="http://tagcrowd.com/" target="_blank">tagcrowd.com</a>.

6. Lester and Bishop's projects were hosted as recently as 2008, but at the time of this publication, they do not appear to be available online.

WORKS CITED

Anoyke, Akua Duky. (2007). Voices of the company we keep. *College Composition and Communication*, 59 (2), 263-275.

Arvidsson, Erik. (2006). Slider (WebFX). Retrieved from http://webfx.eae. net/dhtml/slider/slider.html.

Audeguy, Stéphane. (2005). *The theory of clouds.* (Timothy Bent, Trans.). New York: Harcourt.

Bartholomae, David. (1989). Freshman English, composition, and CCCC. *College Composition and Communication*, 40 (1), 38-50.

Barton, Ellen. (1999). Evocative gestures in CCCC chairs' addresses. In Mary Rosner, Beth Boehm, & Debra Journet (Eds.), *History, reflection, and narrative: The professionalization of composition, 1963-1983* (pp. 235-252). Stamford, CT: Ablex.

Bazerman, Charles. (2009). The wonder of writing. *College Composition and Communication*, 61 (3), 571-580.

Bishop, Todd. (2006, December 29). Microsoft's evolution, in keywords. *Seattle Post-Intelligencer.* Retrieved from http://web.archive.org/web/20090301032602/http://blog.seattlepi.nwsource.com/microsoft/tags/

Bishop, Wendy. (2001). Against the odds in composition and rhetoric [Abstract]. *College Composition and Communication*, 53 (2), 322-335.

Bridwell-Bowles, Lillian. (1995). Freedom, form, function: Varieties of academic discourse. *College Composition and Communication,* 46 (1), 46-61.

Chaplin, Miriam T. (1988). Issues, perspectives and possibilities. *College Composition and Communication*, 39 (1), 52-62.

Cook, William W. (1993). Writing in the spaces left. *College Composition and Communication*, 44 (1), 9-25.

D'Angelo, Frank. (1980). Regaining our composure. *College Composition and Communication*, 31 (4), 420-426.

Davis, Vivian I. (1979). Our excellence: Where do we grow from here? *College Composition and Communication*, 30 (1), 26-31.

Eco, Umberto. (2009). *The infinity of lists.* (Alastair McEwen, Trans.). New York: Rizzoli.

Faigley, Lester. (1997). Literacy after the revolution. *College Composition and Communication*, 48 (1), 30-43.

Gere, Anne Ruggles. (1994). Kitchen tables and rented rooms: The extracurriculum of composition. *College Composition and Communication*, 45 (1), 75-92.

Gilyard, Keith. (2000). Literacy, identity, imagination, flight [Abstract]. *College Composition and Communication*, 52 (2), 260-272.

Glenn, Cheryl. (2008). Representing ourselves. *College Composition and Communication*, 60 (2), 420-439.

Hairston, Maxine. (1985). Breaking our bonds and reaffirming our connections. *College Composition and Communication*, 36 (3), 272-282.

Hesse, Douglas. (2005). Who owns writing? *College Composition and Communication*, 57 (2), 335-357.

Hill, James Lee. (2006). Beyond access to education—Literacy and learning in perspective. In Duane Roen (Ed.), *Views from the center* (pp. 92-103). New York: Bedford-St. Martin's.

Ingold, Tim. (2007). *Lines: A brief history.* New York: Routledge.

Ippolito, Jon & Dietrich, Craig. (2007). Thoughtmesh. *Vectors, 3* (1). Retrieved from http://vectors.usc.edu/projects/index.php?project=84.

Irmscher, William F. (1979). Writing as a way of learning and developing. *College Composition and Communication*, 30 (3), 240-244.

Lee, Rory A. (2009). *Addressing the situation: An analysis of the CCCC chairs' addresses of the last 11 years (1998-2008)* (Master's thesis). Retrieved from http://etd.lib.fsu.edu/theses/available/etd-07132009-125559/.

Lester, Dave. (2007, July 3). American studies tagline: A visual historiography of an evolving discipline. Retrieved from http://web.archive.org/web/20100509224914/http://tagline.davelester.org/.

Lloyd-Jones, Richard. (1978). A view from the center. *College Composition and Communication*, 29 (1), 24-29.

Logan, Shirley Wilson. (2003). Changing missions, shifting positions, and breaking silences [Abstract]. *College Composition and Communication*, 55 (2), 330-342.

Lovas, John C. (2002). All good writing develops at the edge of risk [Abstract]. *College Composition and Communication*, 54 (2), 264-288.

Lunsford, Andrea A. (1990). Composing ourselves: Politics, commitment, and the teaching of writing. *College Composition and Communication*, 41 (1), 71-82.

Macrorie, Ken. (1962). Miscellany. *College Composition and Communication*, 13 (1), 57-61.

McQuade, Donald. (1992) Living in—and on—the margins. *College Composition and Communication*, 43 (1), 11-22.

Mehta, Chirag. (2007). US presidential speeches tag cloud. Retrieved from http://chir.ag/projects/preztags/.

Moretti, Franco. (2000). Conjectures on world literature. *New Left Review*, 1, 54-68.

Moretti, Franco. (2005). *Graphs, maps, trees: Abstract models for a literary history*. New York: Verso.

Mueller, Derek. (2009). *Clouds, graphs, and maps: Distant reading and disciplinary imagination*. (Doctoral dissertation). Retrieved from ProQuest Dissertations and Theses. (Accession Order No. AAT 3385836).

Odell, Lee. (1986). Diversity and change: Toward a maturing discipline. *College Composition and Communication*, 37 (4), 395-401.

Peterson, Jane E. (1991). Valuing teaching: Assumptions, problems, and possibilities. *College Composition and Communication*, 42 (1), 25-35.

Phelps, Louise W. & Ackerman, John. (2010). Making the case for disciplinarity in rhetoric, composition, and writing studies: The visibility project. *College Composition and Communication*, 62 (1), 180-215.

Pickett, Nell Ann. (1998). The two-year college as democracy in action. *College Composition and Communication*, 49 (1), 90-98.

Pough, Gwendolyn. (2011). It's bigger than comp/rhet: Contested and *undis*ciplined. *College Composition and Communication*, 62 (3), 301-313.

Purnell, Rosentene B. (2006). Using language to unlock the limits. In Duane Roen (Ed.), *Views from the center* (pp. 115-131). New York: Bedford-St. Martin's.

Richards, I. A. (1955). The resourcefulness of words. *Speculative instruments*. Chicago: U Chicago P.

Roen, Duane. (Ed.). (2006). *Views from the center: The CCCC chairs' addresses 1977-2005*. Boston, MA: Bedford-St. Martin's.

Royster, Jacqueline Jones. (1996). When the first voice you hear is not your own. *College Composition and Communication*, 47 (1), 29-40.

Schulz, Kathryn. (2011). What is distant reading? *New York Times Sunday Book Review*. Retrieved from .http://www.nytimes.com/2011/06/26/books/review/the-mechanic-muse-what-is-distant-reading.html.

Schütz, Ernst. (2002). *Clouds at noon* [Animated GIF]. Animation of the Sky. Retrieved from .http://www.pbase.com/es839145/image/29707055.

Selfe, Cynthia L. (1999). Technology and literacy: A story about the perils of not paying attention. *College Composition and Communication*, 50 (3), 411-436.

Stewart, Donald C. (1985). Some history lessons for composition teachers. *Rhetoric Review*, 3 (2), 134-144.

Troyka, Lynn Quitman. (1982). Perspectives on legacies and literacy in the 1980s. *College Composition and Communication*, 33 (3), 252-262.

Valentino, Marilyn J. (2010). Rethinking the fourth C: Call to action. *College Composition and Communication*, 62 (2), 364-378.

Villanueva, Victor. (1999). On the rhetoric and precedents of racism. *College Composition and Communication*, 50 (4), 645-661.

Waters, Lindsay. (2007). Time for reading. *Chronicle of Higher Education*, 53 (23). Retrieved from http://chronicle.com/article/Time-for-Reading/10505.

Wootten, Judith A. (2006). Riding a one-eyed horse: Reigning in and fencing out. *College Composition and Communication*, 58 (2), 263-245.

Yancey, Kathleen Blake. (2004). Made not only in words: Composition in a new key. *College Composition and Communication*, 56 (2), 297-328.

APPENDIX: COMPARISON

Using the vertical navigation bar in this space, you can view two clouds at once. This provides an alternative way to compare selected clouds. [Note: To view this comparison, please visit the online version of this webtext, at http://kairos.technorhetoric.net/16.2/topoi/mueller/index.html]

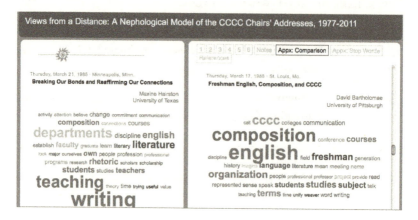

Figure 24 Comparative appendix of all word clouds available on Kairos.

APPENDIX: STOP WORDS

A list of "stop words" limits frequently occuring terms from appearing in the clouds. The list can be adjusted to produce slightly different results in the clouds. A stop list functions to reduce mundane recurrences. The following 429 stop words applied in the making of "Views from a Distance" will not appear in the clouds.

> about above across after again against all almost alone along already also although always among an and another any anybody anyone anything anywhere are area areas around as ask asked asking asks at away back backed backing backs be became because become becomes been before began behind being beings best better between big both but by came can cannot case cases certain certainly clear clearly come could did differ different differently do does done down down downed downing downs during each early either end ended ending ends enough even evenly ever every everybody everyone everything everywhere face faces fact facts far felt few find finds first for four from full fully further furthered furthering furthers gave general generally get gets give given gives go going good goods got great greater greatest group grouped grouping groups had has have having he her here herself high higher highest him himself his how however if important in

interest interested interesting interests into is it its itself just keep keeps kind knew know known knows large largely last later latest least less let lets like likely long longer longest made make making man many may me member members men might more most mostly mr mrs much must my myself necessary need needed needing needs never new newer newest next no nobody non noone not nothing now nowhere number numbers of off often old older oldest on once one only open opened opening opens or order ordered ordering orders other others our out over part parted parting parts per perhaps place places point pointed pointing points possible present presented presenting presents problem problems put puts quite rather really right right room rooms said same saw say says second seconds see seem seemed seeming seems sees several shall she should show showed showing shows side sides since small smaller smallest so some somebody someone something somewhere state states still such sure take taken than that the their them then there therefore these they thing things think thinks this those though thought thoughts three through thus to today together too took toward turn turned turning turns two under until up upon us use used uses very want wanted wanting wants was way ways we well wells went were what when where whether which while who whole whose why will with within without work worked working works would year years yet you young younger youngest your yours

KB JOURNAL

KB Journal takes as its mission the exploration of what it means to be "Burkeian." To this end, KB Journal publishes original scholarship that addresses, applies, extends, repurposes, or challenges the writings of Kenneth Burke, which include but are not limited to the major books and hundreds of articles by Burke, as well as the growing corpus of research material about Burke. It provides an outlet for integrating and critiquing the gamut of Burkeian studies in communication, composition, English, gender, literature, philosophy, psychology, sociology, and technical writing.

KB Journal is on the Web at http://kbjournal.org/

The Meaning of the Motivorum's Motto: "Ad bellum purificandum" to "Tendebantque manus ripae ulterioris amore"

Richard Thames's essay on "The Meaning of the Motivorum's Motto" takes Burke's famous epigraph to A Grammar of Motives, ad bellum purificandum ("toward the purification of war") as its molten center, then follows the many ideas that bubble up from this provocative beginning. They lead Thames to profound insights about Burke's project on human relations, the nature of rhetoric, dialectic, and poetics..

9 The Meaning of the Motivorum's Motto: "Ad bellum purificandum" to "Tendebantque manus ripae ulterioris amore"

Richard H. Thames

ABSTRACT

Why render the Motivorum's motto in Latin? Because ad bellum purifican-dum can be translated "toward the purification of war," but also "toward the purification of the beautiful [thing]," an alternative Burke himself suggests in his unfinished second draft of the Symbolic. In addition, purificandum (associated with transcendence in dialectic) is a neologism Burke probably constructs from purgandum (associated with catharsis in rhetoric and poet-ics). Working back and forth between interpreting the motto and interpreting the text, the relationship between rhetoric (whose end is War) and dialectic (whose end is Beauty à la Plato's Symposium and Phaedrus) can be established and the nature of poetic (which weaves the two together) discerned.

This essay follows on "The Gordian Not: Untangling the Motivorum" (KB Journal Spring 2007).

In memory of Michael Leff—admirer of Burke, scholar of Classical rhetoric, and close reader extraordinaire.

Introduction

AD BELLUM PURIFICANDUM—such was the epigram or motto of Kenneth Burke's proposed multi-volume "Motivorum" found on the opening page of *A Grammar of Motives*, published in 1945. As all Burkeians subsequently noted, the epigram was odd. The typical translation, "Toward the purification of war," seemed to beg the immediate question, "Why not eradication?" And just as quickly the attempt to answer mired all in a myriad of difficulties. The *Grammar* started innocently enough, then abruptly dove into the deep end, examining the paradox of substance, then the paradox of purity. The "purification of war" would be no simple matter, nor the books dedicated to that proposition.

But perhaps the first question truly begged is the more obvious but never asked "Why render the epigram in Latin?" when it's perplexing enough in English. Why complicate the matter further? Because, to echo the Lord's repeated reproach of Satan in "A Prologue in Heaven," it is indeed "more complicated than that" (*RR 277*). *A close reading of the Latin reveals a richness the standard rendering fails to convey.*

I say this with some trepidation. All too often we over-complicate Burke, bifurcating him into early and late; then middle, post-modern, post-structuralist, etc. Actually, Burke is simple in the sense that all great thinkers are—which is not to say easy. Great thinkers thoroughly, relentlessly, and oft times systematically pursue one or two profound ideas for decades or even life.[1] Burke sought to understand language as more than a tool, more than a means to innumerable ends; he thought of *language in and of itself as motivation*. What is required is a representative summation of the system thereafter elaborated, a statement that is simple but not superficial, assuring students and scholars alike that plunging into his work will prove to be not bewildering but bracing and worthwhile.

Such a statement will be offered in conclusion. First, a plunge into paradox.

Burke's Warrant

The warrant for this reading is Burke's own discussion from the unpublished second draft of *A Symbolic of Motives* (left unfinished in 1963)[2] in which there is an early section entitled "Preparatory Etymology" with a subsection on "Beauty and War." Burke notes the Greek root of the word "artistic" (ar-, the source, he says, of "articulate," "aristocracy," and "arithmetic") is related to the Greek word meaning "to join" and even older Sanskrit forms meaning "to attain" and "to fit." Thus, he continues, looking in this etymological direction—

> We may encounter Socrates' notion that the dialectician knows how to carve an idea at the joints, and that dialectics itself begins with two kinds of terms, those that generalize and those that specify. The thought suggests that the work of art will be found, on inspection, to have its own peculiar kind of dialectic, an expert interweaving of composition and division. And in accordance with the genius of this route, when analyzing a poem we are admonished to ask how its parts are related to one another and to the whole. ('63 *SM* ms.32)

Burke further notes that the Greek words for "armament," "Ares" (the god of war), and "virtue" (*arête*) share the same root, as do (obviously) the Latin words *vir* (a man of arms-bearing age) and *virtus*.[3] Contemplating this route, he continues, may suggest reasons for the inclination to consider the tragic cult of the kill as exceptionally "poetic."[4]

Turning to "beauty," Burke observes that

> in pre-classical Latin, a word *duellum* (deriving ultimately from the Indo-European root for "apart" or "two," and meaning "war between two") became transformed into *bellum*, meaning "war." This was related to a word *bonus*, meaning "good" (and derived from an older form, *duonus*, also meaning "good," and similarly related to the root word for "two"). (*SM* ms.33)

Etymologically, then, "beauty" is related to both "war" and "good."

> ("Beauty" is from French *beauté*, that came from an assumed Late Latin word *bellitas*, built from *bellus*, itself modulating from *benulus* to *benus* to *bonus*, the word for "good," and related to *bellum*, the word for "war.") By the same token, when on the subject of artistic felicity, we might well recall that the saintly word "beatitude" apparently bridges us back to the same origins. And inasmuch as the whole story apparently leads to the Indo-European root for the notion of things

apart, or *two* (dva-, dvi-; English two, twice, twilight, twig, twist, twin, twine), it might be relevant to recall also that when St. Augustine wrote his no longer extant tracts on beauty and fitness (*de pulchro et apto*), he apparently constructed his entire theory around a distinction between unity and division . . . (*SM* ms.33-34)

Obviously Burke knew his Latin (from Peabody High School in Pittsburgh) and was well aware that *bellum* was ambiguous, that with the epigram "*ad bellum purificandum*" he was dedicating his *magnum opus* to the purification of both "war" and "the beautiful [thing]" (*bellum* being the accusative form of the noun *bellus*) with suggestions as well of "the good" (the etymologically related *bonus*).

The word *purificandum* is likewise suggestive. Unlike with *bellum*, however, Burke offers no observations concerning its etymology, the term apparently being his own—the post-Augustinian verb *purifico* having been derived from the earlier, more common *purgo* and its non-occurring gerundive form having been derived by Burke himself, perhaps from *purgandum*. The choice of the neologism "purifying" over the vernacular "purging" suggests a preference for *dialectical* processes effecting transcendence over *rhetorical* processes effecting catharsis through victimage (both real and symbolic); at the same time, the etymology suggests some relationship between the two.

Clearly Burke himself warrants closely reading the Latin, though doing so will involve working dialectically back and forth between interpreting the motto and interpreting the text.

Purificandum I

Without doubt one of the most devilishly difficult notions in dramatism is that of "pure persuasion." One need not be ancient in the ways of Burke to beware his invocation of the adjective "pure," tempting him at every dialectical twist and turn to ensnarl in paradox whatever it modifies.

But Burke's discussion represents more than a mere exercise in dialectical deviltry. There is considerable payoff for those with the patience to follow every twist and turn, every image and example. What can be learned concerns the nature of rhetoric and its ultimate possibilities vis-à-vis the human condition.

Burke's analysis of pure persuasion is supposed to be unique, but Aristotle's analysis of money in Nicomachaean Ethics (5.5) and Politics (1.8-10) is remarkably similar and may provide an easier entry.

According to Aristotle, in barter, one commodity is exchanged *directly* for another (wine for wheat). In more advanced markets, money *mediates* exchange; one commodity is sold for money to buy another (wine is sold to buy wheat). But as exchange after exchange extends over time, *the exchange of commodities mediated by money* becomes instead *the exchange of money mediated by commodities* (money buys wine or wheat to be sold in turn for even more money). Ultimately the mediating commodity is dropped and money is exchanged directly for more money still (money is lent for interest—or in modern times made by playing exchange rates, though ancient "bankers" were often money-changers). Thus money, introduced as a *means* to facilitate the *end* of exchange, is transformed into an *end* in itself.

Commodities have *natural ends*—wheat to be eaten and wine to be drunk. There are natural limits to consumption, duration, and therefore acquisition—wheat spoils and wine turns sour. Because there are natural limits to the acquisition of any one thing, as well as many things *in toto*, at some point there will be *enough*. In other words, *wealth* is not unlimited; its natural end is in whatever constitutes enough—not the store of money for exchange, but the stock of real things useful for living the *good life*, achieving *happiness*, realizing *our nature* in the *polis*.

But money as a *means* has no proper *end*. There is no natural limit to its accumulation; no such thing as enough. Its pursuit is therefore *endless, irrational,* and *unnatural.*

Pure persuasion would likewise involve transforming a *means* (persuasion) into an *end* (persuasion for the sake of persuasion alone), thus making pure persuasion *the endless pursuit of a means*.

Burke's point is more than mere word-play, an *end* being not only a *goal* or *purpose* but also a *completion* or *termination*. Therefore pure persuasion as a *means* transformed into an *end* would paradoxically become both *purposeless* and *perpetual*—*purposeless* in that once persuasion's purpose is accomplished, it ceases to be persuasion for the sake of persuasion alone, becoming instead persuasion for the sake of whatever was purposed (*RM* 269-70); and *perpetual* in that once persuasion reaches its goal, it ceases, thereupon becoming something else (*RM* 274).

The perpetual frustration of purpose requires an element of *stand-offishness* or *self-interference*, says Burke (*RM* 269, 271, 274), to prevent persuasion's ever achieving its end. For example, constructing a rhetoric around the key term *identification* means confronting the implications of *division* (*RM* 22). Identification compensates for division, but pure identification could never completely overcome it; identification for the sake of identification alone would require *standoffishness*, the perpetuation of some degree of division for identification to forever overcome. Or, insofar as rhetoric involves *courtship* grounded in biological and/or social *estrangement* (*RM* 115, 208 ff.), pure persuasion would require *coyness* or *coquetry* (*RM* 270)—again a degree of stand-offishness, but more obviously connoting *eros*.

According to Burke, rhetoric is rooted in the use of language to induce *cooperation* as a means to some further end (*RM* 43). Cooperation is always being sought because there is always *competition*. Cooperation for the sake of cooperation alone would require some *interference*, the perpetuation of some degree of competition for cooperation to forever overcome.

Burke's analysis of pure persuasion reveals a *resistance to rhetoric that lies at its very heart*. His point is that analysis of an ultimate form (e.g., pure persuasion) reveals a motivational ingredient present even in the most elemental (*RM* 269, 274)—i.e., *what is ultimately the case is always the case to some degree*.[5] Therefore any rhetorical act would comprise a complex of motives, minimally consisting of (1) persuasion itself compounded with (2) pure persuasion to some degree (i.e., some degree of standoffishness or interference). Rhetoric as rhetoric then can never transcend itself. Rhetoric as rhetoric can never be *salvic*, for *all rhetoric is somewhat self-defeating*.

War constitutes the ultimate instance of pure persuasion—the greatest degree of cooperation perpetuated by the greatest degree of competition, the greatest degree of identification perpetuated by the greatest degree of division.[6] Burke regards war as *diseased cooperation* (*RM* 332) in that complete cooperation cannot be achieved by means of competition, because there must always be something against which we compete; the communion of complete identification cannot be achieved by means of division, because there must always be an enemy from which we are divided, an enemy in opposition to which we stand united.

War, says Burke, is *a special case of peace*—"not as a primary motive in itself, not as *essentially* real, but purely as a *derivative* condition, a *perversion*" (*RM* 20)—like *evil* for Augustine. Little wonder then that Burke writes, the *Rhetoric*

> must lead us through the Scramble, the Wrangle of the Market Place, the flurries and the flare-ups of the Human Barnyard, the Give and Take, the wavering line of pressure and counterpressure, the Logomachy, the onus of ownership, the War of Nerves, the War. It too has its peaceful moments: at times its endless competition can add up to the transcending of itself. In ways of its own, it can move from the factional to the universal. But its ideal culminations are more often beset by strife as the condition of their organized expression, or material embodiment. Their very universality becomes transformed into a partisan weapon. (RM 23)

If war constitutes pure persuasion's ultimate instance, then we are always somewhat at war. If war constitutes *pure persuasion's* ultimate instance,then *war would be the essence of rhetoric.* And the motto "*ad bellum purificandum,*" "toward the purification of war," could be justly translated "toward the purification of rhetoric" as well.

If war perverts cooperation, turning it toward competition, war purified would transform competition, turning it toward cooperation—as in *dialectic*. In rhetoric, says Burke, voices *cooperate in order to compete* (i.e., "cooperative competition"); but in dialectic, voices *compete in order to cooperate* (i.e., "competitive cooperation") (*LSA* 188). If rhetoric is in essence *war*, then dialectic is in essence not *peace* negatively defined as the absence of war but positively defined as *love*—as in Plato's *Symposium* and *Phaedrus* where *Beauty* is the ultimate object of love (or *eros*).

Burke's own etymological analysis supports as much, *bellum* suggesting *war* on the one hand, *beauty* and *good* on the other. The "bellum-bellus" or war-beauty pair suggests the rhetoric-dialectic contrast again, but embodied in *victimage* on the one hand and *eros* on the other. The adjective *bellus* is derived from *benus* and *bonus* meaning "good," once more suggesting Plato's *Symposium* and *Phaedrus* and the dialectical climb to the mystic experience of Beauty "by itself with itself" (*Symposium* 2111b), the Good, the One.

Purgandum

As noted above, the post-Augustinian verb *purifico* is derived from the earlier, more common *purgo*, and its non-occurring gerund *purificandum* apparently derived from *purgandum* by Burke himself. The choice of "purifying" over "purging" suggests his preference for dialectical processes effecting *transcendence* over rhetorical processes effecting *catharsis* through *victimage* (both real and symbolic); at the same time the etymology implies some relationship between them. So, what is that relationship?

Burke actually distinguishes between *dialectical* processes of *purification* and *dramatic* (rather than *rhetorical*) processes of *purgation*. But drama involves both *dialectic* in the sense of thoroughly using language for no purpose other than using language and *rhetoric* in the sense of using language for a particular purpose—e.g. the author's persuading himself and/or his audience vis-à-vis a particular subject, often problematic. For Burke, drama (indeed all literature) is *ceremonial rhetoric* addressing the *timeless* (i.e., speaking to all human beings insofar as they are bodies that have learned language) and the *present* (the here and now, *hic et hunc*, of the author's life and time).

Burke defines human beings as *bodies that are genetically endowed with the ability to learn language.*[7] As such, all humans (though some more than others) take delight in expressing or exercising their being (as in Jerome Kern's lyric from *Showboat*, "fish gotta swim, birds gotta fly"), in doing that which distinguishes them from all other animals, in using language for the sake of using language alone (Rueckert, "Language of Poetry" *Essays* 38). The *internally* directed use of language for its own sake is *dialectical* and *ontological*; the *externally* directed use of language for the sake of something else is *rhetorical* and *historical*, tied to a particular person and a particular place and time (see *SM* ms. 179).

Both dialectic and drama, says Burke, exemplify *competitive cooperation* (as opposed to the *cooperative competition* of rhetoric)—though Burke would appear to be emphasizing the dialectical (rather than rhetorical) aspect of drama insofar as its parts are organically related to the whole. Out of conflicts within a work, "there arises a unitary view transcending the partial views of the participants"—the dialectic of the ideal Platonic dialogue (*LSA* 188).[8]

Both *transcendence* effected by dialectic and *catharsis* effected by ceremonial rhetoric or drama "involve *formal development*," says

Burke; therefore both give us "kinds of *transformation*," operating in terms of a *beyond* in dialectic and *victimage* in rhetoric (or its imitation in drama), though in dialectic there are traces of victimage (i.e., voices left behind), and in drama the cathartic "resolution 'goes beyond' the motivational tangle exploited for poetic enjoyment." Burke even proposes translating Aristotle's famous formula, "through pity and fear *beyonding* the catharsis of such emotions," noting the word normally translated "effecting" or "producing" (*perainousa*) is etymologically from the same root as *peran*, meaning "opposite shore" (*LSA* 298-99).[9]

Transcendence involves building a terministic bridge whereby one realm is transcended by being viewed in terms of a realm *beyond* (*LSA* 189, 200),

> a kind of "translation" whereby the reader is induced to confront a problem in terms that allow of resolutions not possible to other terms of confrontation. Dialectic, we might say, can even effect a kind of "quashed catharsis," or "catharsis by fiat," or "implicit transcendence," since the terms in which a given problem is presented can so setup the situation that a given problem is "resolved in advance," if you can speak of a problem as "resolved" when the terms in which it is treated do not even give it a chance to be expressed in all its problematic aspects. (*SM* ms. 170)

Dialectical purification and dramatic purgation then are both the same and different—the same insofar as the dialectical aspect of drama is emphasized, different insofar as the rhetorical is. And rhetoric and drama are different insofar as the former involves *victimage* and the latter its *imitation* (all the difference in the world to the victim), but they are the same insofar as both are ultimately partisan. Economic, political, and social tensions may be purged by sacrifice upon the stage, but the curtains close and the playhouse doors reopen on a world that remains unchanged. "Hence," says Burke, "tragic purges, twice a year. Such symbolic resolutions must be repeated, since the actual underlying situation is *not* resolved" (*Dramatism and Development* 15).

So ultimately we return to the problematic aspects of rhetoric and Burke's preference for dialectic—though along the way, the idea of dialectic operating in terms of a *beyond* has emerged. Understanding what Burke means unfortunately involves another plunge.

PURIFICANDUM II

The epigram suggests that Burke is prejudiced against rhetorical action, but ultimately *Burke is prejudiced against any action other than linguistic action for its own sake.* All other action would constitute a means to an *external* end that would in its purity be transformed into an end in itself, thereby perpetuating itself by never attaining its intended end; all other action would be to some degree undertaken for its own sake, thereby requiring some degree of interference in accomplishing its external purpose. Thus, *all action is problematic, all action somewhat self-defeating, because what is ultimately the case is always the case to some degree.*

The only action that is not self-defeating is linguistic action for its own sake, because there is *an ultimate end internal to language attained when all that is inherent to language itself has been thoroughly unfolded.* Such pure action is dialectic and its inherent end transcendence—the mystic experience of an ultimate, unitary pantheistic ground *beyond* nonverbal and verbal—*NATURE* (*à la* Spinoza).[10]

Once again, because what is ultimately the case is always the case to some degree, *all other action would also involve an ingredient of linguistic action for its own sake.* All other action would contain some element of language's reaching toward its inherent end.

Normal actions then would comprise a complex of motives consisting of (1) an action undertaken for the sake of its intended external end compounded with (2) some degree of that action undertaken for its own sake (i.e, an element of interference in accomplishing its intended external end); (3) linguistic action for the sake of an external end compounded with (4) some degree of linguistic action undertaken for its own sake (i.e., an element of language reaching toward its inherent, internal end; an element of dialectic culminating in transcendence) —what Burke refers to as a "fragment" of dialect (*RM* 175) and its inherent end, transcendence, and therefore a "fragment" of mysticism.[11]

This complexity of motives can be resolved into a simplicity (banality?) when an act in its purity is transformed from a means into an end in itself. Like pure persuasion, pure actions (other than purely linguistic ones) would be more than fragments of dialectic or mysticism; they would constitute *substitutes* for mysticism, *ersatzmystiken*, as with money, sex, drugs, crime, war—instrumentalities of living transformed into demonic purposes with which one may identify "quite as with mystic communion." Anyone for whom means are thus transformed has "a god" and, "engrossed, enrapt, entranced," can become lost in its godhead (*RM* 331-32).

This perverse internality (eventuating in false mysticism) is counterpart to dialectic's own internality (eventuating in mysticism proper). Their *internality* is in turn counterpart to the *externality* of normal action and linguistic action which constitute means to an external end. Pure action and purely linguistic action constitute *simple* actions that are counterparts to *complex* normal actions. Normal actions, however, in their confusion of motives are ultimately ineffectual—self-defeating (as somewhat pure) and partial (as fragmentary dialectic), their internal ends (between their poles of purity, false and proper) frustrating attainment of their external ends.

The only action by which true transcendence could be achieved would be by dialectic directed toward the internal end of language, devoid of all rhetoric directed toward an external end and therefore defeated by its purity to some degree. The *cooperative competition* of voices in rhetoric is transformed into the *competitive cooperation* of voices in dialectic, says Burke, by the inclusion of one voice that is *primus inter pares*, the foremost among equals, a role performed in Platonic dialogue by Socrates who functions as the summarizing vessel or synecdochic representative of the end or logic of the development as a whole (*GM* 526). Such is the role of the mystic fragment of linguistic action for itself alone that points to the mystic experience of a pantheistic ground *beyond* nonverbal and verbal, body and mind, material and ideal.

BELLUS I

Returning to the epigram, *bellum* suggests Hobbes' *bellum omnium contra omnes*, "the war of all against all," characterizing the rhetorical realm. But as Burke himself suggests, *bellum* can also be the accusative of the noun *bellus*, "the beautiful [thing]." The "bellum-bellus" or war-beauty pair suggests Mars/Ares (god of war) and Venus/Aphrodite (goddess of beauty and sexual love or *eros*) and the rhetoric-dialectic contrast again, but embodied in victimage on the one hand and sexual love on the other. The adjective "bellus" is derived from "benus" and "bonus," meaning "good," once more suggesting Plato's *Symposium* and *Phaedrus* as well as Castiglione's *Courtier* and the dialectical climb to the mystic experience of Beauty, the Good, the One.

So *ad bellum purificandum* can also be translated "toward purification of the beautiful (or beauty)." Such is the dialectical task Burke
sets for himself in the second part of his '63 version of the *Symbolic* at
whose conclusion the manuscript breaks off but whose equivalent can
be found in the chapter from the '58 version on "The Thinking of the
Body," the thorough and thoroughly disgusting "monster" of a chapter
that "wrote itself" in 1951 (Williams, *Unending Conversations* 9 and
24), much to the embarrassment of Burke. That part of that original
chapter was published in 1963 and collected with an equally disgusting essay (*Somnia Ad Urinandum*) in *Language as Symbolic Action* is
testament to a deeply felt need for "expressing or redeeming the fecal
motive" that, according to Burke, is required for transcendence to be
complete (*RM* 309). So, in this alternative translation of the motto, we
spy the *body* that learns language—i.e., we uncover the significance of
embodiment in Burke.

The mystic, says Burke, "invariably aims to encompass conflicting
orders of motivation, not by outlawing any order, however 'inferior,'
but by finding a place for it in a developmental series." The mystic,
for example, treats the body, not as an antithesis to spirit, but as a way
into spirit—"a necessary disciplinary step" for "entry to ultimate communion." Indeed, says Burke, the mystic in his thoroughness employs
body terms for his ultimate experiences (*RM* 189).

Having made his point, Burke arranges the remainder of the *Rhetoric* in a pattern climbing through rhetoric, *beyond* rhetoric in keeping
with the pattern in Castiglione's "paradigmatic" *Book of the Courtier*—
"a series of formal operations for the dialectical purifying of a rhetorical
motive," climbing through dialogues on the endowments of the perfect
courtier, the forms of courtly address, and the code of courtly intercourse between men and women which is Platonically transformed in
the final dialogue concerning the end of the perfect courtier (i.e., the
theme of sexual love dialectically climbing "from woman to beauty in
general to transcendent desire for Absolute union" (*RM* 221)). Burke
begins by considering rhetoric as courtship and dialectically climbs to
considering mysticism as ultimate identification where rhetoric and
the *Rhetoric* end in a vision of Aristotle's God (*RM* 333).

The *end* of rhetoric would be peace, rest, love—and at the same
time *the end* or cessation of rhetoric, when rhetoric *transcends* itself
in dialectic. Rhetoric in its *ideal culminations* would be *love* such as
we find in Augustine, whose "God has made us for Himself," so "our

hearts remain restless until they rest in Him";[12] in Spinoza, whose crowning motive was "the intellectual love of God"; in Plato in the *Symposium* and *Phaedrus* in the love of Beauty and the Good; and in Aristotle whose God is "the motionless prime mover that moves all else not by being itself moved, but by being loved" (*GM* 254). And so rhetoric and the *Rhetoric* end with one of the greatest passages in Burke:

> Finally let us observe, all about us, forever goading us, though it be in *fragments* [emphasis mine], the motive that attains its ultimate identification in the thought, not of the universal holocaust, but in the universal order—as with the rhetorical and dialectic symmetry of the Aristotelian metaphysics, whereby all classes of beings are hierarchically arranged in a chain or ladder or pyramid of mounting worth, each kind striving towards the *perfection* of its kind, and so towards the kind next above it, while the strivings of the entire series head in God as the *beloved* [emphasis mine] cynosure and sinecure, the end of all desire. (*RM* 333)

Purificandum III

Worth noting in the wonder of this concluding passage is the word "mounting," whose range of meanings Burke has considered only a few pages earlier—the kinesthetic sensation of height, social betterment, ethical ascent, fecal matter such as the dung-pile (which might be associated with pyramids, given that ancient Egyptians held the dung-beetle sacred, and thus for Burke the surmounting of the fecal motive), as well as sexual mounting (*RM* 301-13).

Burke, in the final pages, claims the mystic state would have its bodily counterpart. Following neurologist Charles Sherrington (oft-quoted by Burke), he explains how movement is made possible by the coordinated flexing and relaxing of opposed muscles. If conflicting impulses expressed themselves simultaneously, if nerves controlling opposed muscles all fired at once, movement would not be possible. Such a neurological condition could be accurately described in terms of *total activation* (or *pure action*) and/or *total passivity* and plausibly would be involved in the pronounced sense of unity to which mystics habitually testify (*PC* 248; *GM* 294; *RM* 330-31), a oneness as thorough as that experienced in the womb (*PC* 248)—or, dare one suggest, *sexual union.*

Two cautions. First, ideally sexual union would be the consummation, the culmination of courtship; and such would always be the case to some degree. Sexual activity would always involve more for bodies that learn language than it would for other animals. Second, the suggestion is not that sexual union is (always or even sometimes) mystical but that dialectic can lift us to a mystic state which would manifest itself physically in a manner much like sexual union for the body that learns language.

Burke himself hints at *sexual union*—and such an interpretation would explain the mystic's recourse to erotic imagery. For Burke continues, if a taste of new "fruit" is knowledge—or, given the sly allusion to "forbidden fruit," if sexual intercourse is considered (carnal) knowledge—then the experience of a rare and felicitous physical state would be so too. The mystic, reasons Burke, would be convinced his experience was "noetic," conveying a "truth" *beyond* the realm of logical contradiction, constituting a report of something from outside the mind, a "communication with an ultimate, unitary ground" (*RM* 330-31).

Transcendence and catharsis are "rival medicines" (*LSA* 186-89), says Burke—transcendence being effected in terms of a *beyond* and catharsis by imitation of *victimage*. But both are medicines (not metaphorically, though perhaps in contrast to "cookery"), similar enough to suggest the embodiment of transcendence is comparable to the more obvious embodiment of catharsis. So, one should not be surprised when Burke observes that despite discord an audience may be brought by means of dramatic devices to a unitary response. He regards "the tearful outbursts of an audience at a tragedy as a surrogate for sexual orgasm" and 18,000 Athenians weeping in unison as a variant of "what was once a primitive promiscuous sexual orgy" such as "the Dionysian rites from which Greek tragedy developed" (*Dramatism & Development* 14; *LSA* 186; *GM* 229).[13]

Ideas of pity readily attain natural bodily fulfillment in tears, says Burke; and ideas of mirth lead similarly to laughter as well as tears from riotous laughter. Weeping at tragedy and laughing at comedy are akin to love, but not identical. They operate as substitutes for catharsis through erotic love which has its own kind of bodily release (completion, fulfillment). Surely, says Burke toward the end of the 1958 first version of the *Symbolic, the most "cathartic" experience possible would be*

the ability to love everything, without reservation in such bodily spontane-
ity as attains its purely verbal counterpart in ejaculations [sic] of thanks-
giving and praise (*PDC* ms. 322).

A *final caution*—sexual *orgasm* would be cathartic; sexual *union*
need not be (e.g., the Tantric spiritual practice of sexual yoga and
meditation in which orgasm is delayed or withheld). The mystic state
would be more like the moment just prior to release—a neurological
state, Burke speculates, that could be described in terms of *total activa-*
tion and/or *total passivity* in which all nervous impulses "attitudinally
glowed" at once, "remaining in a halfway stage of incipience" (*attitude*
functioning for Burke as a substitute for action or an *incipient* action);
like, he continues appositively, "the *status nascendi*" (not the *act* but
the *state* of being born) of "the pursuit figured on Keats' Grecian Urn"
(*RM* 330-31)[14] (which appropriately for Burke, Keats addresses as "Fair
attitude!"—see *GM* 459).

BELLUS II

Burke's mention of Keats is intriguing but confusing. He mentions
Keats earlier to exemplify pure persuasion—"A single need, forever
courted, as on Keats's Grecian Urn, would be made possible by self-
interference" (*RM* 275). Such interference would prevent persuasion's
ever coming to its end. But persuasion—rhetoric—transcends itself in
dialectic. Linguistic action for itself alone does come to its end, an end
inherent to language itself and a state such as that depicted on the Urn,
a state characterized in a manner suggestive of self-interference—with
a difference.

Pure persuasion, says Burke, would be "as biologically unfeasible as
that moment when the irresistible force meets the immovable body."
It would be psychologically related to "a conflict of opposite impulses"
and philosophically suggestive of "Buridan's extremely rational ass"
starving to death between two equally distant, equally succulent bales
of hay. It would be "the moment of motionlessness . . . uncomfortably
like suspended animation" (*RM* 294).

Noting that if, "as neurologists like Sherrington tell us," the expression of some impulses is contrived by the repression of others, then
there is even on the bodily level an "infringement of freedom" within
us, a sheerly physiological state of "inner contradiction." Thus, he continues, "discord would have become the norm."

> However if going *beyond* [emphasis mine] it, the nervous sys-
> tem could fall [an odd choice of words, but see below] into
> a state of radical passivity whereby all nervous impulses "at-
> titudinally glowed" at once (remaining in a halfway stage of
> incipience, the *status nascendi* of the pursuit figured on Keats'
> Grecian Urn) there could be total "activation" without the
> overt acts that require repressive processes. Hence "contradic-
> tory" movements could exist simultaneously. (*RM* 330-31)

If normal action involves on the bodily level an "infringement of freedom," the state concerning which Burke speculates, the state to which
the purely linguistic act would lift us would be experienced not as
"self-interference" but as "freedom."

And perhaps not as "suspended animation" either, not as *time
stopped* (or interfered with) but as an *eternal present* (*GM* 449). In his
analysis of Keats' poem, Burke writes of "*suspension* in the erotic imagery, defining an eternal prolongation of the state prior to fulfillment—
not exactly arrested ecstasy, but rather an arrested pre-ecstasy." But
what he stresses is "the quality of *incipience* in this imagery." And he
cites G. Wilson Knight's referring in *The Starlit Dome* (295) to "that
recurring tendency in Keats to image [*sic*] a poised form, a stillness
suggesting motion" (*GM* 449-50)—as with total passivity caused by
total activation. Though Keats addresses the Urn as a "still unravish'd
bride of quietness," Burke points to Keats' discovering erotic imagery
("maidens loth," "mad pursuit," "wild ecstasy," and more) everywhere
in the embroidered scene covering it (i.e., the "brede [breed?] of marble
men and maidens overwrought [overly excited?]"), fevered imagery of
ravishment frozen on the Urn, imagery sharing the incipience of the
Bold Lover who never, never wins the kiss (?) but forever loves.

Burke interprets this incipience as a variant of the identification
between sexual love and death typical of 19th century romanticism
(e.g., the "musical monument" of Wagner's *Liebestod*). "On a purely
dialectical basis, to die in love would be to be born to love (the lovers
dying as individual identities that they might be transformed into a
common identity)." Indeed any imagery of a *dying* or a *falling* in common (perhaps why Burke speaks of the nervous system *falling* into a
state of radical passivity—see above) when woven with sexual imagery
"signalizes a 'transcendent' sexual consummation" (*GM* 450-51).[15]

PURIFICANDUM IV

But Burke reminds us that "transcendence is not complete until the fecal motive has in some way been expressed and redeemed" (*RM* 309). Indeed "*the entire hierarchic pyramid of dialectical symmetry may be infused with such a spirit*" (*RM* 311). If we would ascend to the vision of Beauty, beauty must be purified—*ad bellum purificandum*. The mystic—like Keats in the "Ode," like Burke in the *Grammar, Rhetoric,* and *Symbolic*—encompasses conflicting orders of motivation by finding a place for them in a developmental series, treating the body not as an antithesis to but a way into spirit—"a necessary disciplinary step" for "entry to ultimate communion." In his thoroughness the mystic even employs body terms for his ultimate experiences (*RM* 189).

Keats seeks to transcend the body and his own illness[16] ("with the peculiar inclinations to erotic imaginings that accompany its fever"), to redeem by a poetic act his bodily suffering ("death, disease, the passions, or bodily 'corruption' generally (as with religious horror of the body)" being variants of the fecal), by splitting a distraught state into active and passive aspects, so that the benign (purified spiritual activity) remains, while the malign (tubercular—and sexual—fever) can be abstracted and left behind (*RM* 317; *GM* 452-53).

> More happy love! more happy, happy love!
> For ever warm and still to be enjoyed.
> For ever panting, and for ever young
> All breathing human passion far above,
> That leaves a heart high-sorrowful and cloyed,
> A burning forehead, and a parching tongue.

But transcendence is not complete with only a sexual mounting; the urinal and literally fecal must be expressed and left behind as well. Burke claims that sometimes transcendence "may be got by purely tonal transformation" (myriad instances of which can be found in language change and partially codified in Grimm's Laws). Such transformations "would reduce to a single letter or syllable, the process of catharsis, or ritual purging, that is developed at length in tragedy" (RM 310), enabling us to say something without really saying it—like "shucks" (one word, two expletives). Readers of Burke may remember his Great-Gramma Brodie who forbad his saying "G" or "Heck, Holy Smokes, and Darn it" because she knew what they implied (Collected

Poems 242). Nevertheless, he speculates that in the title "urn" may be just such a tonal transformation of "urine" and in the final oracular lines "beauty" a transformation of "body" and "truth" of "turd." Burke cautions, however, that such "joycing" is heuristic or suggestive "though it may put us in search of corroborative observations" (RM 204, 310; "As I Was Saying" 21, an article in which Burke mounts a full defense of his position 20-24).

BELLUS III

According to Burke, the same pattern of transcendence (minus joycing) is evident in Plato's *Phaedrus*. Lysias' reference to a "feast of discourse" on the topic of love functions not merely as a metaphor but a juncture of two levels, the dialogue leading step by step from "feast" on the level of sheerly physical appetite (with an element of sociality introducing a motivation beyond mere hunger) to "discourse" on the level of "purely verbal insemination." In brief, says Burke, "the dialogue is a 'way' from sexual intercourse to the Socratic intercourse of dialectical converse," an instance of the *Socratic erotic*—Plato's cure to rival the playwrights' which he resisted (*GM* 424).

Propounded most directly in the *Phaedrus* and the *Symposium* (which likewise features discourses concerning love on the occasion of a banquet), the *Socratic erotic* is defined by Burke as "an ideological technique whereby bodily love would be transformed into love of wisdom, which in turn would be backed by knowledge derived and matured from the coquettish give and take of verbal intercourse" ("Catharsis—Second View" 132; *PDC* 359); though Burke later observes such coquettish give and take "could be relevantly analyzed as an attenuated variant of the tragic principle ('learning through suffering'), since the victimage involved one's methodic 'suffering' of one's opponent, in order that exposure to such counter-action might thus contribute to the mature revising of one's own position" (*Unending Conversations* 76; *PDC* 372); or, characterizing the Socratic erotic more terministically, Burke says "the seeds of merely bodily love are [so] placed in a terministic context" that "doctrinal insemination" becomes the concern (*Unending Conversations* 71; *PDC* 362).

Catharsis being associated with *drama*, Platonic *transcendence* is in contrast associated with *lyric*, "the kind of arias-with-dance which drama had necessarily subordinated in the very process of becoming drama," says Burke, observing that when drama overstresses thought, it dissolves into exposition, homily, or dialectic ("Catharsis—Second View" 121; *PDC* 342). Burke considers Keats' "Ode on a Grecian Urn" an ideal example of such dialectic adapted to lyric poetry (*Unending Conversations* 76; *PDC* 373; "On Catharsis" 362).

The contrast between lyric and drama is not absolute, however. Both comedy and tragedy can be *partisan*; derisive laughter can be as socially unifying as sacrifice. Both employ *victimage* to some degree—"the butt of humor at whose expense we jointly laugh" as well as the "scape-goat." But comedy involves a "comic blotch" (*hamartema*) rather than a "tragic flaw" (*hamartia*), a foolish blunder rather than a prideful error of judgment. And Aristophanic comedy would culminate in secularized variants of the "sacred marriage" (the hierogamy) and the "love feast" rather than the "kill" ("On Catharsis" 348, 362).[17]

Given that Plato's particular system of cure was based on the Socratic erotic ("Catharsis—Second View" 132; *PDC* 359), the transformations characteristic of dialectic would be more akin to comedy than tragedy, falling on the side of sex rather than victimage—perhaps the reason for Burke's approaching Plato roundabout through Nietzsche (which he does) and Aristophanes (which he planned to do) (*PDC* 359-60, a paragraph added in the *PDC* to "Catharsis—Second View").

PURIFICANDUN V

Burke's positions vis-à-vis dialectic and drama are part of a running argument with Nietzsche's as expressed in the *Birth of Tragedy*. Nietzsche claims that tragedy originates in the struggle between two forces, drives, or principles which he associates with Greek deities— Apollo, embodying the drive toward drawing and respecting boundaries and limits; and Dionysus, the drive toward destroying boundaries and transgressing limits. The purest expression of the Apollonian is Homeric epic poetry and the purest expression of the Dionysian quasi-orgiastic forms is music (especially choral singing and dancing). Applying the one-many alignment, Nietzsche equates the principle of individuation with Apollo and the aristocratic, and "primordial unity" with drunken worshippers of Dionysus and primitive democracy. Tragedy is a merger of aristocratic and popular tendencies (the Chorus "hovering on the edge of riot"), a balance of Apollonian moderation and self-control and Dionysian excess (with the musical, Dionysian element tending to dominate). Tragedy's decline commences, according to Nietzsche, with the arrival of Socrates, a new force dedicated to creating abstract generalizations and attaining theoretical knowledge (*Unending Conversations* 74; *PDC* 369).

Though Burke believes scholarship provides backing for Nietzsche's view of tragedy as "the marriage of conflicting social motives," he disputes Nietzsche's equating the principle of individuation with any one social class, there being democratic as well as aristocratic forms; besides, individuation is not exclusively a social principle. He claims primordial unity is equated with the Dionysian dance when it could be equated with the Apollonian dream as well. And music's equation with Dionysus (an equation central to Nietzsche's argument) could be made more justifiably with Apollo— an equation Burke himself implicitly makes, Apollo's *lyre* being the instrument accompanying *lyric* poetry recited or sung at symposia (though flutes were also common). Burke would appear to align his terms differently, associating Dionysus more with drama and Apollo more with non-dramatic lyric and therefore Platonic dialectic. And while Burke believes Plato did offer a cure in direct competition with both the tragic and comic playwrights, he hardly considered his medicine inferior (*Unending Conversations* 75-76; *PDC* 369-72).

But Nietzsche remains more than relevant for Burke's purposes because, throughout the *Birth of Tragedy*, there runs "a terascopic [*sic*] concern" with what Burke calls "the Daedalian motive"—named for the creator of the Labyrinth on Crete in which the Minotaur (part bull, part man) was kept—given Nietzsche's speaking of trying to find his way through "the labyrinth of the origin of Greek tragedy" (*Unending Conversations* 75; *PDC* 371).

The relation "between articulate form and the inarticulate matter out of which such expression emerges," says Burke, is "labyrinthine" in two senses—"not only is the inarticulate a tangle (at least, as viewed from the standpoint of the articulate); but also articulation itself is a tangle, since any symbol-system sets up an indeterminate range of 'implications' still to be explored." The Daedalian motive—the desire for *articulation*—is cathartic in the non-Aristotelian, Crocean sense of *expression* being cathartic, an experience of *relief* resulting from converting an "inarticulate muddle into the orderly terms of a symbol-system," as well as from finding a *direction* through a *maze* of implications (from a beginning through a middle to an end) ("On

Catharsis" 364). And maintaining his Apollonian alignments, Burke observes, "Regarding dialectical processes in general, any expression or articulation may legitimately be considered as embodying a principle of individuation" (*Unending Conversations* 75; *PDC* 370).

Burke identifies three critical points in the process of purgation or purification—the poet being "cleansed" of his "extra-poetic materiality" when he hits upon his theme and starts tracking down its implications; when "he becomes so deeply involved in his symbol-system" that it takes over, and "a new quality or order of motives" emerges; when he reaches his goal and fulfillment is complete ("On Catharsis" 364).[18]

Contra-Nietzsche, Burke argues Plato may have formulated his medicine *after* the great tragic playwrights had concocted theirs, but "dialectical transcendence is *logically prior* to drama." Any work translating

> the formless tensions of life into an orderly set of systematically inter-related terms (which make possible a treatment of the tension "in principle," in "entelechial perfection") by the same token provides a kind of transcendence, through having "translated" us into the formal realm of a symbol-system. In fact, *any* orderly terminology "transcends" non-terministic conditions (as a medicology can be said to transcend the diseases it diagnoses and prescribes for, or as any theological, metaphysical, political, historical, etc. theory can be said to transcend the non-symbolic motives to which it imparts form by symbolism). Man's first notable step away from the realm of sheer sensation (that is to say, man's first "transcendence") is probably best got by the spontaneous symbolizing of sensation in poetic imagery. (*PDC* 172-73)

Beyond sheer expression, beyond "turning brute impressions into articulate expressions" (*LSA* 188), there is the cathartic process of unfolding, of successively actualizing initially vague potentialities ("On Catharsis" 364). The terms in a symbol-system mutually imply one another in a *timeless (eternal), cyclical, simultaneity* (like notes in a *chord*), but the terms themselves are *future* to one another as a thinker proceeds in a *temporal, linear sequence* from one to the next (like notes in an *arpeggio*), discovering successively how each in turn is implicit in the others. The futurity of an implicational cycle of terms still to be made explicit is "a cause of great unrest," even if the implicational network is built about the cathartic promise of an ultimate rest ("On Catharsis" 364-65). Insofar as such a cycle of terms is without direction, there would be "cathartic" value in the irreversibility of "narrative or dramatic forms, each with its own unique progression." Such development "gives the feel of going somewhere, even though, in the last analysis, the same cyclic tangle broods over any self-consistent symbol system" ("On Catharsis" 366).[19]

But what Burke contends concerning the articulation of any particular work or network is true of the articulation of language in general, its potentialities still to be made actual causing great unrest, though promising nonetheless ultimate rest at the end of their unfolding. To say the human being is a "symbol-using animal" is by the same token to say the human being is a "transcending animal." There is in language itself "a motive force" calling us to transcend a world without language (*RM* 192). And implicit in language as "a means of transcending brute objects" is the idea of God as "the ultimate transcendence". (*RM* 276)

Per linguam, praeter linguam

À la Nietzsche, Burke goes on his own hunt for the origins of tragedy. (In fact, the degree to which Nietzsche's *Genealogy of Morals* and *Birth of Tragedy* inform the *Symbolic* may be greater than at first appears). Like Nietzsche, he turns to Aeschylus, analyzing the *Oresteia* almost line by line.

But his search for the origins of tragedy leads to a search for the origins of language and a focus on the negative as the essence of language. Burke moved rapidly through the early sections of the first draft of the *Symbolic* ("Poetics, Dramatistically Considered") up through the one on Aeschylus' trilogy. In summer 1952, he published "Form and Persecution in the *Oresteia*" in the *Sewanee Review*, then in fall '52 and winter '53 a long four-part essay in the *Quarterly Journal of Speech* on "A Dramatistic View of the Origins of Language," which he identified as part of his *Ethics* years later (1959) in his initial correspondence with William Rueckert—"the damned trilogy" having split along the way into a tetralogy (*Letters* 3). For the next decade he worked back and forth between the proposed *Symbolic* and *Ethics*, publishing parts of each here and there, though the closest he came to publishing either as a complete volume was *Language as Symbolic Action* and *The Rhetoric of Religion*.

The *Sewanee Review* article (collected in *LSA* 125-38) sits halfway between the section of the 1958 first draft that it summarizes and the *QJS* articles. There Burke argues the *Oresteia* (though not reducible to terms so "biologically absolute") is concerned "with the unresolved conflicts between the verbal and the nonverbal" out of which the verbal arises and in which it is necessarily grounded (*LSA* 136). The persecuting Furies and Orestes' mother, Clytemnaestra, are described as the amphisbaena—what Burke takes to be the mythic representation of "the ultimate dreaming worm" (*LSA* 135) "ever circling back upon itself in enwrapt self-engrossment, the 'mystic' dreaming stage of vegetal metabolism in which the taking in and the giving off merge into one another" (*LSA* 310), "the caterpillar" residing at "the roots of our being" ("Art–and the First Rough Draft of Living" 157), "the sheerly vegetating digestive tract that underlies all human rationality, and out of which emerge the labyrinths of human reason" (*LSA* 135). Burke takes the "purely social justice" celebrated in the *Eumenides'* pageantry at the mythic founding of the Acropolis to be a "dialectical transcending of the basic biological worm" (*LSA* 135).

In light of the "sheer physicality" of life, writes Burke, the human animal is but a "digestive tract with trimmings" (*White Oxen* 282), the human organism "simply one more species of alimentary canal with accessories" ("Art–and the First Rough Draft of Living" 157). Somehow, out of this nonverbal tract there emerge linguistic labyrinths in which we lose immediate contact with the sheer materiality of existence. Though the powers of speech may "guide and protect" us in our "tasks of growth, temporary individual survival, and reproduction" (*White Oxen* 282), they also "cause us to approach the world through a screen of symbolism." This screen, forcing us to "approach reality at one remove," distinguishes us from the dreaming worm and makes us the sort of animal human beings typically are ("Art–and the First Rough Draft of Living" 157).

Thus the body that learns language suffers a kind of "alienation" from nature and its own body (*LSA* 52). Language establishes a "distance" between us and the nonverbal ground of our verbalizing, a distance not felt by organisms "whose relations to nature are more direct" (*LSA* 90). The body that learns language exhibits "an unremitting tendency" to make itself over in the image of his distinctive trait, as if aiming to become like "the pure spirit of sheer words, words so essential that they would not need to be spoken" (*PC* 184). Such a tendency denies our animality even though the action of symbolicity depends upon the resources of physical and biological motion.

Prior to language, we are submerged in nature. However, even then a certain kind of individuality is implicit in the sheer physical centrality of the nervous system whereby food a particular body consumes or pains a particular body suffers belong exclusively to that particular body—a view that Burke considers the logological equivalent of the Thomist view of matter as the *principium individualionis* ("Catharsis: Second View" 107). Then come language and the resulting alienation of nonverbal and verbal. Language "strongly punctuates" physical individuality by making us aware of the centrality of the nervous system" (*LSA* 90). Though we may all "go through the same general set of physiological and psychological processes," each of us is still isolated within his own body since "*universality* of that sort by no means removes the *individuality* intrinsic" to the central nervous system ("Catharsis: Second View" 107). Our alienation is exacerbated further as the *material* reality of the human body in physical association with other bodies, human and non-human, becomes submerged beneath the *ideality* of socio-political communities saturated with the genius of language (*White Oxen* 289-90).

The tension created by the vague and vast implications of language yet to be unfolded is released by speech. Thereafter language points down problematic paths, but out of labyrinthine tangles and turns the ultimate course emerges as the thread of language leads up and out in a long climb to its end—by and through language, beyond language, *per linguam, praeter linguam* ("Linguistic Approach to Problems of Education," 263; *Essays Toward a Symbolic of Motives* 266). Such is Plato's Upward Way, the route of dialectical rather than dramatic cleansing by tears or laughter, purification rather than purgation, transcendence rather than catharsis (*Unending Conversations* 70; *PDC* 361)—the way of death and rebirth.

For there is an analogue of dying (and a corresponding rebirth) in the very form of dialectical mounting, the particulars of the senses subjected to progressive transformation whereby their sensuous immediacy and sensory diversity are left further behind with each advance in generalization, the climb complete in the vision of the One—a *mortification* by means of abstraction, (*GM* 429; *Unending Conversations* 74; *PDC* 367) and *death* the final slaying of image by idea. "Death then becomes the Neo-Platonists' One, the completely abstract, which is technically the divine" ("Thanatopsis for Critics" 374).

In Plato's analogy of the cave, the imagery is reversed—we leave behind the shadow realm of death; the cave where we have been imprisoned or entombed becomes a womb giving birth to a new world where we are free at last, a new world in which "everything is, as it were, shined on by the same sun, the unitary principle discovered en route, so that entities previously considered disparate can henceforth be seen as partakers of a single substance, through being bathed in a common light" (*Unending Conversations* 74; *PDC* 367).

How appropriate then that Keats knew, though there was a lust for life in the brede covering the Grecian Urn, there was an aura of death surrounding it as well.[20] An urn after all is a funerary vessel, a chamber pot for life's remains when life is left behind—although the ashes inside may remain from the conflagration of transcendent sexual union rather than cremation. *Sub specie aeternitatis* transcendental fever is transformed into transcendental chill, though Burke cautions that as only the fever's *benign* aspects remained after consumption's *malign* aspects were left behind, so it is on a wholly benign chill that the poem ends (*GM* 458-59). "Cold Pastoral!" writes Keats, describing an unheard melody with a pastoral theme, or the pastoral last rites rendered by a priest, or the pastoral scene of a transcendental ground ("mortality" left behind for "immortality") from which the "silent form" issues its *epiphany*. Then isolation falls away in rapture, and we *know* . . .

Ordinary knowledge comes via the senses, says Burke, so an extraordinary sensory condition (such as one in which "all nervous impulses 'attitudinally glowed' at once" so that we remained "in a halfway stage of incipience, the *status nascendi* of the pursuit figured on Keat's Grecian Urn") would likewise be felt as knowledge.

> The mystic would thus have a strong conviction that his experience was "noetic," telling him of a "truth" beyond the realm of logical conditions, and accordingly best expressed in terms of the oxymoron. And indeed, why would it not be "knowledge"? For if the taste of a new fruit is knowledge, then certainly the experiencing of a rare and felicitous physical condition would be knowledge too, a report of something from outside the mind, communication with an ultimate, unitary ground. (*RM* 331)

Could not a mystic Plato, Keats, or Burke speak of that which in that moment is *revealed*

> 'Beauty is truth, truth beauty,'—that is all
> Ye know on earth, and all ye need to know.

Imago

Burke observes in the closing pages of the *Grammar* that Jowlett, who devoted a great portion of his life to the translating and interpreting of Plato, fully recognized the Platonic *doctrine* of transcendence but never analyzed the dialogues themselves as *acts* of transcendence. "For not only do they *plead* for transcendence; they are so formed that the end transcends the beginning" (*GM* 421). The same might be justly said of the *Rhetoric* and surmised of the *Symbolic*.

The *Rhetoric*'s culminating passage concludes a dialectical climb to a transcendent end. I believe the *Symbolic*'s culminating passage would have concluded a similar climb. I believe the steps can be found in the final sections of the '58 version (itself unfinished), which examines similarities and differences between dramatic catharsis and dialectical transcendence and in Burke's great essay on Emerson which does the same ("I, Eye, Aye—Concerning Emerson's Early Essay on 'Nature,' and the Machinery of Transcendence" published in 1966 and collected in *Language as Symbolic Action*, pp. 186-200).

Burkes writes in "Platonic Transcendence" of

> an "Upward Way" moving towards some "higher" principle of unity; once this principle is found, a whole ladder of steps is seen to descend from it; thus, reversing his direction, the dialectician can next take a "Downward Way" that brings him back into the realm . . . where he began; but on reentering, he brings with him the unitary principle he has discovered *en route* and the hierarchal design he saw implicit in that principle; accordingly, applying the new mode of interpretation to his original problem, he now has the problem "placed" in terms of the transcendent . . . (*Unending Conversations* 71; *PDC* 361-62)

He continues,

> Insofar as reality is non-symbolic and thus outside the realm
> of the symbol-systems by which we would describe it, to that
> extent reality is being described in terms of what it is not. At
> the point where we have gone from sensory images to ideas
> that transcend the *sensory* image, we might next go beyond
> such ideas in turn by introducing a "mythic" image (an image
> that is interpreted not literally but ironically, since it states the
> new position by analogy, and analogies must be "discount-
> ed"). Such use of "myth" as a step in a dialectic may carry
> the development across a motivational gulf by providing a
> new ground of assertion at some crucial point where a further
> advance is not attainable through strictly logical argument.
> (*Unending Conversations* 72; *PDC* 364)

The image of the Urn as an "object" would be *sensory,* says Burke;
the vision of the Urn as "viaticum" would be *mythic* (*Unending
Conversations* 73; *PDC* 366).

Burke's final step in the Emerson essay is his introduction of such
a mythic image (toward which perhaps the whole *Symbolic* moves) by
reference to book six of the *Aeneid* where early in his journey to the
Underworld Virgil descries a wailing throng stranded on the shore opposite death, the land of life behind them; unburied and hence as yet
unferried to their final abode, those shades are said to have "stretched
forth their hands through love of the farther shore"—

> *Tendebantque manus ripae ulterioris amore.*

> That is the pattern. Whether there is or is not an ultimate
> shore towards which we, the unburied, would cross, tran-
> scendence involves dialectical processes whereby something
> HERE is interpreted *in terms of* something THERE, some-
> thing *beyond* itself. (*LSA* 200)[21]

Does not Burke's image suggest we suffer life and long for death; that
life is imprisonment and death a release? Expelled from and wandering the realms east of Eden, are we not like those wretched shades
ourselves, yearning for the life we knew before the Fall, the Life that
would be ours if we should truly Die?

Stretching forth his hands each day—enthralled in tracking down
and contemplating the interrelationships prevailing among terms of a
system ("Poetic Motive" 60), whether another's or his own; constantly

scrutinizing linguistic operations, how they unfold, what they ultimately hold within themselves; aware that wherever the process can be found, even in *traces*, of considering things "in terms of a broader scope" than terms those particular things themselves allow, "there are the makings of Transcendence" (*LSA* 200)—stretching forth his hands from the land of life and language to the silent shore beyond in "*benign* contemplation of death," Burke is led and would lead us likewise to live "a dying life" (*GM* 222-23).

Representative Summations

"Burke's conception of the relationship between language, mind, body, and reality is informed by (a) *naturalism*, the mean between an anti-scientific idealism and a reductive materialism; and (b) *organicism* (*biology*), the source for hierarchy (an organism's organization) and entelechy (its development). Language is the entelechy of the human organism, generating the mind, the highest (meta-biological) level of a body genetically endowed with the ability to learn language. Language itself mirrors biology (a terminology generating a hierarchy on the path to its entelechy) and possesses its own entelechy (an all-inclusive "nature . . . containing the principle of speech," or NATURE."[22] The system resulting is basically Aristotelian.

However, though Burke's system is Aristotelian, his concept of rhetoric is Platonic. There is no "fall" for Aristotle, but there is for Plato and a corresponding fall for Burke, the consequence of which is a "false" or "fallen" consciousness regarding the relationship between body and mind, nonverbal and verbal, material and ideal, as well as ourselves and others. Being primarily *ontological* rather than *historical*, this fallen consciousness can be characterized on the one hand as Platonic; being a fall into the *ideal* world of language rather than the *material* world, it can be characterized on the other as Marxoid; but being *naturalistic* (i.e., being primarily neither idealistic as with Plato nor materialistic as supposed with Marx, but acknowledging both the material and the ideal as *natural*), it is more Aristotelian than either (unless like Burke one considers Marx a naturalist and an Aristotelian).[23]

Consistent with Plato, *rhetoric* leaves us mired in this fallen realm; only *dialectic* can mystically lift us from it. All rhetoric (i.e., action for the sake of some purpose) is always to some degree self-defeating; every attempt to compensate for or overcome the imbalances and conflicts that characterize the human condition leads to but further imbalance and conflict. Only dialectic (i.e., linguistic action for itself alone) leads to true, though momentary, transcendence. No linguistic action is ultimately efficacious other than *purely* linguistic action effecting transcendence through dialectic (the preferred route) or catharsis through drama (the less preferred in that drama mixes dialectic and rhetoric). The problem being language, the only solution is more of the same—rhetoric's giving way to dialectic (i.e., a true and transcendent Rhetoric as with Plato) that overcomes the imbalance or conflict between body and mind, nonverbal and verbal, material and ideal, the conflict between ourselves and others, and for the moment makes us whole.

The *cause* of this fall can be traced to language which in its thorough ("cathartic") operation turns distinctions (such as mind and body) into divisions. The remedy is likewise found in language which in its thorough (dialectical and in the Crocean sense "cathartic") operation overcomes divisions. The cause is too much language, the cure more of the same—a "homeopathic" approach Burke characterizes as Aristotelian.

But the *ultimate cause* must be traced to the very nature of things (the existence of time and space and thus of distinction and potential division between parts which language in its thorough operation makes actual)—a "proto-fall" for which language provides no remedy. The ultimate remedy lies only in an end to the nature of things—the *escaton*. Language provides temporary solace by generating an experience of wholeness through drama and (preferably) dialectic. But the experience of wholeness is shattered by (linguistic) action of any kind. The experience can be maintained only by a constant repetition of drama or dialectic. The eternal repetition which at first provides solace eventually becomes a source of despair from which *death* is the only escape, a position characteristic of Zen Buddhism in which the Nirvana of *nothingness* and *oblivion* is sought. Thus, action is depreciated by Burke, the only action sanctioned being incipient (or more accurately, substitutive): an *attitude* of Neo-Stoic resignation *à la* Spinoza.

NOTES

1. The question of how systematic Burke actually may be is subject to ongoing debate. Burke's system is not readily apparent because he was an autodidact with a dense and difficult highly personal (not to say jargon-laden) style. Had he stayed at Columbia he might have proven easier to categorize

and read, but within the strait-jacket of academe he might never have become the protean thinker beloved by his admirers. From the *Grammar* on Burke clearly thinks he is being systematic, the question thereafter being whether he abandoned "dramatism" following the *Rhetoric* with the development of "logology," though Burke himself claims dramatism is his ontology and logology his epistemology ("Dramatism and Logology," *The [London] Times Literary Supplement*, August 12, 1983, p. 859). Burke's never publishing his proposed *Symbolic* is also supposed as grounds for arguing he abandoned dramatism. Clearly the author believes otherwise. Burke's thought is systematic though its expression may be more like that of a poet than a philosopher, more Plato than Aristotle.

2. Correspondence, partial publication, and the manuscript itself indicate the bulk of the unfinished second draft of the *Symbolic of Motives* (hereafter the *SM* for "Symbolic," its running header) can reasonably be dated 1961-63, though the history of the complete manuscript is complex going back to the last sections of the first draft (hereafter the *PDC* for "Poetics, Dramatistically Considered," the manuscript's title). In a sense Burke was already revising the first draft before distributing it in 1958. Not only does Burke indicate the first draft is incomplete (*PDC* ms. p 374); in addition "The Poetic Motive," the last section of the first draft (*PDC* ms. pp 375-391) becomes the first section of the second draft (*SM* ms. pp. 1-17) with virtually no change. The section is published in *Hudson Review* 11 (Spring 1958): 54-63. Other parts of the *PDC* published after 1958 with virtually no change (e.g., "Catharsis (Second View)," *Centennial Review of Arts and Science* 5 (Spring 1961): 107-32) may have been intended like "The Poetic Motive" for the revised *SM*.

Burke indicates to Malcolm Cowley in a series of letters from 1961 that he is now working hard on revising the *Symbolic* (see David Williams, "Toward Rounding Out the *Motivorum Trilogy*," *Unending Conversations*, p. 16). On the other hand 1963 appears to be the date for Burke's completion of "Part Two" of the second draft covering *SM* ms. pp. 223-269 (the point at which the manuscript breaks off). "Part Two" is a major revision of "The Thinking of the Body" section from the first draft covering ms. pp. 76-179. The essay "The Thinking of the Body (Comments on the Imagery of Catharsis in Literature)," published in *Psychoanalytic Review* 50 (Fall 1963) and collected in *Language as Symbolic Action* (pp. 308-343), is drawn almost entirely from the *PDC* except for most of the last two sections (*LSA* pp. 308-30 and 330-43, respectively). There Burke writes (*LSA* p. 341) that as he works he is living on a Florida key—in fact Englewood, Florida from the end of December 1962 through the middle of March 1963, where he was working on the *Symbolic* among other things. Burke specifies in the *SM* (ms. p. 265) exactly what he has cut out of the section from the *PDC* and indicates he plans to publish the material in a separate monograph (i.e., the above mentioned essay). Burke has probably completed the *SM* material too, since he receives news on March 4th that William Carlos Williams has died. Thereafter he appears to be caught up in innumerable projects, especially those involving his budding relationship with the University of California Press, and from 1967 until her death in 1969 his wife's illness.

3. A similar though less thorough discussion can be found in the *PDC*—e.g., "Embracing such words as 'arms' and 'articulate,' the root of the word 'artistic' is apparently related to a Greek word meaning 'to join.' (Further back, in Sanskrit, there were related roots meaning 'to attain' and 'to fit.')" Summing up the discussion of previous pages Burke says, "the etymological inklings in the word 'artistic' point towards *dialectic*, or *articulation*, with appropriate modes of generalization and specification—and this trend would come to a head in principles of *classification* (as with the order of the terms in a Platonic list of classes arranged like the rungs of a ladder)" (4-5).

4. Burke adds parenthetically, "Later in this text, we shall consider Poe's proposition that 'the most poetical topic for the ideal lyric is a beautiful woman dead" (*SM* 32-33)—suggesting the *SM* will turn ultimately to the consideration of "beauty" (traditionally the end of poetics and aesthetics) and "death" (which Burke associates with perfection and the end of dialectic as well as "rebirth.")

5. Burke's exact phrasing is important given the claim: "though what we mean by pure persuasion in the absolute sense exists nowhere, *it can be present as a motivational ingredient in any rhetoric*" (*RM* 269); and "as the ultimate of all persuasion, its form or archetype, there is pure persuasion. . . . The important consideration is that, *in any device, the ultimate form (paradigm or idea) of that device is present, and is acting*. And this form would be the 'purity'" (*RM* 273-74). Emphases mine.

6. See also *RM* 218 where Burke discusses Shakespeare's *Venus and Adonis* and the "antinomian yet intimate relation between love and war" where he characterizes the marriage between Venus and Mars as "a love match that is itself a kind of war."

7. Burke phrased his definition in precisely this manner during a dinner conversation with Barbara Biesecker and me among others on November 5, 1987 at the SCA Convention in Boston. Burke's phrasing echoes his 1985 essay "In Haste" (p. 330): ". . . our bodies being physiologically in the realm of nonsymbolic motion, but genetically endowed with the ability to learn a kind of verbal behavior I call symbolic action." See also his 1978 essay "(Nonsymbolic) Motion/(Symbolic) Action" (pp. 811-12): " . . . our anthropoid ancestors underwent a momentous mutation. In their bodies (as physiological organisms in the realm of motion) there developed the ability to learn the kind of tribal idiom that is here meant by symbolic action." And ". . . the mutation that makes speech possible is itself inherited in our nature as physical bodies." See also his 1981 essay "Variations on 'Providence'": "But unlike all

other earthly animals (to our knowledge) the human kind is *genetically, physiologically, materially* endowed with the ability to learn the kind of language which Logology would call 'symbolic action'" (*On Human Nature* 274).

8. Burke goes on to observe both dialectic and drama "treat of persons and their characteristic thoughts"—though the dialectic of Platonic dialogue stresses the thoughts held by persons, while drama stresses the persons holding the thoughts. Still, "in both forms the element of personality figures"—though "dialectic can dispense with formal division into cooperatively competing voices." The thoughts can still be "vibrant with personality," but they are considered "various aspects of the same but somewhat inconsistent personality, rather than as distinct characters in various degrees of agreement and disagreement" as in Platonic dialogue (*LSA* 188).

9. See also *LSA* 125, fn 1.

10. In a critical passage in the *Rhetoric* (180—the end of "Part II"), Burke distinguishes between the *nonverbal* (by which he means the "visceral"), the *postverbal* ("the unutterable complexities to which the implications of words themselves give rise") and the *superverbal* (whatever would be the "jumping-off place" if we went "through the verbal to the outer limits of the verbal")—i.e., the superverbal not as "nature minus speech, but nature as the ground of speech, hence *nature as itself containing the principle of speech*," an all-inclusive nature that would be not less-than but more-than-verbal (or NATURE to make the distinction clear and the phrase concise), Burke's equivalent to Spinoza's "God or Nature" (though the elements or attributes are reversed).

Unlike Spinoza, however, Burke does not forget the phenomenal character of his starting point. Spinoza describes the finite in terms of the infinite, his metaphysical propositions assuming the character of assertions about external reality; his one infinite divine substance possesses an infinite number of attributes of which we know but two, *thought* and *extension* ("God" and "Nature" being the names we respectively give them), *mind* and *body* constituting their finite modifications or modes. Burke describes the infinite in terms of the finite, his metabiological propositions being projections of the human; his infinite "*nature* [equivalent to *extension*] . . . containing the principle of *speech*" [equivalent to *thought*] is an extension of the finite "*body* genetically endowed with the ability to learn *language*" [equivalent to *mind*] —i.e., our phenomenally limited (anthropocentric) view of ultimate being is of human being writ large.

11. Burke does not seem altogether consistent in his use of the term "fragments" in the *Rhetoric*. Of course one could always argue (as Burke himself undoubtedly would) that however the notion is named, the idea is still inherent in the system. Still it is instructive to examine Burke's usage.

Burke says, for example, "Empirically, what theologians discuss as the ultimate Oneness of God is equivalent to the ultimate oneness of the linguistic principle." And from what has been argued, he would seem to suggest here that that principle operates in part or as a "fragment" in all language use. But he goes on, "Rhetoric is thus made from fragments of dialectic." His explanation: Expression "as persuasion, seeks to escape from infancy by breaking down the oneness of an intuition into several terms, or voices. It defines by partisanship, by determination. These terms may bring clarifications that are themselves confusions on another level" (*RM* 175-76). The discussion calls to mind an earlier discussion: "The notion of the Son as bringer of light seems in its essence to suggest that the division of the part from the whole is enlightening, a principle that might be stated dialectically thus: Partition provides *terms*; thereby it allows the parts to comment upon another. But this 'loving' relation allows for the 'fall' into terms antagonistic in their partiality, until dialectically resolved by reduction to 'higher' terms" (*RM* 140). In these passages and others, "fragments" suggests pieces divorced from or *apart from* the whole.

But elsewhere "fragments" suggests pieces that retain some aspect of the whole, that are somewhat or somehow connected to or *a part of* the whole—in which two cases (*RM* 331) the term is bracketed in quotation marks. Burke, for example, contrasts mysticism and its "fragments" with "substitutes" for mysticism that involve "the transforming of means into ends"—false mysticisms of money or crime or drugs or *war* (*RM* 331-32).

Overall, the term seems to retain the ambiguity of the rhetoric-dialectic relationship, of voices *cooperating in competition* versus voices *competing in cooperation*, of *opposition* versus *apposition*.

The ambiguity of mysticism versus false mysticism (and the ambiguity of "fragments" as well) continues to the end of the *Rhetoric*: "Mysticism [including false mysticism?] is no rare thing. True, the attaining of it in its pure state is rare." Does Burke mean a "true" or "real" state as opposed to a false one? or some other kind of state such as "pure" versus "impure," that is, mixed with the *ersatz*? He continues: "And its secular analogues [the "secular" contrasted with the "sacred" or "pure"? the "social" contrasted with the "cosmic"?], in grand or gracious symbolism, are rare. But the need for it, the itch, is everywhere [*à la* Augustine?—see fn. 12 below]. And by hierarchy it is intensified." (*RM* 332-33)

Mysticism (?), says Burke, can exist "under many guises" in hierarchy. Anagogically the conditions of the "divine," the goadings of "mystery" reside in hierarchy (*RM* 333). In his "Definition of Man" Burke says that in his *Rhetoric* he tried to trace the relationship between social hierarchy and mystery. He concedes that should the fourth clause of his definition, "goaded by the spirit of hierarchy," sound too weighted, he could settle instead for "moved by a sense of order." He then points to E. M. Forster's *A Passage to India* "for its ingenious ways of showing how social mystery can become interwoven with cosmic mystery"; and Castiglione's *Book of the Courtier* for nicely bringing out two kinds of "worship," kneeling on one knee to the sovereign and on both knees to God; and the ancient Roman application of the term *pontifex maximus*to the Emperor to specifically recognize his "bridging" relationship as the head of the social hierarchy and as a god (*LSA* 15-16).

But given that "the mystery [social and cosmic?] of the hierarchic is forever with us," writes Burke in the final paragraph of the *Rhetoric*, let us

> scrutinize its range of entrancements, both with dismay and in delight. And finally let us observe, all about us, forever goading us, though it be in fragments [meant in all its ambiguity?], the motive that attains its ultimate identification in the thought, not of the universal holocaust, but of the universal order—as with the rhetorical and dialectical symmetry of the Aristotelian metaphysics, whereby all classes of being are hierarchically arranged in a chain or ladder or pyramid of mounting worth, each kind striving towards the perfection of its kind, and so towards the kind next above it, while the strivings of the entire series head in God as the beloved cynosure and sinecure, the end of all desire. (*RM* 333)

12. Burke's own system can be profitably considered in regard to Augustine's famous aphorism and modern theologian Paul Tillich's rendering of it—God is the end of all our striving, that with which we are ultimately concerned. For Augustine and Tillich the *theistic* motive (though it may not be recognized as such) inspirits all aspects of our lives, so no account of human motivation is complete without it. The motive might be misdirected toward other ends (wealth, power, glory—other "gods") but no substitute could fully satisfy. The theistic motive in Augustine and Tillich is apparently secularized as the *hierarchic* motive in Burke. The end of all striving is not God but a principle (such as money) that infuses all levels of a particular hierarchy and functions as God. Thus sheerly worldly powers take on the attributes of secular divinity and demand our worship. For Burke, though, the hierarchic motive itself is ultimately *linguistic*. And the linguistic motive is ultimately *natural*—meaning the natural world would encompass more than the merely material (see *RM* 180). The end of all linguistic striving then would be that NATURE which gives birth not simply to our bodies but also to language and our minds. Thus the *theism* of Augustine and Tillich is transformed into the *naturalism* of Burke in which it is NATURE that has made us symbol-using animals and our hearts are restless until our symbols bring us to rest in IT. See Thames, "The Gordian Not" 29.

13. Burke's contention is particularly apt given Mircea Eliade's analysis of the centrality of sex and victimage in his study of the archaic ontology implicit in myth and ritual (*Myth of the Eternal Return*; see also Richard H. Thames, *Mystical Ontology in Kenneth Burke* [dss.])

According to Eliade, myths testify to archaic man's terror of losing contact with *being* (the eternal and sacred) by allowing himself to be overwhelmed in the process of *becoming* (the temporal and profane). When archaic man repeats an archetypal gesture (at essential moments such as a New Year, birthday or anniversary; a rite of passage; a founding) his action not only repeats but also coincides with an archetype initiated by the gods *ab origine*, at the beginning of time. By repeating such a gesture he escapes from becoming and maintains contact with being; he abolishes and projects himself out of profane into primordial or mythic time: he returns and is witness to *Creation*. Thus his rituals evince a thirst not only for the *ontic* but also the *static*. Such repetition enables him to maintain contact with being in all its plenitude; such repetition enables him to live like the mystic in a continual, atemporal present by generating a cyclical structure for time.

According to Eliade, "sex" and "victimage" were central to primitive festivals in which time and space were ritually abolished and regenerated. Both constitute repetitions of the *cosmogony*—the act of Creation. *Sexual intercourse* ritually repeated the *hierogamy*, the union of heaven and earth resulting in the cosmos' birth. In the Babylonian New Year festival the king and a temple slave reproduced the hierogamy, a ritual to which there corresponded a period of collective orgy. Intercourse and orgy represent chaos and a rebirth of the universe. It was also during New Year festivals that demons, diseases, and sins were expelled in ceremonies of various types, all involving some form of *victimage*. According to Sir James Frazer (in that part of the *Golden Bough* entitled the *Scapegoat*) the "riddance of evil" was accomplished by transferring it to something (a material object, an animal, or a human being) and expelling that thing (now bearing the faults of the entire community) beyond inhabited territory. With the scapegoat's sacrifice, chaos was slain. Such ritual purification means a combustion, an annulling of the sins and faults of the individual and the community as a whole—not a mere purifying, but a regeneration, a new birth.

Both sex and victimage repeat the cosmogony. Both represent attempts, in the words of Eliade, "to restore—if only momentarily—mythical and primordial time, 'pure' time, the time of the 'instant' of the Creation" (*Myth* 54). *In illo tempore* the gods had displayed their greatest powers, the cosmogony being "the supreme divine manifestation, the paradigmatic act of strength, superabundance, and creativity." Religious man, says Eliade, thirsts for the real. "By every means at his disposal, he seeks to reside at the very source of primordial reality, when the world *was in statu nascendi*" (*The Sacred and the Profane* 80).

Burke argues that Aristophanic comedy culminates in secularized variants of the "sacred marriage" (the hierogamy) and the "love feast" whereas tragedy culminates in ritual sacrifice, victimage, the "kill" ("On Catharsis" 348, 362).

See endnote 14 below.

14. See endnote 13 above. The mystic state would involve annulment of the here and now and absorption into the Absolute which would be formless as opposed to form in time and space and therefore chaotic as the ground of creation, nothing as opposed to all that is, the womb of plenitude out of which the world is born—pure being.

15. Later in his analysis Burke adds in a footnote

In the light of what we have said about the deathiness of immortality, and the relation between the erotic and the thought of a "dying," perhaps we might be justified in reading the last line of the great "Bright Star!" sonnet as naming states not simply alternative but also synonymous:

And so live ever—or else swoon to death.

This use of the love-death equation is as startlingly paralleled in a letter to Fanny Brawne:

I have two luxuries to brood over in my walks, your loveliness and the hour of my death. O that I could take possession of them both in the same moment. (*GM* 456)

16. See Burke's own piece, "The 'Anaesthetic Revelation' of Herone Liddell" (*White Oxen* 255-310), cited by Burke himself ("Catharsis—Second View" 119-20; *PDC* 340), in which the protagonist,

a "word-man" recovering from the ill effects of surgery, becomes engrossed in studying the death of Keats, as revealed through Keats's letters. Here, by critically re-enacting the death of a "perfect" poet, the word-man in effect uses Keats as cathartic victim. But the cathartic principle is broken into other fragments also, as for instance, in shell-gathering, in speculations on the sea as life-giving charnel house, and in the change of scene, itself designed to be curative.

Burke takes the title from William James' *Varieties of Religious Experience* from which Burke takes excerpts of excerpts, assembling the "cullings into one consecutive, dithrambic but rambling account, which should give a composite portrait of the experience, [the] mystic state" (*RM* 328-29).

17. "On Catharsis or Resolution, with a Postscript" (*Kenyon Review* 21 (Summer 1959): 337-75) is commonly supposed to have been drawn from the *PDC* section on "Catharsis (First View)" written in 1951 (ms. pp.38-56). Actually parts of the essay are taken verbatim from the first draft, but parts can also be found verbatim in the second! In 1959 Burke indicated in his first exchange with William Rueckert (*Letters from Kenneth Burke to William H. Rueckert: 1959-1987*, p. 4) that the "Symbolic" was somewhat delayed

because unfortunately "some other possibilities turned up—and I couldn't resist tracing them down." Still he hoped to complete the Poetics' "final bits" in the fall of that year—"a section on comic catharsis, for instance, though the general lines [were] already indicated" in his essay "On Catharsis." He also hoped "to make clearer the relation btw. dramatic catharsis and Platonic (dialectic)/ transcendence" though he thought Rueckert would also agree that he had "already indicated the main lines in that connection," again in "On Catharsis" as well as elsewhere (e.g., the final sections of the *PDC*). Burke appears to have thought the "Symbolic" through to the end and did not anticipate its taking much longer to finish.

Burke adds at the end of "Platonic Transcendence" in the *PDC* (375):

> We may not be able, at this time, to complete our remarks on Comedy. [How ironic that *Burke's remarks are incomplete and Aristotle's lost*, a situation Burke surely found fitting.] But here is, roughly, the sort of things to be treated: First, by using as [a] model the three comedies of Aristophanes on peace, we shall be able to dwell on the pleasing antics of peace. We want to consider the relation between wholly cathartic laughter and derision. We want to ask in particular about the role of "body-thinking" in Aristophanic comedy. We want to inquire further about laughter, tears, and appetite, as regards the materials of poetic form. (*Unending Conversations* 77; *PDC* 374)

Burke's comment about completing "a section on comic catharsis" coincides with plans from the *PDC* but his comment about hoping "to make clearer the relation between dramatic catharsis and Platonic (dialectic)/ transcendence" takes things a step further. Clearly then, the essay is of considerable importance, indicating the direction the unfinished second draft may have taken.

In fact the distribution of the PDC in the Summer of 1958; the publication of "The Poetic Motive" (the essay included at the end of the PDC and moved to the front of the SM) in Spring 1958; the publication of "On Catharsis" in Summer 1959 and the presence of verbatim sections in the SM; and Burke's comments in the letter to Rueckert on 8 August 1959 vis-à-vis material in "Beyond Catharsis" and "Platonic Transcendence" as well as comments on what remains to be done on page 375 of the PDC, suggest that pages 362-68 from "On Catharsis" may constitute a sketch for the remainder of "A Symbolic of Motives."

Other essays published between 1959 and 1966 may contain additional clues—e.g. "Rhetoric and Poetics" (a talk presented at a Symposium on the History and Significance of Rhetoric under the auspices of the UCLA Classics Department in May 1965 and collected in *LSA* 295-307) as well as the extensive footnotes in *LSA*.

18. Burke continues: "Corresponding stages may be ascribed to the reader, or to the work itself, as with the different qualities of beginning,

peripety, and end, analyzed without reference to either reader or writer" ("On Catharsis" 364).

19. Such translation of the logical into the temporal is the subject of Burke's essay on Poe's "The Philosophy of Composition" which he promises to discuss later (*SM* 129). He does discuss Poe's essay in his own "The Principle of Composition" (*Poetry* 99, October 961, 46-53) which he tells Rueckert will be used in some form in the *Symbolic* (*Letters* 31-32). See also "Poetics in Particular, Language in General" (*LSA* 25-43).

20. Burke quotes Bernard Blackstone who in *The Consecrated Urn* (332) observes that in the original draft the line "And silent as a consecrated urn" read "And silent as a corpse upon a pyre" (see "As I Was Saying" 21).

21. The first reference to this image appears on p. 363 of the essay "On Catharsis"; Burke describes it again in "Rhetoric and Poetics" (*LSA* 298); and he expands on it in the Emerson essay published in 1966 about the time he would have been returning to the *Symbolic* after finishing *LSA* and prior to the diagnosis of his wife's malady sometime between late 1966 and early 1967.

22. See Thames, "The Gordian Not: Untangling the *Motivorum*. Part One: Seeking the Symbolic." *KB Journal* (*Kenneth Burke Society Journal* online at *kbjournal.org*), Spring 2007.

23. In his *Grammar* (200-14) Burke argues that, so far as dramatistic terminology is concerned, Marxist philosophy begins by grounding *agent* in *scene* but requires a systematic featuring of *act* given its poignant concern for ethics; in other words, that Marx, an "idealistic materialist," should be grammatically classified with Aristotle and Spinoza as a "realist" (or "naturalist")—like Burke! Consequently, Burke offers "a tentative restatement of Marxist doctrine formed about the act of class struggle"—a "somewhat Spinozistic" characterization consistent with Soviet philosophical thought during the 1920s and '30s but also with Burke's own philosophical stance. (See G. L. Kline, *Spinoza in Soviet Philosophy*, London: Routledge Kegan Paul, 1952.)

Burke accepts the idealistic-materialistic dialectic as descriptive of the dynamic underlying social change but not the Marxist escatology—*sub specie aeternitatis* all revolutions are essentially the same, ultimately leading to but another revolution, one system of inequality being replaced by another perhaps for some period more adequate to the demands of a particular time and place. (See Thames, "The Gordian Not: Untangling the *Motivorum*. Part One: Seeking the Symbolic.")

Not only does Burke assimilate Marx to Spinoza and Aristotle and the naturalist tradition in the *Grammar*, he assimilates him to Plato and the dialectical development of terms in the *Rhetoric* (183-97). There Burke distinguishes between three orders of terms: the *positive* that names visible and tangible things which can be located in time and place; the *dialectical* (i.e., says Burke, dialectical "as we use the term *in this particular connection*") that permeates the positive realm but is itself more concerned with ideas than things, more with action and attitude than perception, more with ethics and form than knowledge and information; and the *ultimate* (or *mystical*) that places the dialectical (actually from context, the rhetorical—see above) competition of voices in a hierarchy or sequence or evaluative series, a developmental series ordered by a "guiding idea" or unitary principle, transforming the competing voices into "successive positions or moments in a single process" (*RM* 183-87). The dialectic development typical of Platonic dialogue is the instance *par excellence* of the third order (see the discussion above in "*Bellus*").

Burke contends the Marxist dialectic gains much of its strength by conforming to an *ultimate* order. Rather than confronting one another merely as parliamentary voices representing conflicting interests, various classes are instead hierarchically arranged, each with a disposition or "consciousness" matching its peculiar set of circumstances, "while the steps from feudal to bourgeois to proletarian are grounded in the very nature of the universe" (*RM* 190).

The assimilation of Marx to Spinoza and Plato are both examples of Burke's tendency to de-historicize—to *essentialize the temporal* rather than *temporize the essential* (see Trevor Melia's "Scientism and Dramatism" in *The Legacy of Kenneth Burke*, edited by Herbert W. Simons and Trevor Melia, Madison: University of Wisconsin Press, 1989, pp. 66-67).

WORKS CITED

Blackstone, Bernard. *The Consecrated Urn, An Interpretation of Keats in Terms of Growth and Form.* London: Longmans Green, 1959; reprint 1962.

Burke, Kenneth. "The Anaesthetic Revelation of Herone Liddell." *Complete White Oxen: Collected Short Fiction of Kenneth Burke.* Berkeley: University of California Press, 1968. 255-310.

— . "Art—and the First Rough Draft of Living." *Modern Age* 8 (1964): 155-65.

— . "Beyond Catharsis." "Poetics, Dramatistically Considered." Ms., 1958. 281-320. Also in *Unending Conversations: New Writings by and about Kenneth Burke.* Eds. Greig Henderson and David Cratis Williams. Carbondale: Southern Illinois University Press, 2001. 52-64.

— . *Collected Poems: 1915-1967.* Berkeley: University of California Press, 1968.

— . *The Complete White Oxen: Collected Short Fiction of Kenneth Burke.* Berkeley: University of California Press, 1968.

— . "Catharsis—Second View." *Centennial Review of Arts and Science* 5 (1961): 107-132.

— . "Dramatism." *Communication: Concepts and Perspectives.* Ed. Lee Thayer. Washington, DC: Spartan Books, 1967. 327-352. Also abridged in *International Encyclopedia of the Social Sciences 7.* New York: Macmillan and Free Press, 1968. 445-452.

— . "Dramatism and Logology." *Times Literary Supplement.* 12 August. 1983: 859.

— . *Dramatism and Development.* Barre, MA: Clark University Press with Barre Publishers, 1972.

— . *A Grammar of Motives.* Berkeley: University of California Press, 1969.

— . *Language as Symbolic Action: Essays on Life, Literature, and Method.* Berkeley: University of California Press, 1966.

— . "Linguistic Approach to Problems of Education." *Modern Philosophies and Education.* Ed. Nelson B. Henry. National Society for the Study of Education Year Book 54. Chicago: National Society for the Study of Education; University of Chicago Press, 1955: 259-303. Also abridged in *Essays Toward a Symbolic of Motives, 1950-1955.* Ed. William H. Rueckert. West Lafayette, IN: Parlor Press, 2006. 261-282.

— . "On Catharsis, or Resolution, with a Postscript." *Kenyon Review* 20 (1958): 337-375.

— . "The Orestes Trilogy." *Essays Toward a Symbolic of Motives: 1950-1955.* Ed. William H. Rueckert. West Lafayette, IN: Parlor Press, 2006. 103-147.

— . *Permanence and Change: An Anatomy of Purpose.* 3d ed. Berkeley: University of California Press, 1984.

— . "The Poetic Motive." *Hudson Review* 40 (1958): 54-63.

— . "Poetics, Dramatistically Considered." Ms., 1958.

— . "The Principle of Composition." *Poetry* 99 (1961): 46-53. Also in *Terms for Order.* Ed. Stanley Edgar Hyman with the assistance of Barbara Karmiller. Bloomington: Indiana University Press (A Midland Book), 1964. 189-98.

— . *A Rhetoric of Motives.* Berkeley: University of California Press, 1969.

— . *The Rhetoric of Religion: Studies in Logology.* Berkeley: University of California Press, 1970.

— . "A Symbolic of Motives." Ms., 1963 (?).

— . "Thanatopsis for Critics: A Brief Thesaurus of Deaths and Dying." *Essays in Criticism* 2 (1952): 369-375.

Eliade, Mircea. *The Myth of the Eternal Return: Cosmos and History.* Princeton, NJ: Princeton University Press (Bollingen paperback), 1971.

— . *The Sacred and the Profane.* New York: Harcourt, Brace & World (Harvest Book), 1959.

Henderson, Greig and David Cratis Williams (eds). *Unending Conversations: New Writings by and about Kenneth Burke.* Carbondale: Southern Illinois University Press, 2001.

Kline, G. L. *Spinoza in Soviet Philosophy*. London: Routledge Kegan Paul, 1952.

Knight, G. Wilson. *Starlit Dome: Studies in the Poetry of Vision*. London: Methuen, 1941.

Nietzsche, Friedrich. *The Birth of Tragedy and Other Writings*. Raymond Geuss and Ronald Speirs (eds). Cambridge: Cambridge University Press, 1999.

Rueckert, William H. (ed). *Essays Toward a Symbolic of Motives: 1950-1955*. West Lafayette, IN: Parlor Press, 2006.

— (ed). *Letters from Kenneth Burke to William H. Rueckert: 1959-1987*. West Lafayette, IN: Parlor Press, 2002.

Rueckert, William H., and Angelo Bonadonna (eds). *On Human Nature: A Gathering Where Everything Flows, 1967-1984*. Berkeley: University of California Press, 2003.

Simons, Herbert W. and Trevor Melia (eds). *The Legacy of Kenneth Burke*. Madison: University of Wisconsin Press, 1989

Thames, Richard. "The Gordian Not." *Kenneth Burke Journal*, Spring 2007.

— . "Mystical Ontology in Kenneth Burke: Consequences for His Theory of Rhetoric." Dissertation. University of Pittsburgh. 1979.

— . "Nature's Physician: The Metabiology of Kenneth Burke." *Kenneth Burke and the 21st Century*. Ed. Bernard L. Brock. SUNY Series in Speech Communication. Albany: State University of New York Press, 1998. 19-34.

Walker, Jeffrey. *Rhetoric and Poetics in Antiquity*. Oxford: Oxford University Press, 2000.

An earlier shorter version of this paper was presented at the 2011 Southern States Communication Convention in Little Rock, Arkansas.

PEDAGOGY

Pedagogy is on the Web at
http://dukeupress/pedagogy

As a journal dealing exclusively with pedagogical issues, *Pedagogy* is intended as a forum for critical reflection and as a site for spirited and informed debate from a multiplicity of positions and perspectives. It strives to reverse the long-standing marginalization of teaching and the scholarship produced around it and instead to assert the centrality of teaching to our work as scholars and professionals."

Writing Time: Composing in an Accelerated World

Jeanne Marie Rose's article explores how composition courses might address contemporary capitalism's strain on students' time resources through a classroom practice of temporal awareness. The piece discusses two related dimensions of this approach. The first involves incorporating students' considerations of time into course content; the second, rooted in teacher inquiry, asks writing instructors to examine how time mediates the pedagogical relationships developed within their courses. As Rose writes succinctly about the purpose of her project,

> With students at all kinds of institutions confronting capitalism's cultural acceleration, compositionists have a shared stake in making time a central concern of writing pedagogy. This project complements scholars' ongoing

attention to the economics of English studies, particularly the privatization of the university (Downing, Hurlbert, and Mathieu 2002; Ohmann 2003) and the casualization of academic labor (Schell 1998; Schell and Stock 2001; Bousquet, Scott, and Parascondola 2004). It also extends compositionists' recent attention to students' working lives (Bousquet 2008; Lu and Horner 2009; Scott 2009). My goal in this essay, while linked to these broader investigations, is to situate time in the context of our interactions with our students and our classes.

Rose's essay asserts the centrality of pedagogy within the very material lives of faculty and students. By focusing on the materiality of time, she asks us to question our assumptions about best practices (e.g., process pedagogy) while also placing the discussion within contemporary attention to the economics of English studies.

10 Writing Time: Composing in an Accelerated World

Jeanne Marie Rose

Barreling down the highway on my way to campus, weighing the odds of getting a speeding ticket versus being late for class, I glimpsed a billboard advertisement for my college: "It's Your Time," it announced. Glancing again at my dashboard clock, I wondered, "Time for *what?*" Educators in English are profoundly aware that it is not a particularly advantageous time to be a college student. It is a time when time itself has become a dwindling resource for students, who increasingly define themselves as employees, parents, practiced multitaskers, and wary victims of downsizing and less as individuals whose primary identification is as students. Just as I should have known better than to assume I could make up for lost time by driving faster, I cannot help but think that we in English studies should be doing more to develop writing pedagogies that address students' experience of time in an era of global capitalism.

We understand that speed and efficiency are necessary to the worldwide circulation of goods, services, and finance; we are familiar with the "just in time" arrival of products and materials to eliminate idle time in warehouses. Nevertheless, many faculty members persist in viewing teaching and learning as humanist pursuits free of market forces. Geographer David Harvey (2005) provides a helpful frame for recognizing the extent to which capitalist constructions of time permeate our classrooms. Harvey associates the push to efficiency with a neoliberal political system wherein states profess an abiding faith in the regulatory capabilities of the market. In the name of political freedom, Harvey explains, neoliberalism purports to champion minimal state interference, except in cases where state intervention enables the privatization of formerly public sectors—such as education—and allows for the creation of new markets and increased circulation of capital. As Harvey points out, the neoliberal values of speed, efficiency, individual freedom, and competition are consequently "incorporated into the common-sense way many of us interpret, live in, and understand the world" (3). Socialized within a neoliberal system that values ever-faster production and consumption, today's students often come to college hoping to expend minimal time to accrue maximum capital—grades, future employment, and a salary that allows them to pay off their student loans. As this market logic infuses pedagogical relationships and shapes classroom community, writing pedagogy's commitment to process, revision, and collaboration becomes particularly vulnerable.

In recent years, scholars in composition have been steering the field toward an increased awareness of the dissonance between writing process pedagogy as it is conventionally imagined and contemporary students' experience of time. As Bruce Horner (2000: 35) has observed, composition scholarship needs to pay more attention to students' "unmet material needs," including "lack of time." Johnathon Mauk (2003: 372) raises similar concerns about community college students' "ongoing race through time." Amy Robillard (2003: 75), writing in response to the long-range time horizons invoked in Lynn Z. Bloom's "Freshman Composition as a Middle-Class Enterprise" (1996), asks composition studies to recognize that the "different ways of conceiving of time are class-based." Implicit in these assertions is an awareness that composition pedagogy, with its characteristic treatment of writing as a recursive process requiring multiple drafts, demands more time than many students possess. One community college instructor puts it bluntly: "We can say, 'Writing is a process' until we're purple, but when people have a full-time job, all these kids, three other classes . . . [t]hey sit down and crank it out the night before because that's all the time they got" (Mauk 2003: 373).

Although composition studies has tended to associate time limitations with working-class populations like Mauk's students, privileged students are also having to compress many activities into a single day, often in the interest of graduating as competitive candidates in an unpredictable job market. This career anxiety and its ramifications for students of varying class identifications can be attributed to the "neoliberalization" Harvey discusses (2005: 165–72). As the continuous expansion of the market runs the risk of eventual saturation, employers favor short-term contracts as a means of maximizing profit and maintaining flexibility. Conditions once associated with factory laborers facing plant closures are increasingly the norm for the professional-managerial class with which college students identify or aspire to join. In their quest for future employment, students learn to adopt those qualities capitalism prioritizes: flexibility, speed, and an ability to keep pace with technological innovation. Unfortunately, market values are often at odds with the sustained reflection necessary for writing and learning. PBS's *Frontline* program "Digital Nation" (aired February 2, 2010), for example, profiled students at highly "wired" schools such as MIT and Stanford, indicating that the multitasking associated with abundant communication technology compromises students' focus on their writing. These students expressed a tendency to view their papers as chunks or paragraphs, citing an inability to think about their work holistically.

With students at all kinds of institutions confronting capitalism's cultural acceleration, compositionists have a shared stake in making time a central concern of writing pedagogy. This project complements scholars' ongoing attention to the economics of English studies, particularly the privatization of the university (Downing, Hurlbert, and Mathieu 2002; Ohmann 2003) and the casualization of academic labor (Schell 1998; Schell and Stock 2001; Bousquet, Scott, and Parascondola 2004). It also extends compositionists' recent attention to students' working lives (Bousquet 2008; Lu and Horner 2009; Scott 2009). My goal in this essay, while linked to these broader investigations, is to situate time in the context of our interactions with our students and our classes.

In so doing, I aim to grapple with Julie Lindquist's (2010: 175–76) assertions that "writing teachers generally don't know our students very well" and "at the bottom of it all is the problem of *time*." While Lindquist's solution lies in long-term ethnographic research,[1] I am interested in posing an alternative approach to the problem of time, rooted in classroom practice. To that end, I recommend that composition courses address the current strain on students' time by fostering *tempo-ral awareness*, a materialist approach to time that locates individual time resources within larger sociocultural contexts. I discuss two dimensions of this reflective approach. The first involves incorporating students' considerations of time into course content, making time a subject of writing courses. The second, which uses time to fuel teacher inquiry, requires writing instructors to examine how time mediates the peda-gogical relationships developed within composition courses. Facilitat-ing temporal awareness for students and teachers alike, I argue, is an essential piece of the work we must do as twenty-first-century litera-cy educators, work that recognizes time's significance to composition courses and accordingly strives to foster a more equitable and informed writing pedagogy.

The Materiality of Time

The work of writing instruction—responding to large numbers of pa-pers and looking at multiple iterations of drafts, often at multiple insti-tutions and often for inadequate compensation—puts writing teachers in a unique position to identify the material conditions that constrain their use of and access to time. An instructor who does only a cursory read of the last few papers in a stack might understand this practice as a necessary evil of having too many papers to grade. A faculty member who takes longer than she would like to return papers because she was revising an article for publication might see herself as prioritizing job responsibilities. On the one hand, these practices are part of the commonsense understanding of work and productivity that Harvey (2005: 39–41) attributes to neoliberalism. Writing teachers view the paper load—and the scrambling to get through it—as an unavoidable reality of our work; efficiency, in turn, becomes a naturalized part of our professional lives. On the other hand, these examples demonstrate the utility of isolating time from other resources, even as we acknowl-edge its connection to them. Focusing on time gives us a heuristic for examining how values such as speed, efficiency, productivity, and expediency "can be mobilized to mask other realities" (Harvey 2005: 39), such as the university's myth of synonymous working conditions among all faculty members. Because the demands of our teaching and scholarship give writing teachers considerable experience negotiating time, I am asking composition teachers to extend this insight to their pedagogical practice—in other words, to collaborate with students to examine how time resources shape people's ways of working, writing, and relating to one another. This process, which places individual time resources in the context of broader social, cultural, and economic dynamics, enables writing courses to spur temporal awareness.

My approach grows out of the historical materialist understanding of writing and writing instruction articulated by Horner (2000) and, more recently, by Tony Scott (2009). An historical materialist stance, which derives from Marx and Engels, maintains that economic conditions and cultural circumstances profoundly shape human experience. According to this formulation, writing emerges within the conditions surrounding its production, or, as Horner (2000: 59) puts it, writing is "material social practice in which structure and agency meet." Horner implores composition studies to conceptualize students' writing as work, stressing the need for a fuller understanding of that work as it is both constituted by and constitutive of composition courses. As he explains, a materialist perspective enables writing teachers to stop looking at students' writing as an isolated product: instead, we need to ask, "What does it mean, in the context of a required composition course, for the writer of the . . . paper to write as he has? What practices is he engaged in? How do these interact with what specific conditions? What work is going on?" (61). Much like Harvey's critique of commonsense values, Horner's line of questioning challenges writing teachers to consider the full complexity of students' production. He asks us to associate students' writing with their material lives within and beyond the writing classroom, to take stock of their current resources and prior educational opportunities, and to locate these within particular courses at particular institutions.

Working in a similar vein, Scott (2009) contributes a political economic perspective to composition's existing materialist scholarship. Pointing to composition studies' tendency to overlook the material distinctions among disparate student and faculty populations, Scott calls for "more radically material and politically aware conceptions of pedagogy and discourse" (8). This activist stance asserts the inextricability of students' financial realities from postsecondary writing instruction.[2] As Scott discusses in detail, a large percentage of today's college students are employed in the service economy. When not in school, these students are waiting tables, scanning groceries, or making lattes. "They move from job to job," he explains, "often working for employers who have obviously built high turnover into their business plans" (3). We see this in his discussions of Jenny and Karen, two of his multiple examples. A twenty-two-year-old senior, Jenny has already held seven jobs (139), while Karen, who works at a retail chain, has a hard time learning her coworkers' names because of rapid turnover (150). While these work experiences are characteristic of many of today's undergraduates, Scott is concerned that higher education in general and composition studies in particular continue to downplay students' material realities. His discussion therefore urges compositionists to more comprehensively account for the relationship between students' resources and their writing.

Taken together, Horner's and Scott's materialist orientations remind us that the work of writing courses is contingent upon students' material realities, institutions' funding and facilities, and the complex social relations that converge in first-year composition. For today's student populations, the material relations of writing pedagogy and writing classrooms coalesce around considerations of time. With its inherent connection to social and economic conditions, time drives individual students' writing. Students' time resources, while complex and shifting, also number among the tangible markers of difference among students and across institutions. I thus view attention to students' temporal experiences as foundational to a materialist writing pedagogy that sees students' creativity as "at once enabled and constrained by the available 'stuff' of daily life" (Scott 2009: 149). To that end, I am asking composition teachers to view students' writing as not only a site of temporal negotiation, in which students work within and make decisions about their time resources, but also a space for the active inquiry and exploration that promotes a broader awareness of the relationship of temporal conditions to market forces.

Time, Tools, and Technology

My students often talk about time, frustrated that they do not have enough of it. Making time a topic for a composition course, however, places it in a new, defamiliarized frame: in addition to being a material resource necessary *for* writing, time becomes a subject *of* that writing. Studying time allows writing classes to engage such issues as accelerated productivity, contemporary employment and communication trends, and the busyness, fatigue, and, occasionally, opportunity that can accompany all of the above. In this way, composition courses challenge neoliberalism's insistence that personal responsibility determines success (Harvey 2005: 65) and guide students to understand their temporal experiences in the context of a broader capitalist system. These explorations of time do not supersede attention to writing; rather, the two are complementary. As Anne Beaufort (2007: 185) has indicated, theme-based writing courses such as mine allow for "joint intellectual inquiry . . . that in some small way approximates other discourse communities." As I discuss, addressing time directly, with an eye toward temporal awareness, has enabled my writing courses to become more responsive to my students' demanding lives while challenging them to confront the naturalized understandings of time that surround them.

To illustrate this approach, I describe Time, Tools, and Technology, a 2009 composition course taught at a branch college within a larger state university system. The suburban campus, located in eastern Pennsylvania, enrolls approximately twenty-seven hundred students, predominantly at the first- and second-year levels. The institution offers fifteen four-year degrees, with robust enrollment in its business, mechanical engineering, applied psychology, and education majors. Most entering students intend to complete their degrees at the university's main campus, though many opt to stay with us because of the smaller class sizes and less expensive tuition. Two-thirds of the students are commuters, giving the campus a predominantly regional population. In an effort to recruit location-bound adult students, the college has been aggressively marketing its four-year programs. The students in my two sections of Time, Tools, and Technology therefore showed varying levels of social privilege.[3] While not all students could be understood as working class, nearly all balanced school with outside employment. Despite students' diversity, they held common concerns: juggling work, school, and family life; covering tuition costs; and finding the time to meet their multiple responsibilities.

Anticipating students with this range of educational histories and life experiences, I developed the course theme to generate critical examinations of time while also appealing to students' shared realities. The syllabus constructed the theme broadly, using time as a window into other material considerations, much like Scott (2009: 3) does in writing courses examining work. I selected course texts that served not only to model reflective inquiry into time but also to stimulate class discussion. As might be expected, many readings questioned the normative value of productivity: a New York Times cover story relating the dangers of texting and driving cautioned against multitasking behind the wheel (Richtel 2009); a Malcolm Gladwell (2005) excerpt explored police action during the "seven seconds in the Bronx" that preceded the fatal shooting of Amadou Diallo; and a Jeanne Marie Laskas (2009) article characterized the split-second decision making required of air traffic controllers. Taken together, these readings showed that efficiency can lead to dangerous—and sometimes fatal—consequences. While works like these connected technology to accelerated interpersonal exchanges, others put timekeeping in the context of individual and cultural values, such as Randy Pausch's 2007 "last lecture" on time management, delivered during Pausch's battle with terminal pancreatic cancer. In addition to stressing the significance of family time, Pausch, a computer scientist, took a decidedly pro-efficiency position that enabled the class to approach the course theme from an alternative perspective.

The course's writing assignments similarly challenged students to interrogate temporal experiences. Of the five major writing assignments, three of which I discuss in detail here, all but one addressed the course theme. In each case, time served as a catalyst for critical thinking; writing about time, in turn, became a form of active inquiry designed to complicate commonsense understandings such as "everyone is busy," "technology saves time," or "faster is better." I did not overtly introduce terms such as neoliberalism or capitalism into the course (though the latter was frequently implied). I was hopeful, however, that asking students to explore why people are perpetually crunched for time or to weigh the ramifications of technologies that enable us to do things faster would spur consideration of the market's role in our daily lives.

The course opened with a profile unit, intended to make the course theme concrete by associating it with real people's ways of negotiating time. Our first essay assignment required students to choose an interview subject and investigate that person's time through a "day in the life" approach. I encouraged students to profile a family member, roommate, coworker, or friend. In this way, students could use their existing familiarity with their subject—and the authority they could derive from that knowledge—as a basis for deeper inquiry. While I had initially considered an autobiographical piece for this first assignment, I believed students would be more apt to observe and reflect if they were examining someone else's timekeeping. Meanwhile, the "day in the life" approach provided a degree of structure without being too prescriptive. Like all course assignments, the profile involved drafting and revision, along with peer review and in-class writing.

The texts assigned in this unit, both of which profiled young adults, modeled the critical thinking I hoped students would bring to their profiles. The first, an excerpt from Eric Schlosser's Fast Food Nation (2007), depicted Elisa Zamot, a teenager who opens a McDonald's every Saturday and Sunday. Schlosser documents Elisa's eight-hour shift, during which she carries supplies from the basement, stocks paper products, and reheats frozen breakfast items, all prior to "seven hours of standing at a cash register" (67–68). As Schlosser reflects on Elisa's time, he equates her employment with "throughput," the rapid production that epitomizes the fast food industry (68). The second profile, Cynthia Selfe's "Students Who Teach Us: A Case Study of a New Media Text Designer" (2004), describes Selfe's former student David John Damon. As she explains, David's sophisticated new media literacy, which he allocated his time to developing and sustaining, was at odds with conventional academic literacies: "As David continued devoting the majority of his days to online design work, spending weekends travelling to consult with his Web design fraternity clients," he eventually failed out of the university (49). In keeping with the goals of the profile unit, Schlosser's and Selfe's pieces showed students the value of using time as a lens for examining people's daily experiences. These profiles also established the dialectical relationship between individuals' allocation of time resources—Elisa's choice to work weekends, David's choice to develop his business—and the larger social structures—Elisa's family finances, David's inconsistent educational background, their status as racial minorities—that drive these choices.

If students' profiles are any indication, the readings contributed to the class's understanding that time, like writing, is a site where "structure and agency meet" (Horner 2000: 59).[4] Several profiles made connections between workplace productivity and societal assumptions about human value. Many students foregrounded their parents' employment situations, noting that their jobs entailed long hours, competitive working conditions, and personal and familial costs. Some observed that their parents were constantly rushing around, chronically distracted and short tempered. If too little time was a burden for some profile subjects, too much time was also a concern, particularly for individuals who had been downsized. These profiles equated the lack of productivity that accompanies unemployment with shame, anxiety, and malaise. A related rationale manifested itself in profiles addressing commuters. Some featured students with long commutes, forced to spend time between classes in noisy libraries or napping in their cars. Others looked at professionals who spend several hours a day commuting to work through some combination of car, bus, and train. These profiles routinely referenced productivity that was contingent upon extensive travel and troubling periods of "wasted" time.

I recognize that these examples could be said to invoke stock narratives of labor exploitation. I am also aware that any attempt to identify definitively students' thought processes or to interpret their writing is limited from the start (Horner 2000: 31). It is quite possible that students' profiles, written in a course that featured time, illustrate their compliance with a professed agenda. Other profiles seem to have taken the opposite tack, celebrating their subjects' unique accomplishments and affirming the notion of individual freedom that the course's emphasis on time sought to problematize. Indeed, asking students to interview friends or family members may have encouraged students to look at their profile subjects in this way—as, for example, the best-ever multitasking mom rather than one of many working women navigating what Arlie Hochschild (1989) calls "the second shift." Nevertheless, several students' careful attention to their profile subjects' material conditions persuades me that time functioned as a valuable tool for exploration, particularly for this initial essay assignment.

Accordingly, Sierra's profile of her sister exemplifies the temporal awareness that writing courses can elicit. Throughout, Sierra describes how Grace, a married mother of two, negotiates her schedule within a particular material context. The piece opens by detailing the family's modest, single-bathroom home. Each morning, Sierra explains, the family "gather[s] into their small bathroom" like "clowns in a car." The profile goes on to convey the time-intensive work of parenting four-year-old Logan and two-year-old Kimberly. Because Logan "refuses to open his mouth until they practically force him to," brushing his teeth "takes about ten minutes." Breakfast, which Grace calls "one of the worst parts of the day," typically results in Kimberly strewing her breakfast all over the house. Through her extensive detail, Sierra shows that her sister spends every moment chasing a child or doing a chore. Grace's only "time to herself" coincides with the children's naps; she uses this time doing laundry and developing her freelance graphic design business. By midday, writes Sierra, Grace "catches herself glancing at the clock every few minutes waiting for [her husband] to get home." If at times the profile reads as a valorization of an older sibling, it nevertheless makes visible the labor of home and child care that is minimized through our culture's indifference to domestic work. In this way, Sierra accomplished what the assignment was designed to have students do: closely examine an individual's time as a means of acknowledging larger social structures, most notably the extent to which cultural notions of work and productivity infuse private life.

To varying degrees, students' profiles show that explicit attention to time fosters the critical thinking and cultural critique that fulfill core values in writing studies. Such assignments draw attention to temporal experiences that are generally invisible or unremarkable. If looking at people's time—real people that students knew and cared about—was a constructive starting place for building temporal awareness, turning our attention to the technologies people use to "save time" posed a logical next step.

To that end, the profile section was followed by a cultural analysis unit that asked students to "read" technological devices and services. This unit aimed to extend the profile's interrogation of taken-for-granted notions of time: ideally, examining the "bigger picture" surrounding time-saving appliances and services would encourage students to shift from an individual to a collective emphasis while conceptualizing the relationship between them. I sought to engage the cultural push to acquire newer, faster, and "better" gadgets; particular groups' access to and exclusion from technology; and individuals' use of technologies in both prescribed and innovative ways. Once again, our course readings raised the kinds of questions I hoped students would pursue in their writing. In addition to the previously mentioned *New York Times* cover story about texting and driving (Richtel 2009), we read articles about the Kindle (Baker 2009) and about Japan's emerging genre of cell-phone novels (Goodyear 2008). Each reading placed technology in the context of human users. The Richtel piece, for example, prompted us to question why so many Americans—some of us included—persist in texting while driving, convinced that we are saving time even if we are endangering lives. Meanwhile, Baker's article depicted subway commuters reading on Kindles, as if to suggest that reading no longer merits its own time and place but lends commuters a sense of productivity during their "dead time." Goodyear's piece was especially interesting to the class, as it presented cell phones not as a device for instant communication, as most students use them, but as a word-processing tool for creative writers.

The unit's writing assignment, a cultural analysis essay loosely modeled on the assigned readings, asked students to examine a technology or service in order to reveal cultural habits, practices, and priorities. Whereas the profile assignment directed students explicitly to study their subjects' time, the analysis approached time indirectly. On the whole, students' essays showed growing awareness of the relationship between technological innovation, the faster circulation of goods and services, and consumers' costs and demands. Doug's essay, for example, explained how Netflix's promise to eliminate the late fees associated with movie rentals implies cost savings. "To rent three movies at a time it is only $16.99," he notes, indicating that he can select films from his eighty-five-movie queue and keep them as long as he would like. His essay goes on to show that this strategy provides Netflix with a predictable income stream regardless of subscribers' viewing patterns: "Say for instance that I did not want to rent a movie this month. I'm [still] stuck paying $16.99." Significantly, Doug identifies the reciprocal benefits of this arrangement, commenting on the ways Netflix appeals to customers who seek the convenience of an at-home movie service.

Other papers foregrounded the interpersonal consequences of technology. Ericka looked at the microwave's effects on household dining habits. While families might have previously come together to prepare and enjoy meals, she states, the microwave enables family members to eat separately, either by reheating leftovers or cooking prepackaged, nutritionally suspect meals. With support from outside sources, she equates the microwave with parents' long work hours, which leave little time for family dinners yet enable people "to pay for conveniences such as the microwave." Mark's essay on HotSchedules, an online scheduling platform commonly used in the restaurant industry, did similar work. Through HotSchedules, he explains, employees can view their schedules, request particular shifts and time off, and trade hours with coworkers. Despite facilitating clear communication and effective scheduling, HotSchedules, Mark observes, also reinforces workplace hierarchies: "Managers have special access to HotSchedules of which a typical employee is wholly unaware." He goes on to discuss how the software promotes workplace surveillance. In addition to monitoring employees' online actions, managers can use the time that they would have spent scheduling "pay[ing] more attention to each individual employee and their working habits." In both cases, students acknowledged the freedoms afforded by technology—the flexibility of quick meal preparation after a long day at work and the convenience of scheduling shifts online. Yet they also called attention to technology's reduction of face-to-face interactions. In this way, their papers associated the contemporary workplace's efficiency with diminished social relationships, whether familial or collegial, observations consistent with Harvey's (2005: 3) assertion that contemporary capitalism "seeks to bring all human action into the domain of the market."

Analysis essays such as these, nuanced explorations of the trade-offs inherent in adopting technologies and services, suggest that the course succeeded in cultivating temporal awareness. While many students' analyses showed growth beyond the profiles, a handful of students did rely on uncritical observations, almost as if they were marketing the latest gadget's speed and ease rather than evaluating a technology. If essays like these indicate that the course was sometimes falling short of its goals, they serve as valuable illustrations of students' socialization as neoliberal subjects, an issue I take up in my next section.

As my discussions of the profile and the cultural analysis units indicate, critical examinations of time generate insights about resources, privilege, convenience, and capitalism. A midsemester definition unit, in which students explored terms such as *time management* and *procrastination*, functioned similarly. Because time drives writing classes more palpably than other courses—a result of steady, time-intensive assignments—writing professionals have a collective investment in sponsoring this awareness. Integrating such work into first-year composition courses helps students to recognize that their struggles to balance employment, relationships, and school are representative of widespread cultural conditions rather than individual problems to be surmounted or concealed. This recognition may be especially significant for working-class students, who, as Nancy Mack (2006: 54) reminds us, "need writing assignments in which they can occupy an authoritative position." Unlike the "assignments that render working-class students powerless" (54), assignments geared toward temporal awareness welcome students, like mine, having a range of socioeconomic backgrounds and identifications. Writing about time equips students to examine the factors impinging upon their own writing time, including tuition costs that force them to work long hours or social media sites that purportedly save time through instant communication. It teaches them to negotiate their writing within and against the barriers that constrain it. Engaging time in this way moves writing courses and writing students beyond time management—working efficiently, writing quickly, and valorizing task completion—and toward a more conscious and informed writing practice.

TEACHERS' TEMPORAL INQUIRY

Just as students have a stake in thinking critically about time, teachers, too, need to approach time—particularly students' time—comprehensively. When students tell us, "I only had a half hour before class, so I didn't have time to proofread" or "I worked on my paper during my two fifteen-minute breaks, and I wanted to talk about X, but I didn't get to it," teachers often balk, seeing such comments as evidence of students' irresponsibility. Rather than penalizing students for a lack of time or accusing them of having a mercurial attitude toward it, however, we might link these comments to the cultural circumstances limiting students' resources. We might do more to acknowledge the ways in which standardized testing at all grade levels and easy-to-evaluate, sometimes machine-scored, five-paragraph essays socialize students into an efficiency habit well before they enroll in college. We might consider the extent to which students' work experiences teach them to consolidate tasks, to pull shots of espresso while taking drive-thru orders or to field calls while doing data entry. In this way, we learn to recognize that students who resist a recursive writing practice do not necessarily see themselves as doing hasty or insufficient work; these students are conditioned to take pride in working under pressure, delivering product in a timely manner, and—in a clear correlate to corporate productivity—expending minimal resources to accomplish an objective. Teachers who contextualize their students' writing in this way will be in a better position to help students do the same. With that goal in mind, I describe a kind of reflective teacher inquiry—itself a form of temporal awareness—that offers insights into students' "ways of conceiving of time" (Robillard 2003: 75).

Jasbir K. Puar's Terrorist Assemblages (2007) provides a lens for the temporal inquiry I propose. Theorizing queer identity in the context of Western nationalism and Islamophobia, Puar articulates a useful distinction between the "paranoid temporality" endemic to neoliberal capitalism and the "anticipatory temporality" that resists accommodation to market values (xix–xxi). Paranoid temporality, Puar explains, "attempts to ensure against future catastrophe" (xx); as such, it galvanizes the fear—of terrorist others, but also of unemployment and financial instability—that secures compliance with capitalist values such as competition and individual freedom. The "It's Your Time!" billboard I passed on my way to school, for example, exploits paranoid temporality as a marketing strategy. Displayed in January 2010, concurrent with the New Year's resolution season, the advertisement treats time as a resource that must not be squandered while appealing to and reinforcing popular assumptions that equate timely entry into college with the acquisition of training, jobs, and success. Conversely, Puar's anticipatory temporality relies upon a "critical creative politics," a willingness to take risks in the interest of forging social arrangements beyond the market's domain (xx). In an effort to guide students toward the creative agency Puar associates with anticipatory temporality, writing teachers can replace "the frenetic speeds of crisis and urgency" we bring to our work with deeper thinking about students' writing (xxi). While we need to guard against reading students' texts as definitive evidence of their temporal subjectivities, their papers enable us to make provisional observations that can infuse our writing pedagogy.

To illustrate this approach, I explore constructions of temporality invoked in the final assignment for Time, Tools, and Technology. A process analysis assignment, this paper asked students to describe a process integral to their college experience and chart the steps in enacting it. While previous assignments had engaged the course theme as an overt subject, this assignment integrated time into its method: as a process analysis, it was inherently concerned with timing and sequencing; students had to address time in some way, especially because the assignment's subject of "college experience" involved considerations of time allocation and time to degree. Students chose topics ranging from how to find a parking space to how to study for a calculus exam. Because they provide an accessible venue for investigating students' temporal experiences, I use two papers about time management to model my inquiry. My case studies feature work by Tara, an eighteen-year-old African American soccer player, and Jake, a thirty-eight-year-old white security guard. I emphasize their demographic information here because it informs my discussion of their texts. Knowing, for example, that Tara is arranging her schedule as a varsity athlete who lives on campus while Jake must coordinate his as a part-time commuter student who works nights situates their respective time-management practices.[5] To be clear, however, notions of time and temporality inform writing done in many composition classes, not only in those that treat time as an explicit theme. Common reflective writing assignments—such as portfolio cover letters, self-assessments, and literacy narratives—invite discussions of timekeeping and time constraints and are thus well suited to teachers' temporal inquiry.

In "How to Be a Student-Athlete and Still Maintain a Social Life," Tara expresses a commitment to time management indicative of the received wisdom that emerges from paranoid temporality. To that end, her process analysis associates effective time management with individual empowerment and future employment; she constructs student-athletes as competitive preprofessionals who must learn to manage, in multiple senses of the word, their time. "A key to being successful during this busy [sports] season," she writes, "is having the best organization skills/technique that you probably will ever have to have as a college student." Tara goes on to list several habits suggestive of a managerial ethos, including her practice of dividing work "into two separate categories, one being light weight, the other heavy weight." As she explains, "light weight assignments such as answering a few questions on a homework assignment, doing a section of [online math problems], editing a paper, and reading something for a course can be done after your sporting activity. Assignments as such won't require much energy or time." Success, according to this formulation, means allocating one's time resources for maximum productivity. It involves assessing one's quantity of time, anticipating how much time one will have after a game or practice, and weighing how mental or physical fatigue might affect the quality of it. The ostensible goal of this strategic time management, according to Tara, is to allow for a social life: "making friends, going to different events, building relationships." Tara notes that "free time comes less than often," so one might need to "meet up with your friends to eat or do homework." Consistent with this multitasking, the piece recommends building extracurricular activities into one's schedule: "Social networking is vital in college! Build relationships with people, and don't be afraid to step outside your box to talk to new people and participate in various events. You never know what the future holds; the people you meet and the experiences you have may end up playing an important role in your status in the future." Like the previous delineation of lightweight and heavyweight tasks, this advice for campus engagement, which evokes buzz phrases such as relationship building and think outside the box, intimates Tara's internalization of capitalist discourse and the values inherent in it.

As I reflect on Tara's writing, I recognize student-athletes' need for careful timekeeping as they balance daily practices, coursework, and games that involve evening and weekend travel. On my campus, a recent addition to the National Collegiate Athletic Association, student-athletes are akin to employees. Paid in the form of athletic scholarships, they must devote their time to maintaining a required grade-point average, training rigorously, and remaining in good health. It is not surprising, then, that Tara's discussion likens college to professional employment. With the campus's burgeoning sports program likely to bring increasing numbers of student-athletes, it is constructive for me to weigh the implications of Tara's remarks, which apply to nonathletes as well. Treating time as a professional, her paper suggests, means ranking and classifying academic activities, emphasizing task completion over learning, and determining—before even beginning—which tasks deserve energy and attention. Writing a paper counts as heavyweight, but editing it—even if that process could bring new insights that deepen and complicate the paper—merits only negligible time. Meanwhile, if professionalizing one's time involves pursuing recreational activities with an eye toward one's future status, an ethic of networking could similarly inform the peer exchange foundational to writing courses. Concerned that this expediency stands to compromise intellectual discovery and interpersonal relationships, I leave my reflection troubled by this discourse of professional time management yet hopeful that my course's attention to time will enable students to recognize, interrogate, and potentially resist it.

Tara's process analysis makes for an interesting comparison to Jake's essay, "What It Takes to Balance School and Work." While Tara's vision of professional time management asserts individual control, Jake's theme of managed time foregrounds individual limitations. As he writes in his introduction, "Many individuals, who have just graduated high school, as well as working adults, are considering going back to school to obtain an advanced degree because of the recent downturn in the economy. People are finding it difficult to obtain a good job without some type of advanced degree. The main problem people are having is how to adjust their schedules accordingly in order to get back into the classroom."

Notably, this process analysis stresses the barriers that returning students, already employed but perhaps precariously, face in coming to college. Recognizing these challenges, Jake writes, "There is only so much time in a day," and the paper encourages adult students to be realistic about their time: "Live within your means; do not over-schedule yourself." To that end, Jake's paper offers strategies for negotiating one's work commitments. "Allow support from your employer," he writes, "this can be a large help with maintaining a good rapport and respect in the workplace." Whether the support is financial or moral is not specified, yet Jake's advice, like Tara's, implies the employment anxiety characteristic of paranoid temporality: one must make sure one's employer is on board with one's educational goals, his paper indicates, so as to maintain workplace harmony (and perhaps more pragmatically to ensure scheduling flexibility). One's time, according to this construction, is not one's own.

In a seeming contradiction that actually reinforces the supervisor/worker dichotomy, Jake cites the need to "learn to say no" to extra shifts: "Keep in mind in the work place you are only a number and they can replace you at any time. Only take extra time when it is convenient to you." This attention to overtime speaks to employees who, having little control over their jobs and facing uncertainty about their employment, can claim their time by declining additional shifts. Jake's simultaneous regard for and suspicion of his employer is resonant of the distrust students bring to the faculty-student relationship. Some students view their course instructors as bosses; indeed, some of my colleagues' syllabi tell their students to do just that. I think about students who become adversarial when I distribute assignment guidelines, and I wonder if they see me as managing their time. Is such resistance students' attempts to assert themselves in classroom situations with unequal power relations, a way to refuse "extra time," so to speak?

Despite Tara's appeal to a corporate ethos and Jake's wariness of the downsizing that corporate efficiency elicits, both students articulate an acceptance of neoliberal thinking. Each sees college as a route toward financial security, a stance Scott (2009: 137–38) identifies as a persistent motivator for today's students. This belief, along with the papers' mutual attention to status in the workplace—future or present—is a reminder that higher education, for all its alleged egalitarianism, fuels paranoid temporality. Reflecting on students' texts, in turn, reveals the extent to which college classrooms are compliant with capitalist competition. Some students, like Tara, live on campus and occupy a place of relative privilege that affords access to institutional resources, opportunities for extracurricular involvement, and a sense of jurisdiction over their schedules; others, like Jake, come to campus for brief periods of time, often during their work day, and must obtain permission from employers to do so. As I weigh this inequity, I consider practical measures that could accommodate students' various timetables, such as rotating due dates across days of the week to offer employed students a more equitable work flow; students who work weekends, for example, would not always face Monday deadlines. Alternatively, I could introduce sliding due dates wherein students set their own schedules. While only a modest step, this attempt to disrupt competitive norms gestures toward the creative problem solving that can reinvigorate market-driven pedagogical relationships.

My consideration of Tara's and Jake's papers, along with my attendant observation that economic anxieties inform students' ways of negotiating time, risks stating the obvious, yet this obviousness is precisely why writing teachers need to pay more attention to students' individual and collective temporalities: to disrupt and denaturalize the commonsense understandings of time that stifle creative critical thinking. This cognizance of students' complex relationship to all forms of capital, temporal or economic, seems to be what Lu and Horner (2009: 114) are seeking when they remind us that "to ignore students' financial concerns is unconscionable." Examining such concerns in the context of our students' writing both unmasks and localizes them. The generalized apprehensions of all college students everywhere become the particular realities of the students with whom we meet a few times a week, discuss and develop writing, share parking lots and cafeterias, and e-mail regularly. We learn that some students come to our classes under the auspices of institutional sponsorship, while others must make significant sacrifices to be there. Teachers' temporal inquiry, in other words, puts a face on students' time constraints. When we are open to learning from our students' writing, to gaining insights into the ways cultural discourses about time speak to and elicit career concerns, we preserve the interpersonal engagement that has been a hallmark of writing pedagogy; we are able to modify our curricula to work with, even as we complicate, the temporal resources and perspectives our varied undergraduate populations bring to our classrooms. By pursuing temporal inquiry, we begin to promote anticipatory temporality within academic spaces that leave little time for it.

Toward Temporal Awareness

As indicated, the circumstances today's undergraduates face—the assiduous time management involved in balancing their school and work schedules, the need to fit coursework into pockets of time, and the drive to do things faster—all create conditions, albeit conditions that are experienced in dynamic ways by students and institutions, to which writing pedagogy must be accountable. While my own approach has been to facilitate temporal awareness through writing courses that treat time as an explicit topic, I recognize that composition's appropriate subject matter remains a contested issue. Two decades ago, for example, scholars debated literature's role in composition courses, weighing the relative merits of literary analysis versus academic argument (Elbow 1990; Lindemann 1993; Tate 1993; Scholes 1998); today, literature continues to be studied in writing courses at a range of institutions (Anderson and Farris 2007; Isaacs 2009). More recently, composition studies has turned its attention to transfer, attempting to identify specific content and approaches that enable rhetorical knowledge developed in first-year writing to be carried beyond the confines of a particular class (Beaufort 2007; Downs and Wardle 2007). The diverse populations taking and teaching composition courses, coupled with institutions' distinct programmatic cultures, suggest that the field will not soon come to a resolution regarding course content. I therefore close by suggesting ways various incarnations of first-year writing might incorporate critical examinations of time.

Given the scarcity of time resources, all composition courses stand to benefit from some attention to time and temporality. Writing courses using literature, for instance, might consider texts' representations of time, locating these culturally and historically and comparing literary depictions to students' own temporal experiences. This approach is especially well suited to composition courses that pursue "the study of literature for social, cultural, and political inquiry" (Isaacs 2009: 110). Explorations of time also are a useful accompaniment to the metareflective assignments and activities characteristic of first-year composition classes designed to facilitate transfer. This tack works well with Downs and Wardle's (2007) introduction to writing studies approach, which emphasizes writing theory and writing research; students enrolled in such courses might compose auto-ethnographies that chart the ways time shapes their literacy practices or conduct research projects that survey how much time each week their classmates spend texting. Students' inquiries into time are also likely to illuminate the discourse community knowledge that Beaufort (2007) sees as foundational; as students learn to situate different genres within discourse communities, they could link textual conventions, expectations, and social functions to temporal circumstances, such as the succinct phrasing and structure typical of business communities or journalists' fast-to-read inverted pyramids. In all cases, students' work could be reinforced through class discussions that associate timekeeping with material conditions, thereby spurring consideration of time's relationships to broader social and economic structures.

Teachers' temporal inquiry can similarly be adapted for multiple settings. We might take a cue from Rebekah Nathan (2005), whose ethnography *My Freshman Year*—in which Nathan enrolled as a student at her own university—speaks to faculty members' lack of appreciation for students' time pressures. As she learned, "going to school . . . was a time-management nightmare; student life required much more and a very different kind of juggling than my life as a professor" (111). Although Nathan's embedded ethnography is not feasible, students' discourse poses a rich site for inquiring into their time, whether instructors undertake reflective analysis of students' texts or informal explorations. Teacher inquiry might involve jotting notes during class discussions of time-oriented topics, identifying trends, and meditating on these during office hours or while proctoring tests or quizzes. It could involve taking a temporal inventory when grading; because my students submit papers electronically, I have excerpted key passages, such as the depictions of technology and efficiency in the cultural analysis assignment, and combined them in a single document that I then discussed with the class. Metareflective assignments are particularly useful catalysts for teacher reflection. Additionally, we can ground our observations within empirical data that illuminate students' timekeeping, including institutional administrations of surveys such as the National Survey of Student Engagement or the frequency and timing of log-ins to our course management sites.

Because our local conditions lend themselves to different kinds of temporal inquiry, my intent is not to be prescriptive; rather, I want to stress the significance of temporal awareness, regardless of the form it takes. Students need to examine the materiality of time and weigh its consequences for their lives as writers, students, workers, and citizens. We as teachers, meanwhile, need to be open to learning about our students' particular ways of experiencing time, and we need to bring this awareness to our course design and delivery. To paraphrase the billboard with which I opened this essay, it is our time as English educators to pay more attention to time. In an educational climate increasingly shaped by capitalist efficiency, we can no longer stop our explorations of time with simple assertions of busyness; we must instead use our collective time constraints as the starting place for an overdue pedagogical conversation.

NOTES

I am grateful to *Pedagogy* editors Jennifer L. Holberg and Marcy Taylor and two anonymous readers for their valuable feedback on this essay. I thank my composition students for lending their voices—and, by extension, their time—to my work.

1. Lindquist and her Michigan State colleague Bump Halbritter are currently pursuing ethnographic research along these lines in *LiteracyCorps Michigan*, a digital video project that conducts artifact-based interviews with students (Lindquist 2010).

2. Collectively, contemporary college students face considerable financial challenges. The National Center for Education Statistics (2009) reports that 65.6 percent of all undergraduates received some financial aid during the 2007–8 academic year, with 79.5 percent of all full-time students receiving aid. According to the Project on Student Debt (2010), 67 percent of 2008 graduates from four-year colleges and universities carried student loan debt at an average rate of $23,200 per graduating senior.

3. According to registration data, slightly more than half of the thirty-four students who completed the course were first-semester, first-year students who had matriculated directly after high school. Six students were designated adult learners. Seven students fell into a more nebulous category; generally in their early twenties, students in this group had an advanced semester standing indicative of transfer credit or noncontinuous enrollment. Twenty-four students were male (71 percent) and 10 were female (29 percent), a departure from the college's overall ratio of 55 percent male to 45

percent female. Meanwhile, twenty-seven students identified as Caucasian, five as African American, and one each as Latino and Asian.

4. Students cited in this essay signed informed consent forms in accordance with the university's policy for the ethical treatment of human subjects. I disguise identifying features throughout my discussion, referring to students and their profile subjects pseudonymously and modifying distinguishing characteristics where appropriate.

5. Although writers' social and material locations are arguably just as significant to the profiles and cultural analyses, I opted not to disclose demographic information because the assignments did not ask students to address their own experiences and expertise.

Works Cited

Anderson, Judith H., and Christine R. Farris, eds. 2007. *Integrating Literature and Writing Instruction: First-Year English, Humanities Core Courses, Seminars.* New York: Modern Language Association.

Baker, Nicholson. 2009. "A New Page." *New Yorker,* 3 August. www.newyorker.com/reporting/2009/08/03/090803fa_fact_baker.

Beaufort, Anne. 2007. *College Writing and Beyond: A New Framework for University Writing Instruction.* Logan: Utah State University Press.

Bloom, Lynn Z. 1996. "Freshman Composition as a Middle-Class Enterprise." *College English* 58: 654–75.

Bousquet, Marc. 2008. *How the University Works: Higher Education and the Low-Wage Nation.* New York: New York University Press.

Bousquet, Marc, Tony Scott, and Leo Parascondola, eds. 2004. *Tenured Bosses and Disposable Teachers: Writing Instruction in the Managed University.* Carbondale: Southern Illinois University Press.

Downing, David B., Claude Mark Hurlbert, and Paula Mathieu, eds. 2002. *Beyond English Inc.: Curricular Reform in a Global Economy.* Portsmouth, NH: Heinemann/ Boynton-Cook.

Downs, Douglas, and Elizabeth Wardle. 2007. "Teaching about Writing, Writing Misconceptions: (Re)Envisioning 'First-Year Composition' as 'Introduction to Writing Studies.'" *College Composition and Communication* 58: 552–85.

Elbow, Peter. 1990. *What Is English?* New York: Modern Language Association.

Gladwell, Malcolm. 2005. *Blink: The Power of Thinking without Thinking.* New York: Back Bay.

Goodyear, Dana. 2008. "I ⬚ Novels." *New Yorker,* 22 December. www.newyorker.com/reporting/2008/12/22/081222fa_fact_goodyear.

Harvey, David. 2005. *A Brief History of Neoliberalism.* Oxford: Oxford University Press.

Hochschild, Arlie, with Anne Machung. 1989. *The Second Shift: Working Parents and the Revolution at Home.* New York: Viking.

Horner, Bruce. 2000. *Terms of Work for Composition: A Materialist Critique.* Albany: State University of New York Press.

Isaacs, Emily. 2009. "Teaching General Education Writing: Is There a Place for Literature?" *Pedagogy* 9: 97–120.

Laskas, Jeanne Marie. 2009. "Traffic." *Gentleman's Quarterly*, April.

Lindemann, Erika. 1993. "Freshman Composition: No Place for Literature." *College English* 55: 311–16.

Lindquist, Julie. 2010. "What's the Trouble with Knowing Students? Only Time Will Tell." *Pedagogy* 10: 175–82.

Lu, Min-Zhan, and Bruce Horner. 2009. "Composing in a Global-Local Context: Careers, Mobility, Skills." *College English* 72: 113–33.

Mack, Nancy. 2006. "Ethical Representation of Working-Class Lives: Multiple Genres, Voices, and Identities." *Pedagogy* 6: 53–78.

Mauk, Johnathon. 2003. "Location, Location, Location: The 'Real' (E)states of Being, Writing, and Thinking in Composition." *College English* 65: 368–88.

Nathan, Rebekah. 2005. *My Freshman Year: What a Professor Learned by Becoming a Student.* Ithaca, NY: Cornell University Press.

National Center for Education Statistics. 2009. "Fast Facts: Statistics on Financial Aid." US Department of Education. http://nces.ed.gov/fastfacts/display.asp?id=31 (accessed 7 March 2011).

Ohmann, Richard. 2003. *Politics of Knowledge: The Commercialization of the University, the Professions, and Print Culture.* Middletown, CT: Wesleyan University Press.

Pausch, Randy. 2007. "Time Management." YouTube. www.youtube.com/watch?v=o TugjssqOT0&feature=related (accessed 21 September 2009).

Project on Student Debt. 2010. "Quick Facts about Student Debt." Institute for College Access and Success. http://projectonstudentdebt.org/files/File/Debt_Facts_and _Sources.pdf (accessed 7 March 2011).

Puar, Jasbir K. 2007. *Terrorist Assemblages: Homonationalism in Queer Times.* Durham, NC: Duke University Press.

Richtel, Matt. 2009. "Driven to Distraction: Drivers and Legislators Dismiss Cellphone Risks." *New York Times*, 19 July, national edition.

Robillard, Amy E. 2003. "It's Time for Class: Toward a More Complex Pedagogy of Narrative." *College English* 66: 74–92.

Schell, Eileen. 1998. *Gypsy Academics and Mother Teachers: Gender, Contingent Labor, and Writing Instruction.* Portsmouth, NH: Heinemann/Boynton-Cook.

Schell, Eileen, and Patricia Lambert Stock, eds. 2001. *Moving a Mountain: Transforming the Role of Contingent Faculty in Composition Studies and Higher Education.* Urbana, IL: National Council of Teachers of English.

Schlosser, Eric. 2007. *Fast Food Nation: The Dark Side of the All-American Meal.* New York: Harper.

Scholes, Robert. 1998. *The Rise and Fall of English: Reconstructing English as a Discipline.* New Haven, CT: Yale University Press.

Scott, Tony. 2009. *Dangerous Writing: Understanding the Political Economy of Composition.* Logan: Utah State University Press.

Selfe, Cynthia. 2004. "Students Who Teach Us: A Case Study of a New Media Text Designer." In *Writing New Media: Theory and Applications for Expanding the Teaching of Composition*, ed. Anne Francis Wysocki, Johndan Johnson-Eilola, Cynthia L. Selfe, and Geoffrey Sirc, 43–56. Logan: Utah State University Press.

Tate, Gary. 1993. "A Place for Literature in Freshman Composition." *College English* 55: 317–21.

REFLECTIONS

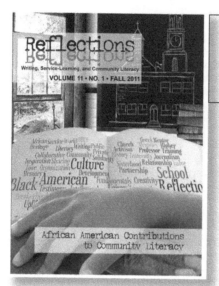

Reflections: A Journal of Public Rhetoric, Civic Writing, and Service is on the Web at http://reflectionsjournal.net/

Reflections, a peer reviewed journal, provides a forum for scholarship on civic writing, service-learning and public rhetoric. Originally founded as a venue for teachers, researchers, students and community partners to share research and discuss the theoretical, political and ethical implications of community-based writing and writing instruction, *Reflections* publishes a lively collection of essays, empirical studies, community writing, student work, interviews and reviews in a format that brings together emerging scholars and leaders in the fields of community-based writing and civic engagement.

Daughters Making Sense of African American Young Adult Literature in Out-of-School Zones

Melvette Melvin Davis' "Daughters Making Sense of African American Young Adult Literature in Out-of-School Zones" was chosen because the article considers the value of young adult literature in the literacy development of adolescents. Davis' account of an out-of-school reading group for adolescent African American girls illustrates the contemporary work that African American reading groups still perform for developing youth. Her research contends that reading groups, such as these, function as "homeplaces," spaces where diverse, relevant, and realistic African American experiences are shared, validated, and explored. However, the work is enjoyable as much for its rigorous methodology, as for its contributions to African American literacy research. She is clear about her standpoint and detailed in observations. Her work models a robust approach to an empirically based activist research model.

11 Daughters Making Sense of African American Young Adult Literature in Out-of-School Zones

Melvette Melvin Davis

> **Bria:** Some people get out at two o'clock; parents don't get home til' five. Dat's a long amount of time when they're sittin' home by themselves, and homework don't take dat long, and some people don't even do it. So, you got kids, but no time. They need to get their kids involved in stuff.
>
> **Nakia:** And get her some books. Like, if I wasn't here, I'd probably be layin' down on the phone with some boy or somethin."
>
> **Melvette:** Okay.
>
> **Nakia:** I'm just tellin' the truth!

Adolescence is a time when male and female youth begin to mature physically and also explore and define their cultural, gendered, and otherwise social selves. For African American girls, in particular, adolescence can also be a time of learning to cope with racial and gender oppressions (Ladner; Wade-Gayles; Collins, "The Meeting of Motherhood"; Crew; Groves; Paul). Elaine Kaplan describes coming of age for African American girls as "a time when Black girls, striving for maturity, lose the support of others in three significant ways. First, they are abandoned by the educational system; second, they become mere sexual accompanists for boys and men; third, these problems create a split between the girls and their families and significant others" (10). Additionally, the sexist and racist practices that female adolescents of color encounter in urban and predominately white classrooms undermine and often silence their voices (Fordham *Blacked Out*). Much attention has been given to ways young people's social, cultural, and educational needs, such as those mentioned by Kaplan, can be addressed in the classroom, but lacking are studies and discussions that explore ways after-school or out-of-school programs might help address these vital needs (Mahiri and Sablo; Alvermann, Young, and Green; Mahiri). These types of discussions are critical because not only do out-of-school time programs supplement academic learning, connect young people with caring adults, support young people's development, and add productive time to a young person's day (The American Youth Policy Forum), but in a time when school reform highly prioritizes standardized assessment, these types of programs also offer an opportunity for youth to develop their academic, cultural, social, and personal literacies without the threat of failing to pass a test or be promoted to the next grade level. These types of programs, no doubt, help keep young people from being overcome by self-destructive activities well known to youth just needing "something to do."

In light of the coming-of-age research that characterizes adolescence for African American girls as a time when they must grapple with racial, gender, and sometimes, economic biases that may frustrate their adolescent experiences, I organized and facilitated a book club during the 2005-2006 school year with a group of ninth and tenth grade girls participating in the Umoja Youth Empowerment Program in an effort to address the young women's need for a) positive role models and b) Black female-centered spaces where discussions of issues such as Black female identity, voice, relationships, cultural awareness, and educational development can take place in order to help African American girls navigate adolescence (Sullivan; Cauce et al.; Pastor; Leadbeater and Way; Gilligan, Lyons, and Hanmer). This book club provided an opportunity for teen girls to read and discuss with peers and adult mentors young adult texts written by African American female authors. In this article, I discuss the issues in the African American young adult (AAYA) texts we read that stimulated discussion, the ways readers responded to these issues, and the ways readers made use of the opportunity to discuss AAYA literature in an out-of-school context.

AAYA LITERATURE WRITERS: BLACK-EDUCATIONIST-ACTIVIST AUTHORS

African American youth's engagement with literature that portrays diverse African American experiences has the potential to inspire their imaginations, affirm their literacy, gender, and cultural identities, and challenge them to think critically about the world around them (Bishop; Johnson; Groves). Pamela Groves argues that strong, young adult, Black female protagonists allow youth to see people like themselves resisting defeat and resolving issues. She declares, "One of the goals of young adult novels written with African American female protagonists is to resolve the rage and restore the selves of these girls by offering strategies of resistance as they work toward liberation" (64). She asserts that African American coming-of-age stories offer readers a chance to "identify with individual characters as well as the larger group in these stories and [offer them] new ways of defining themselves. They can view themselves and their lives in a safe, nurturing place, before having to confront an oppressive world" (64).

Like Groves, I believe it is vital for young readers to read about realistic situations and to be able to see other young adults work through not-so-perfect lives. With this in mind, I chose works by contemporary YA literature authors for the young women to read in the book club. A preliminary investigation of select works by authors Sharon Flake (*Who Am I Without Him?*), Rita Williams-Garcia (*Blue Tights*; *Like Sisters on the Homefront*), and Connie Porter (*Imani All Mine*) revealed that these authors featured contemporary, relatable stories about African American adolescent girls and that they wrote from an insider's perspective[1]. Additionally, my analysis of book reviews, interview responses, and biographical texts about these women revealed powerful information about not only the value they place on the work they do as authors, but also the commitment they have to tell stories, stimulate conversations, and provoke action concerning real issues affecting African American youth and families.

I also gleaned from this examination that these authors function as activists, or advocates, for youth. They use literature as a medium to explore critical social and cultural issues relevant to African American girls. Their use of literature to highlight African American girls' experiences demonstrates an interest in and commitment to providing young adult readers with relevant and realistic stories about African

American girls and their experiences. Sharon Flake explains the importance of speaking back to negative images and giving families and communities hope through stories:

> I feel so strongly about telling the experiences of African-Americans because I think some people still see us in stereotypical ways. They equate the inner city with crime, violence, unwed mothers, and uncontrollable black boys. They don't see that inner city mothers also cook and care for their kids and take pride in their neighborhoods. They don't seem to see the many young black kids who, although under enormous social disadvantages, still choose the right path. (Hyperion)

Similarly, Rita Williams-Garcia conveys a calling to promote literacy and tell stories that young people want to read. She explains, "Writing stories for young people is my passion and my mission. Teens will read. They hunger for stories that engage them and reflect their images and experiences" (Williams-Garcia *Homepage*). In *Imani All Mine*, author Connie Porter courageously undertook writing the story of an inner-city, African American girl who was determined to survive through academic, familial, and personal struggles including rape, pregnancy, stereotypes, and prejudices. Both Flake's *Who Am I Without Him?* and Williams-Garcia's *Like Sisters on the Homefront* have won Coretta Scott King Honors, and Porter's 1999 novel *Imani All Mine* is a Black Caucus of the American Library Association (BCALA) Honor Book.

I argue that these authors also function as educators as they employ strategies that coincide with those used by exceptional teachers of African American children. Through their stories, these authors demonstrate an ethic of caring; promote a communally-centered atmosphere; make learning entertaining, interesting, engaging, and relevant; and validate and extend students' literacy and cultural identities (Ladson-Billings; Howard; Irvine; Ware). Also, because of the socially and culturally relevant themes these women address, I argue that they function as the "socially responsible othermothers" that they depict in some of their stories (Collins "The Meaning of Motherhood"). In viewing these authors' writings as "community work" ("The Meaning of Motherhood"), we are challenged to move beyond accepting these texts as simply didactic in nature to receiving them as the life-informing and life-transforming tools that they are (Coles; McGinley and Kambrelis; Meier).

BACKGROUND & THEORETICAL FRAMEWORK

Participants in the book club were in the ninth or tenth grade, or age 14 or 15, and they were recruited from a youth empowerment program called Umoja[2]. Umoja is a non-profit, community-based, youth empowerment program in Maryland. The program promotes racial harmony and uses history to empower and encourage youth to abstain from pre-marital sex, drugs and alcohol, and violence. All ninth and tenth grade girls in Umoja did not participate, only those who volunteered and had parental consent for the project. This yielded a group of seven young women. The combination of the girls' educational interests, diverse personalities, perspectives, and familial experiences, as well as their willingness to share, listen, and ask questions, helped shape the unique space in which the girls, and we mentors, responded to issues in African American women's YA literature. This space became known as The Umoja Book Club.

I collected data for this project using participant observation, field notes, book club session recordings, one-on-one interview recordings, and collection and analysis of participants' written responses to book club readings. For organizing and coding, I drew on practices that promoted a recursive analysis of data. This approach involved a cycle of collection, preliminary analysis, organizing and coding, checking for evidence, interpreting, categorizing, recognizing subjectivities, and writing results (Purcell-Gates; Bryman; Creswell; Moss). I interpreted data using a culturally-relevant (Lee; Ladson-Billings; Hale; Manley and O'Neill; Smitherman and Cunningham; Davis; Meier), Black feminist (Foss and Foss; Fordham *Blacked Out*; Collins *Black Feminist Thought*; Beuboeuf-Lafontant) and reader-response (Rosenblatt; Wilhelm) framework. Interpreting data through these lines of thinking allowed me to view and write about the girls' literacy experiences in a way that valued their knowledge, their experiences, their literacies, and their identities.

Cheryl, the director of the Umoja program, co-facilitated the book club with me. Cheryl's assistance was invaluable as she already had a rapport with the students and was actively mentoring the girls, so she was familiar with the needs and issues I hoped to address by creating a space and opportunity for the girls and mentors to connect through literature. Acting as a facilitator provided a chance for me to be a part of the discussions, learn from the girls participating, and adopt identities outside of researcher such as that of a book club co-participant, facilitator, and mentor. Also, I was interested in the significance of a certain type of approach to book club facilitation and implementation, a culturally relevant approach, and I, as the researcher and facilitator, was most familiar with this type of approach.

My idea of a culturally relevant approach to an out-of-school book club included several unique context and content elements related to adolescent development principles discussed by Signithia Fordham (*Blacked Out*); Elaine Kaplan; and Patricia Hill Collins (*Black Feminist Thought*) and principles of culturally relevant theory as related by Gloria Ladson-Billings; Tyrone Howard; Tamara Beauboeuf-Lafontant ("A Womanist Experience"), Jacqueline Irvine; and Franita Ware. The four content elements consisted of: 1) a community and communally-centered book club. The book club meetings were held outside of school, located in homes of mentors or parents who had volunteered to host the book club, and the group interactions took place in cozy, homelike settings; there were three book club meetings, and they each occurred at someone's home. For the first session, the parent coordinator for Umoja volunteered her home. The second session was hosted in the home of one of the participants, Danielle. Danielle's mother volunteered their home after the first session. The third session was held in the home of the assistant director for Umoja; 2) books read for and discussed in book club were African American young adult texts, particularly those that featured African American female protagonists and were authored by African American women; 3) the book club offered a space that valued African American young adult girls' ways of reading and being—their thoughts, feelings, ideas, interests, issues, and talk; and 4) the book club included discussion with and facilitation by African American adult, female mentors.

I did not approach this project from an outsider's standpoint. I grew up in the same communities as many of the girls that I worked with in the book club, so I had a personal connection and history with the community in which I conducted this research. Additionally, I had, and still have, a personal history with the youth empowerment program that I recruited participants from, as I was a participant when I was in high school. This made my researcher/observer/participant/ facilitator/mentor role often difficult to navigate. The opportunity to research in a community that I was familiar with came with many difficulties especially because, like Gretchen Generett and Rhonda Jeffries, I was constantly faced with the dilemma of how to "understand the 'other' when [I was] the 'other' and few have been able to articulate a definition of 'other' that is acceptable to [me] and from which [I] can begin the understanding process" (3). However, scholars like Karen Foss and Sonja Foss; Fordham ("Dissin' 'the Standard'"); Collins (*Black Feminist Thought*), and Beauboeuf-Lafontant ("A Womanist Experience") showed me that there is a community of scholars who value women's knowledge, experiences, and scholarship and helped me to conscientiously write as an African American woman who had the privilege, and challenge, of interacting with and learning from a group of girls about their experiences as readers and as young, African American daughters trying to navigate adolescence. I hope this work helps to give voice to the young, gifted, and Black girls of the Umoja Book Club and demonstrates to community and academic circles the value in connecting with and cultivating young people's literacies in out-of-school spaces.

BOOK CLUB CONVERSATIONS: DAUGHTERS MAKING SENSE OF/WITH YA LITERATURE

Louise Rosenblatt characterizes reading as a transaction, a back and forth, between reader(s) and text(s). In contrast to viewing reading as "receiving meaning in texts," this transactional view "regard[s] reading as the creation, in concert with texts, of personally significant experiences and meanings" (Wilhelm 24). Rosenblatt asserts that with each experience with a text, new meanings will emerge: "Even if the reader immediately rereads the same text, a new relationship exists, because the reader has changed, now bringing her memory of the first encounter with that text and perhaps new preoccupations" (*Making Meaning* x). In Wilhelm's *You Gotta Be the Book!*, he draws on Rosenblatt's transactional theory as well as his years of classroom teaching and research with students concerning their reading practices in order to help him uncover the various ways adolescents read. Wilhelm's research gleaned ten dimensions of response that adolescent readers drew upon as they transacted with texts, and he describes these dimensions in the context of three categories: *evocative, connective*, and *reflective*. The *evocative* dimensions classify transactions that point to an interest in the story and the characters. The *connective* dimensions describe ways that readers connect personally with characters and begin to extend their thinking, talking, writing, and relating beyond the world of the story. Finally, the *reflective* dimensions point to readers' ways of evaluating the significance of the author and text.

In this section, I combine the Black feminist theoretical lens that undergirds this project with Wilhelm's reader-response framework to analyze the ways the young ladies of the Umoja book club "changed their own words"[3] about literature, life, and themselves. The sections are organized thematically according to the most popular topics in the book club: relationships with mothers, relationships with boys, and support and guidance in the lives of girls.

Bria: "That mother was crazy."

Group responds: "Yes."

Melvette: "Which mother was crazy?"

Bria: "The mother who kicked her daughter out. But, see, her problem was, she favored her son too much, and she was like, 'Okay Imma do everything for my son,' and she didn't care nuttin' about her daughter."

Cheryl: "What do you think about the fact that she was like, 'You're going to get an abortion?'"

Nakia: "You don't do that [get an abortion]. If you went out and did what you did, then you have to pay for the consequences. Sometimes the consequences may be bad, sometimes it could be a blessing at the same time."

Bria: "I think, with her mother, I think if you're gonna make a child do somethin', you need to tell them a reason. And that's one thing I've been tryin' to get across to my motha. She needed to tell her 'why' because she didn't even understand what was even happening."

The experiences of daughters and mothers in-and-out-of-relationship with each other was a topic that resonated deeply with the girls in the book club. In the example above, Bria criticizes the character Ruby from *Homefront* for her approaches to disciplining her daughter Gayle. She describes Ruby as "crazy," and the other girls agree with this assessment. Although Ruby's character is not physically present throughout the novel, discussion of her character was dominant throughout this particular book club meeting. Ruby was especially criticized by the girls for her lack of communication with her daughter about serious issues, namely sexuality, abortion, and the risks and possibilities associated with sexual activity. In the above exchange, Bria not only evaluates Ruby's actions, but she also identifies with a critical issue in Ruby and Gayle's situation that the girls brought to light throughout their conversations, the lack of communication between mothers and daughters.

Analyses, personal connections, and reflections such as these permeated our discussions as the girls sought to better understand their lived experiences as well as the fictionalized mother-daughter relationships. The girls extracted meaning from and constructed meaning with the texts as they drew on their personal, social, and cultural ways of knowing and being and used the stories and their characters as a springboard from which to launch their criticisms, testimonies, and solutions for daughters and mothers.

For book club participant Nakia, asserting her personal beliefs about social and familial issues and relating her personal experiences to the text was essential to making the story come alive for her (Wilhelm). The following is an example of her taking a *connective* stance. She relates her personal experiences to the text, and she shares a story about herself and her cousin to help support her argument about the importance of open communication between mothers and daughters.

> **Nakia:** "Like, I'm not sayin' my motha was encouraging me to have, um, sex, but she said, 'Well, what I can say is, I can tell you not to do it,' she said, 'but you have your own mind-set.' She said, 'I'm just sayin' not to do it.' Like, I know my cousin, wit' her motha, when her motha, my cousin, her motha didn't know whether or not she was havin' sex. She said, 'Well, if you are, just tell me so I can get you on birth control pills and take you through the steps of what to do and what not to do and how to carry it.' She said, 'I can't tell you no and yes, if you have your own mentality.' She said, 'But what I can tell you is what to look out for and what not to do and stuff like dat.' She said, 'Maybe if I tell you the consequences, that you'll listen.' She said, 'But I know if I tell you yes or no, you not goin' listen.' And, my cousin, she took the advice."

Here, Nakia identifies with Gayle as a daughter whose mother takes the "just don't do it approach." Yet, she is careful not to have her mother confused with the "crazy" mother in the text. She tries to share her mother's direct words, rather than paraphrasing them for the group. Additionally, she contrasts Gayle's and her own situation with her cousin's and demonstrates the significance of a mother sharing advice, not just giving directives. This more explanatory and advisory approach, Nakia explains, was well received by her cousin and made a difference in her cousin's decisions about sex.

Throughout our discussions, Nakia was confident in her beliefs, and she seemed comfortable sharing her thoughts and critiques about the actions of characters and the situations that arose in the text. Although Nakia had not read *Homefront*, her outspoken stance demonstrated her interest in the story and the issues brought to light by it. In the following example, Nakia takes an *evocative* stance and moves from identifying with an issue and sharing a related personal experience to "becoming" a character and taking on the role of Gayle's mother.

> **Nakia**: "Now, see, if I was a mother of her, I would say, 'Okay, you decided to do this. I will help you, but later on, you gonna get a job.'"
>
> **Cheryl**: "You would help her after the first one?"
>
> **Nakia**: "I would help her."
>
> **Cheryl**: "She was thirteen. She came home the first time pregnant, and you helpin' her wit the first baby . . ."

Bria, Jamilah and Danielle talk simultaneously about adoption as an option.

> **Jamilah**: "Don't kill the baby."
>
> **Nakia:** "She could get child support."
>
> **Bria**: "My motha done gone through so much tryin'a get child support. That don't do nuthin'. She's . . . it's been I don't know how many years. She still don't get it. My fatha don't care."
>
> **Nakia**: "My father just started paying a few years ago."
>
> **Cheryl**: "Okay, so you understand and know that child support is not a definite or a given . . . and WIC can run out."

> **Nakia**: "As a child, I'd rather my father spend time with me."

> **Cheryl**: "Yeah, but time, sweetheart don't clothe you, nor does it feed you."

Here, Nakia effortlessly moves from speaking as character Ruby, a mother, to speaking from her personal perspective as a daughter. She connects real-world options and possibilities to the circumstances in the text. Though Nakia begins to role-play, Bria's and co-facilitator Cheryl's knowledge and experiences seem to prevent them from believing in the promise of Nakia's approach to dealing with the situation. However, when Cheryl challenges Nakia, she does not hesitate to use her identity, knowledge, and personal experience as a daughter to support her point-of-view. Although Nakia goes back and forth connecting personally and imagining characters' life possibilities, her responses consistently speak to the importance of open communication between mothers and daughters.

Nakia was not the only participant who weaved in and out of roles and reading strategies. In the exchange below, Courtney and Danielle use a *reflective* lens as they try to understand the significance of Earlene and Tasha's relationship in *Imani All Mine*. Danielle goes back and forth analyzing Earlene and Tasha. Finally, she puts herself in Tasha's shoes and concludes what she would do in the situation.

> **Courtney**: "I wanna know does her mom just talk to her that way just because she feels like it, or does she have a purpose for not tellin' her daughter some things. It seems like she's kinda evil like ever since she had the child. It seem like she's been kinda distressed or somethin' like dat. I wanna know did somethin' happen to her when she was young that makes her like, tough on Tasha."

> **Danielle**: "I wanna know why Tasha didn't tell her mother that she was raped and that she wasn't like fast. That's what her mother was thinking. I was like mad that she didn't say anything."

> **Melvette**: "When somethin' like, you know, that serious and detrimental happens to you, you need to tell."

Courtney: "But like, I think she might have not told her because she probably just felt like it was her fault. 'If you wasn't so fast or whatever you might not have been raped.'

Danielle: "Me, if I was raped, I would not tell my mother. But, if she sittin' there callin' me fast anyway, you might as well tell her because she goin' say the same thang."

Courtney: "I would. I definitely would 'cause my mom, she would probably go crazy, but not because of me, because I was raped."

Melvette to Danielle: "But that wouldn't be your fault, like, why wouldn't you tell her? You feel like, she would be judgmental? You feel like you did somethin', or you would be ashamed?"

Danielle: "I would be ashamed."

Melvette: "So, you would let that keep you from tellin' your mother?"

Danielle: "I would be afraid of like, hurtin' her. Like, this is what I did."

Melvette: "You mean, if you had sex willingly, or if you were raped?"

Danielle: "If I was raped."

Cheryl: "Dat's deep Danielle. I'm tryin' to process this. Let me process this. Give me a minute."

By putting herself in Tasha's world, Danielle realizes the difficulty of having to relate to a mother like Earlene. In the girls' eyes, Earlene is "judgmental," "selfish," "mean and bitter," didn't "listen," and does not "give [Tasha] advice." In Danielle's view, these attributes are a hard battle to contend with. She wonders, "How you sit there and cuss at somebody then all of a sudden wanna give them advice. I wouldn't listen to her either." Danielle's declaration that she would not tell her mother if she were raped concerned both co-facilitator Cheryl and me, and we talked seriously with the girls about dealing with a situation like that. Although Danielle had just read the story and saw the potential consequences of a girl her age not telling her mother about a rape, she still empathized and related personally to Tasha enough to believe that she wouldn't tell her mother either. Danielle's response underscores the detrimental effects of mother-daughter relationships with strained communication and confirms the need for women and spaces that welcome girls' concerns (hooks; Leadbeater and Way; Collins, *Black Feminist Thought*).

As the girls made connections with the texts and expressed frustration in dealing with similar experiences, they, in some ways, treated the texts as instruction manuals, not just for girls such as themselves, but for their mothers. They recognized the ability of the texts to convey the feelings and thoughts they had often tried to express to their mothers and grandmothers. *Homefront*, especially, became recognized by the girls for highlighting the need for communication and sincere engagement between daughters and mothers.

From the first session to the last, the girls' conversations emphasized the communication disconnects that complicate the bonds between daughters and mothers, and they used their texts and their testimonies to demonstrate the seriousness of the social, personal, and familial issues affecting adolescent girls. In addition to making connections between the literature and their lives, they recognized in their analyses the experiences of girls in their families, schools, and communities. They drew on their personal pools of knowledge and experience and poured into the lives of each other as they thought independently and collaboratively about ways to solve the life puzzles affecting adolescent and adult women's fictional and non-fictional lives.

In these book club conversations, the girls interrogated the AAYA texts and contrasted the textual representations with their lived experiences. They used the book club as an opportunity to make and share meaning with peers, and through their recalling of other relevant fictional tales and their retelling of personal stories, they created their own YA texts. They co-constructed a framework for negotiating relationships with male peers and voiced their beliefs about self-esteem and self-assertion in male-female relationships. They also shared their struggles to establish relationships with male peers while negotiating their parents' rules and behaviors. While the YA texts served to initiate discussion, the girls' conversations were dominated by their personal testimonies of efforts to reconcile autonomy and respect for parental rules with their increasing interest in romantic relationships and their need for realistic advice about dealing with these relationships.

In addition to recalling their relationship experiences with boys and emphasizing the need for attention, affection, and conversations from mothers to daughters about sexuality, self-esteem, and relationships, the girls spent a significant amount of time pointing out the need for a network of caring adults to support girls as they journeyed through adolescence and transitioned into womanhood. In their conversations, they discussed the paths that girls sometimes find themselves walking, and they recounted the difficulties that trouble adolescent waters.

BOOK CLUB AS HOMEPLACE

The girls used the Umoja Book Club not only as a space to discuss issues that arose in the texts, but especially as a space to speak on behalf of themselves and other teenage daughters about these personal, familial, and social issues. They shared their frustrations and personal testimonies, and they sometimes became the voice of daughters who struggled with issues in the texts. The girls also used the book club as a space to reflect on their principles and beliefs and as a space to problem solve and challenge their peers, parents, and families to learn from past and present experiences, to dialogue about issues, and to consider the implications of one's decisions. The girls read, reflected on, and discussed their connections with, and critiques of, African American YA literature in a space that was outside a context of "questions or requirements" (Rosenblatt, *Making Meaning*) and within a context of safe spaces and relationships (Rosenblatt, *Making Meaning* ; Groves; Pastor).

The girls' exposure to the contemporary fiction by authors Porter, Flake, and Williams-Garcia, described previously as Black-educationist-activist authors, stimulated response practices that paralleled the educationist-activist sentiments of the writers. The social, personal, and familial issues highlighted in the texts, relationships with mothers, relationships with boys, and support and guidance for girls, resonated with the girls to the extent that a significant portion of their responses focused on thinking of ways to aid teen girls and families struggling with issues. Throughout our meetings the girls consistently 1) *analyzed*: critiqued the stories, characters, topics, and sometimes authors, and shared their perspectives, 2) *testified*: drew upon and connected their life experiences to the texts and characters, and 3) *problem solved*: brainstormed ways to help fictional and non-fictional mothers and adolescent girls work through personal and relationship issues.

According to bell hooks, Amy Sullivan, and Patricia Hill Collins (*Black Feminist Thought*), girls' and women's relationships thrive off of opportunities to listen to, speak with, and learn from each other. These opportunities, Richardson and Pough note, are often characterized by the literacies that African American girls and women draw upon as they express themselves in personally, socially, and culturally significant ways. The girls made the Umoja book club a "home," not in a traditional sense, but in the sense of a nurturing place where they were able to, with peers and understanding adults, freely voice and weave together their ideas about literature and life (Pastor).

CULTURALLY RELEVANT PEDAGOGIES IN OUT-OF-SCHOOL ZONES: IMPLICATIONS FOR PRACTICE

As evidenced by the participants' responses, the girls found value in the texts, and even in the space of a community-based book club, the girls used a critical reading lens to make sense of the stories. Our group reading experiences seemed to validate the girls' personal knowledge and literacies as revealed by Danielle's impromptu recitation of her favorite piece, "Our Deepest Fear." She wowed the mentors and her peers during our last session when she recited this well-known excerpt in response to an exercise that asked her to brainstorm a relevant book topic that would appeal to her peers. We all listened as she encouraged us with the words, "Our deepest fear is not that we are inadequate. Our deepest fear is that we are powerful beyond measure. It is our light, not our darkness that most frightens us. We ask ourselves, 'Who am I to be brilliant, gorgeous, talented, and fabulous?'Actually, who are you not to be?...."

This study highlights only a small sample of readers and texts over a short period of time, but the Umoja Book Club gave this group of teenage girls license to reflect on and talk about their life experiences and frustrations, to learn from each other and mentors, and to brainstorm ways to address adolescent girls. From this research, we gain an example of how community-based resources might create spaces for girls that engage them in critical discussions about life with peers and mentors. We are also able to observe how this out-of-school program addressed African American adolescent girls' coming-of-age needs in a culturally responsive way. By reaching beyond the academic task of analyzing and theorizing about literature and integrating the social and cultural themes explored by AAYA literature authors, the Umoja Book Club was able to give a group of African American girls the opportunity to read, write, and discuss literature that "affirms who they are" (Harris 553) and convey to them the value of literature outside the classroom and within their lives. The sense of social consciousness and activism that was cultivated through our readings and discussions highlights the value in affirming spaces and points to a need for these types of spaces in and out of school.

Elyse Eidman-Aadahl and Glynda Hull and Katherine Schultz challenge literacy theorists not to stop at theorizing but to reach out in conversation and in practice to the myriad of community-based organizations across the nation to capitalize on our passion, experience, knowledge, and understanding and to create the engaging literacy environments that we all strive for. By first acknowledging young people's multiple literacies, racial, gender, and economic challenges, and their diverse development needs, those of us interested in supporting young people's literacy development can address their circumstances with better judgment and confidence. We must explore the attributes of spaces that aid positive adult mentorship and nurture adolescent voices. Then we must create and recreate environments that are safe, nurturing, and fulfilling for young people. By recognizing and implementing effective classroom *and* community-based practices, we can begin to carve out homeplaces in spaces familiar and unfamiliar to young people—living rooms, classrooms, libraries, and even boardrooms. The possibilities are endless.

NOTES

1 African American women writing about experiences of African American girls and women and issues affecting African American girls and women (Boston and Baxley).

2 Pseudonyms are used in this article for the organization and for participants.

3 This is a reference to Cheryl Wall's text, *Changing Our Own Words: Essays on Criticism, Theory, and Writing by Black Women.*

WORKS CITED

Alvermann, Donna P., Josephine P. Young, and Colin Green. "Adolescents' Negotiations of Out-of-School Reading Discussion." *National Reading Research Center Reading Research Report* 77 (1997): 1-28. Print.

American Youth Policy Forum. *Helping Youth Succeed Through Out-of-School Time Programs.* Washington, DC: American Youth Policy Forum, 2006. Print.

Beauboeuf-Lafontant, Tamara. "A Womanist Experience of Caring: Understanding the Pedagogy of Exemplary Black Women Teachers." *The Urban Review,* 34.1 (2002): 71-86. Print.

—. "Womanist Lesson for Reinventing Teaching." *Journal of Teacher Education,* 56.5 (2005): 436-445. Print.

Bishop, Rudine Sims. "Walk Tall in the World: African American Literature for Today's Children." *Journal of Negro Education* 59.4 (1990): 556-565. Print.

Boston, Genyne and Traci Baxley. "Living the Literature: Race, Gender Construction, and Black Female Adolescents. *Urban Education,* 2.6 (2007): 560-581. Print.

Bryman, Alan. *Social Research Methods.* Oxford: Oxford University Press, 2004. Print.

Cauce, Ana, et al. "African American Mothers and Their Adolescent Daughters: Closeness, Conflict, and Control." *Urban Girls: Resisting Stereotypes, Creating Identities.* Eds. Bonnie Leadbeater and Niobe Way. New York: New York University Press, 1996. 100-116. Print.

Coles, Robert. *The Call of Stories: Teaching and the Moral Imagination.* Boston: Houghton Mifflin, 1989. Print.

Collins, Patricia Hill. "The Meaning of Motherhood in Black Culture and Black Mother-Daughter Relationships." *Double Stitch: Black Women Write about Mothers and Daughters.* Eds. Patricia Bell-Scott, et al. Boston: Beacon Press, 1991. 42-60. Print.

—. *Black Feminist Thought: Knowledge, Consciousness, and the Politics of Empowerment.* New York: Routledge, 2000. Print.

Crew, Hilary. "Feminist Theories and the Voices of Mothers and Daughters in Selected African-American Literature for Young Adults." *African-American Voices in Young Adult Literature: Tradition, Transition, Transformation.* Ed. Karen Patricia Smith. Metuchen, N.J.: Scarecrow Press, 1994. 79-113. Print.

Creswell, John. (1998). *Qualitative Inquiry and Research Design: Choosing Among Five Traditions.* Thousand Oaks: Sage Publications, Inc, 1998. Print.

Davis, Olga Idriss. "The Rhetoric of Quilts: Creating Identity in African American Children's Literature." *African American Review* 32.1 (1998): 67-76. Print.

Eidman-Aadahl, Elyse. "Got Some Time, Got a Place, Got the Word: Collaborating for Literacy Learning and Youth Development." *School's Out: Bridging Out-Of-School Literacies with Classroom Practice.* Eds. Glynda Hull and Katherine Schultz. New York: Teachers College Press, 2002. 241-260. Print.

Flake, Sharon. *Who Am I Without Him? Stories about Girls and the Boys in Their Lives.* New York: Jump at the Sun, 2004. Print.

Fordham, Signithia. *Blacked Out: Dilemmas of Race, Identity, and Success at Capital High.* Chicago: The University of Chicago Press, 1996. Print.

—. "Dissin' 'the Standard': Ebonics as Guerilla Warfare at Capital High." *Anthropology & Education Quarterly,* 30.3 (1999): 272-93. Print.

Generett, Gretchen, and Rhonda Jeffries. "Black Women as Qualitative Researchers: Performing Acts of Understanding and Survival—An Introduction." *Black Women in the Field: Experiences Understanding Ourselves and Others through Qualitative Research.* Eds. Gretchen Generett and Rhonda Jeffries. Cresskill, NJ: Hampton Press, 2003. 1-10. Print.

Gilligan, Carol, Nona Lyons, and Trudy Hanmer, eds. *Making Connections: The Relational Worlds of Adolescents Girls at Emma Willard School.* Cambridge: Harvard University Press, 1990. Print.

Groves, Pamela E. "Coming-of-Rage: Young, Black, and Female in America." *Mosaics of Meaning: Enhancing the Intellectual Life of Young Adults through Story.* Kay Vandergrift. Ed. Lanham, Maryland: Scarecrow Press, Inc., 1996. 47-66. Print.

Hale, Janice E. *Unbank the Fire: Visions for the Education of African American Children.* Baltimore: Johns Hopkins University Press, 1994. Print.

—*Learning While Black: Creating Educational Excellence for African American Children.* Baltimore: Johns Hopkins University Press, 2001. Print.

Harris, Violet J. "African American Children's Literature: The First One Hundred Years." *Journal of Negro Education* 59.4 (1990): 540-555. Print.

Hyperion Books for Children. *Sharon Flake Biography.* Hyperion Books for Children. 2003. Web. 15 Jan. 2008.

Howard, Tyrone. "Telling Their Side of the Story: African-American Students' Perceptions of Culturally Relevant Teaching." *The Urban Review,* 33.2 (2001): 131-149. Print.

hooks, bell. *Yearning: Race, Gender, and Cultural Politics.* Boston: South End Press, 1990. Print.

Hull, Glynda, and Katherine Schultz. *School's Out: Bridging Out-Of-School Literacies with Classroom Practice.* New York: Teachers College Press, 2002. Print

Irvine, Jacqueline. "African American Teachers' Culturally Specific Pedagogy: The Collective Stories." *In Search of Wholeness: African American Teachers and Their Culturally Specific Classroom Practices.* Ed. Jacqueline Irvine. New York: Palgrave, 2002. 139-146. Print.

Johnson, Dianne. *Telling Tales: The Pedagogy and Promise of African American Literature for Youth.* New York: Greenwood Press, 1990. Print.

Kaplan, Elaine. *Not Our Kind of Girl: Unraveling the Myths of Black Teenage Motherhood.* Berkeley: University of California Press, 1997. Print.

Ladner, Joyce A. *Tomorrow's Tomorrow: The Black Woman.* New York: Doubleday & Company, Inc., 1971. Print.

Ladson-Billings, Gloria. *The Dreamkeepers: Successful Teachers of African American Children.* San Francisco: Jossey-Bass Publishers, 1994. Print.

Leadbeater, Bonnie, and Niobe Way, eds. *Urban Girls: Resisting Stereotypes, Creating Identities.* New York: New York University Press, 1996. Print.

Lee, Carol. *Signifying as a Scaffold for Literacy Interpretation: The Pedagogical Implications of an African American Discourse Genre.* Urbana: National Council of Teachers of English, 1993. Print.

Mahiri, Jabari, and Soraya Sablo. "Writing for Their Lives: The Non-School Literacy of California's Urban African American Youth." *The Journal of Negro Education* 65.2 (1996): 164-180. Print.

Mahiri, Jabari. *Shooting for Excellence: African American and Youth Culture in New Century Schools.* Urbana: National Council of Teachers of English, 1998. Print.

Manley, Anita, and Cecily O'Neill. *Dreamseekers: Creative Approaches to the African American Heritage.* Portsmouth, NH: Heinemann, 1997. Print.

McGinley, William and George Kamberelis. "*Maniac Magee* and *Ragtime Tumpie*: Children Negotiating Self and World through Reading and Writing." *Research in the Teaching of English*, 30.1 (1996): 75-113. Print.

Meier, Terry. "Kitchen Poets and Classroom Books: Literature from Children's Roots." *The Real Ebonics Debate: Power, Language, and the Education of African-American Children.* Eds. Theresa Perry and Lisa Delpit. Boston: Beacon Press, 1998. 94-104. Print.

Moss, Beverly. "Ethnography and Composition: Studying Language at Home." *Methods and Methodology in Composition Research.* Eds. Gesa Kirsh and Patricia A. Sullivan. Carbondale: Southern Illinois University Press, 1992. 153-171. Print.

Pastor, Jennifer, Jennifer McCormick, and Michelle Fine. "Makin' Homes: An Urban Girl Thing." *Urban Girls: Resisting Stereotypes, Creating Identities.* Eds. Bonnie Leadbeater and Niobe Way. New York: New York University Press, 1996. 15-34. Print.

Paul, Dierdre Glenn. "Images of Black Females in Children's/Adolescent Contemporary Realistic Fiction." *Multicultural Review* 8.2 (1999): 34-41, 59-65. Print.

Porter, Connie. *Imani All Mine*. Boston: Houghton Mifflin Company, 1999. Print.

Pough, Gwendolyn. "Girls in the Hood and Other Ghetto Dramas: Representing Black Womanhood in Hip-Hop Cinema and Novels." *Check it While I Wreck it: Black Womanhood, Hip-Hop Culture, and the Public Sphere*. Gwendolyn Pough. Boston: Northwestern University Press, 2004. 127-161. Print.

Purcell-Gates, Victoria. "Ethnographic Research." *Literacy Research Methodologies*. Eds. Marla Mallet and Nell Duke. New York: Guilford Press. 92-113. Print.

Rosenblatt, Louise. *Literature as Exploration*. New York: Noble and Noble, 1968. Print.

—. *The Reader, the Text, the Poem: The Transactional Theory of the Literary Work*. Carbondale: Southern Illinois University Press, 1978. Print.

—. *Making Meaning with Texts: Selected Essays*. Chicago: Heinemann, 2005. Print.

Smitherman, Geneva and Sylvia Cunninghman. "Moving Beyond Resistance: Ebonics and African American Youth." *Journal of Black Psychology* 23.3 (1997): 227-232. Print.

Sullivan, Amy. "From Mentor to Muse: Recasting the Role of Women in Relationship with Urban Adolescent Girls." *Urban Girls: Resisting Stereotypes, Creating Identities*. Eds. Bonnie Leadbeater and Niobe Way. New York: New York University Press, 1996. 226-249. Print.

Wade-Gayles, Gloria. "The Truths of Our Mothers' Lives: Mother-Daughter Relationships in Black Women's Fiction." *SAGE: A Scholarly Journal on Black Women* 1.2 (1984): 8-12.

Wall, Cheryl. "Introduction: Taking Positions and Changing Words. *Changing Our Own Words: Essays on Criticism, Theory, and Writing by Black Women*. Ed. Cheryl Wall. New Brunswick: Rutgers University Press, 1989.1-15. Print.

Ware, Franita. "Black Teachers' Perceptions of Their Professional Roles and Practices." *In Search of Wholeness: African American Teachers and Their Culturally Specific Classroom Practices*. Ed. J.J. Irvine. New York: Palgrave, 2002. 33-45. Print.

Wilhelm, Jeffrey. *"You Gotta Be the Book": Teaching Engaged and Reflective Reading With Adolescents*. 2007. New York: Teachers College Press, 2008. Print.

Williams-Garcia, Rita. *Blue Tights*. New York: Lodestar Books, 1988. Print.

—. *Like Sisters on the Homefront*. New York: Lodestar Books, 1995. Print.

—. *Rita WG.Com: Homepage*. Ritawg.com. n.d. Web. 15 Jan. 2008.

About the Editors

Steve Parks is an Associate Professor of Writing and Rhetoric at Syracuse University. He is the author of *Class Politics: The Movement for a Students' Right To Their Own Language* and *Gravyland: Writing Beyond the Curriculum in the City of Brotherly Love*. With Paula Mathieu and Tiffany Rousculp, he co-edited *Circulating Communities: The Tactics and Strategies of Community Publishing*. Working with Samantha Blackmon and Cristina Kirklighter, he has co-edited *Listening to our Elders: Writing and Working for Change*, a research project supported by NCTE. He has also published in *College English*, *Journal of College Composition and Communication*, and *Community Literacy Journal*. Over the past ten years, he has directed New City Community Press (newcitypress.com).

Beverly Moss is an associate professor of English at The Ohio State University in Columbus, Ohio. Her scholarly interests focus on literacy in African American community spaces and in composition theory and pedagogy. Her publications include *Everyone's an Author* (co-authored with Andrea Lunsford, Lisa Ede, Carole Clark Papper, and Keith Walters), *A Community Text Arises: A Literate Text and A Literacy Tradition in African American Churches, Literacies across Communities* (edited collection), and *Writing Groups Inside and Outside the Classroom* (co-edited with Nels Highberg and Melissa Nicolas).

Julia Voss is an assistant professor in the Department of English at Santa Clara University. She teaches classes in college writing and digital composing and studies studies composition and literacy using qualitative methodologies and multimodal presentation formats. Her current projects focus on strategies for teaching digital composing in a constantly-evolving literacy ecology and on the writing practices and pedagogies occurring in different spaces across college campuses.

Brian Bailie is a PhD candidate in the Composition and Cultural Rhetoric program at Syracuse University. His work focuses on the intersections of protest and media, technology and transnationalism, identity and material rhetoric, and the ways activists exploit, expand, resist, and utilize these intersections to their advantage. Bailie has served as contributor, associate editor, and special issue editor for *Reflections: A Journal of Writing, Service-Learning, and Community Literacy.* His most recent publications have appeared in the *KB Journal* nd *Composition Forum.*

Heather Christiansen is a PhD student in the Rhetoric, Communication and Information Design program at Clemson University. Her research interests include visual rhetoric, the rhetoric of branding, identity, user experience design, consumer behavior and social influence. She currently serves as the managing editor for *The WAC Journal.*

Stephanie Ceraso received her PhD in English from the University of Pittsburgh, specializing in rhetoric and composition, pedagogy, sound and listening, and digital media. Her work examines listening as a full-bodied, multimodal practice and aims to expand conventional notions of listening that emphasize the ears while ignoring the rest of the body. She is generally interested in how more fully embodied modes of listening might deepen our knowledge of multimodal engagement and production. Steph currently teaches at Georgetown University but will be joining the faculty at the University of Maryland, Baltimore County in the fall. You can find more about her research, projects, and teaching at www.stephceraso.com.

www.ingramcontent.com/pod-product-compliance
Lightning Source LLC
Chambersburg PA
CBHW031236050326
40690CB00007B/824